Therapy's Best

*Practical Advice
and Gems of Wisdom
from Twenty Accomplished
Counselors and Therapists*

Therapy's Best
Practical Advice and Gems of Wisdom from Twenty Accomplished Counselors and Therapists

Howard Rosenthal, EdD

Routledge
Taylor & Francis Group
New York   London

First published by
The Haworth Press, Inc., 10 Alice Street, Binghamton, NY 13904-1580.

This edition published 2013 by Routledge

Routledge
Taylor & Francis Group
711 Third Avenue
New York, NY 10017

Routledge
Taylor & Francis Group
27 Church Road
Hove, East Sussex BN3 2FA

PUBLISHER'S NOTE
The development, preparation, and publication of this work have been undertaken with great care. However, the publisher, employees, editors, and agents of The Haworth Press are not responsible for any errors contained herein or for consequences that may ensue from use of materials or information contained in this work. The opinions expressed by the author(s) are not necessarily those of The Haworth Press, Inc.

Cover design by Jennifer M. Gaska.

Library of Congress Cataloging-in-Publication Data

Rosenthal, Howard, 1952-
    Therapy's best : practical advice and gems of wisdom from twenty accomplished counselors and therapists / Howard Rosenthal.
        p. cm.
    Includes bibliographical references.
    ISBN-13: 978-0-7890-2474-9 (hard : alk. paper)
    ISBN-10: 0-7890-2474-8 (hard : alk. paper)
    ISBN-13: 978-0-7890-2475-6 (pbk. : alk. paper)
    ISBN-10: 0-7890-2475-6 (pbk. : alk. paper)
    1. Psychotherapy. 2. Counseling. 3. Psychotherapists—Interviews. 4. Counselors—Interviews I. Title. [DNLM: 1. Psychotherapy—Interview. 2. Counseling—Interview. WZ 112.5.P6 R815 2006]

RC480.R6653 2006
616.89'14—dc22

                                                                        2005033378

CONTENTS

ABOUT THE AUTHOR

Howard G. Rosenthal, EdD, is the coordinator of the Human Services Program at St. Louis Community College at Florissant Valley and teaches graduate classes for Webster University. Dr. Rosenthal received his master's degree from the University of Missouri, St. Louis and his doctorate from St. Louis University. He has over 20 years experience doing psychotherapy, including his work at the Midwest Stress Center. He is the author and editor of a string of successful books. Most counselors are familiar with Dr. Rosenthal, as helpers from coast to coast have used and praised his academic bestseller the *Encyclopedia of Counseling,* his text the *Human Services Dictionary,* and his 18-hour audio licensing preparation program for the National Counselor Examination. His book *Favorite Counseling and Therapy Techniques: 51 Therapists Share Their Most Creative Strategies* is a publisher's bestseller, while the sequel *Favorite Counseling and Therapy Homework Assignments, Leading Therapists Share Their Most Creative Strategies* features contributions from more famous helpers than any book of its kind.

Dr. Rosenthal's humorous, reader-friendly writing style landed him an interview—along with other influential authors such as Barry Sears of the Zone Diet books and Mark Victor Hansen, coauthor of the Chicken Soup for the Soul series—in Jeff Herman's book, *You Can Make It Big Writing Books: A Top Agent Shows You How to Develop a Million Dollar Bestseller.*

Dr. Rosenthal has lectured to over 100,000 people, making him one of the most popular speakers in the Midwest. He has been the recipient of awards for his teaching as well as his clinical work. His Web site is www.HowardRosenthal.com.

Preface

Lessons from the Legends
of the Couch

You are about to embark on a fascinating journey where you accompany me as I pick the brains of a select group of elite helpers. Make no mistake about it. These are not interviews with Joe Average Therapist, or Jane Average Therapist, or even the therapist next door. Herein you will discover encounters with some of the best and the brightest helpers who have ever walked the face of the planet. Collectively, these legends have written enough books and articles to capsize a small battleship.

Just for the record, lest the reader accuse me of sensationalism, I must mention that I am not using the word *legends* loosely. Two of my interviewees (Albert Ellis and Al Mahrer) have been given the American Psychological Association's Division of Psychotherapy's coveted "Living Legends of Psychotherapy" award.

I'M DR. HOWARD ROSENTHAL
AND I APPROVED THESE QUESTIONS!

Rather than using a cookie-cutter approach and asking every expert the same questions, I fine-tuned my inquiries to find out what makes these interventionists such outstanding helpers, their theories so popular, and perhaps most important, what makes them tick. I often ask controversial questions, sometimes based on my personal insider information in the profession, in order to reveal heretofore-unknown information conspicuously missing from the majority of our textbooks, classes, and seminars. Yes this book is entertaining.

Nonetheless, I firmly believe that every professional helper, individual undergoing or contemplating psychotherapy, and person with an overwhelming interest in human behavior, will walk away from this book as a better, more productive, competent, wiser, and happier human being.

Each interview contains fascinating, unexpected insights and authentic gems of wisdom. At times, you will find the experts' revelations novel, iconoclastic, brutally frank, crude, humorous, and in direct opposition to the material you were taught (or perhaps are teaching) in your classes or textbooks. There is nothing, dry, dull, stuffy, or boring about these scholarly exchanges.

Perhaps the most inaccurate assumption you as the reader can make is: "Oh, I've heard all the stuff before." My comment: Don't bet on it! For example, within these pages you will discover little known facts such as:

Dr. Albert Ellis, arguably the greatest living clinical psychologist and psychotherapist of our time, reveals that a major impetus for the creation of rational emotive behavior therapy (REBT) revolved around a homework assignment he prescribed for himself. As a result of carrying out his self-appointed psychotherapeutic task over 100 women turned Ellis down for a date! Check it out! But wait, there's more. When Ellis initially created his REBT theory—now universally praised and taught in virtually all individual and group psychotherapy and counseling classes—the vast majority of psychiatrists, psychologists, and social workers were against him and did everything they could to stop him from writing and lecturing about this approach. Finally, his highly acclaimed self-improvement and bibliotherapeutic work *A Guide to Rational Living* (co-authored with Robert Harper) might never have succeeded without the ardent work of a lay hypnotist and direct marketing genius named Melvin Powers who believed in the power of rational thinking.

Dr. William Glasser, who founded reality therapy and choice theory, told me that "I don't believe in brain drugs and can never remember prescribing any," despite the fact that he is a psychiatrist. This is even more remarkable when one considers that Glasser also has a very heavy background in chemistry. He also shares the number one blunder most therapists make.

Remember those five stages of death and dying you committed to memory to please your professors, pass your exams, and become a more adept helper? One of our experts forthrightly asserts that he could *never* remember a client he worked with that fit into these stages. We could dismiss this individual's remarks, except that they come from none other than *Dr. Edwin Shneidman,* known to many as the foremost expert on suicide prevention, suicidology (a term, I might add, he personally coined), and thanatology (i.e., death studies).

The book also includes a thought-provoking interview with *Richard Nelson Bolles,* the man who took career and vocational counseling beyond the halls of the counselor education departments of our graduate schools and into the confines of the average home, with his book *What Color Is Your Parachute?.* Over eight million copies have been sold. But here again, don't prematurely assume you know what will be revealed. Bolles shares with us the surprising fact that a résumé is not the best way to get a job and that he puts precious little stock in our scientific career inventories and tests.

In an interview that some prepublication readers have dubbed "the most honest interview with a counseling expert ever," it is comforting to hear *Dr. Jeffrey Kottler,* author of over fifty books, admit that at times he "authentically does not feel like a pro" when conducting therapy. He further relates an incident where he was asked to lecture on the steps for good counseling and could not remember nearly half of them. Kottler's interview is a little like watching Tiger Woods miss an "easy" two-foot putt. It reaffirms what we know, but often fail to admit: Simply, that all of us, even the top experts in the helping field, are normal, fallible human beings just like the rest of us. That, in and of itself, is comforting.

Ever wonder how marriage counseling experts who write the textbooks decide in their own lives who is *the one* for them? You'll find out in a husband/wife encounter with *Drs. Dorothy and Ray Becvar.*

What will psychotherapy be like in the year 2050? Psychotherapy scholar *Dr. Raymond Corsini* looks into his crystal ball and tells us in his interview. Hint: It's *not* what you think; the client can perform the sessions without a therapist with just a minimal amount of training. I take it a step further and interview with the creator of this iconoclastic, futuristic approach, *Dr. Al Mahrer.* On the lighter side, can you guess which internationally known therapist sent Corsini a note during a conference with a picture of a women on a couch that said in upper case letters DR. CORSINI, WILL YOU KISS ME? Corsini also shares his personal recollections about the late, great Carl R. Rogers.

Dr. Jon Carlson, who has snared two doctorates in the field, written thirty books, and over 100 articles, will tell us what gems of wisdom he has gleaned from videotaping over two hundred of the best living therapists. This is practical information you can immediately begin using to improve the quality of your therapy sessions.

Ready to hear something new and creatively exciting? Sure cognitive therapy is beneficial, but is it counterproductive or perhaps even inappropriate in some case? *Les Greenberg,* the father of emotion focused therapy (EFT) shares his thoughts.

Ever think of writing your own self-help book? Let *Dr. Robert Alberti,* the owner of a serious self-improvement publishing company, give you a few hints. Dr. Alberti—also one of the key pioneers in the assertiveness training movement—talks about the early days of the movement and the evolution of assertiveness training.

Is there any truth to the accusation leveled in the 1980s that Sigmund Freud copped out and changed his theory to save face with his peers? I go one-on-one with noted psychoanalyst *Dr. Nancy McWilliams,* who answers this question and discusses a host of other issues related to psychodynamic treatment. She'll also share her views on the pros and cons of the new brief strategic therapies and why every therapist can be a better helper by integrating analytic techniques. Dr. McWilliams also explains why things are looking up for analysts *without* medical degrees.

You'll discover that learning to talk to yourself in the second person (in a manner that is clearly distinct from REBT or other cognitive therapies) can be therapeutic. In a unique father/daughter interview with *Drs. Robert and Lisa Firestone,* I'll explore a valuable modality known as voice therapy, created by Dr. Robert Firestone. Voice therapy has been used with an array of problems from child abuse, to suicide, to relationship difficulties. I have personally used one of Dr. Robert Firestone's training videos in numerous training sessions I have conducted and can attest to the validity of his ideas. To my knowledge, the interview herein is the most comprehensive to date related to his work. We'll also find out from Lisa what it is really like growing up with a famous psychologist as your father! (Don't worry, it seems extremely positive.)

Finally, I'll spend some time taking a sentimental journey with *Muriel James* who is still going strong some thirty-plus years after she helped make transactional analysis (TA) and gestalt therapy household words with the publication of her wildly successful book *Born to Win* (co-authored with Dorothy Jongeward) that has now sold over four million copies in twenty-two languages (some of which Muriel admits she's never heard of). This book—which she was told would never take off in a big way—was one of the few publications that flourished in the self-help arena *and* in serious behavioral sciences classes and countless therapists' library collections.

The aforementioned synopses are merely teasers, appetizers to the main course, if you will, to the actual interviews . . . and other interviews with experts who are not mentioned because of space limitations.

By rubbing elbows with these consummate professionals, their theories, ideas, and experiences, we can truly learn more about ourselves to help us help others. And in the final analysis, isn't that what life is really all about?

Enjoy the journey!

Chapter 1

The Svengali Interviews

The old red brick office building was hardly pretentious. As I climbed the creaky, rickety stairs to the second floor I couldn't help thinking that this structure was well past its prime. The door to the office was thin wood and was in dire need of a new coat of paint. The upper portion of the door sported an opaque glass window that would have been right at home in an old Humphrey Bogart detective movie. A shabby little business card affixed to the door and sporting the words "The Stop Smoking with Hypnosis Center," scribbled with an unsharpened number 2 lead pencil, told me I was in the right place. My heart began to beat a little faster as I anticipated that the key to my future was just behind the door.

I was certain that a professionally painted sign would be brimming from the door in short order. I knocked.

"Rosenthal, I presume. Hi, I'm Jed Wren. Have a seat and make yourself comfortable." Jed appeared to be in his early fifties. His white shirt had a yellowish tint and his hair looked a bit unkempt. Unlike my own tie that had been obsessively knotted to perfection, his had seen more than its share of coffee stains and hung at half-mast.

To say I was excited would be putting it mildly. This is what it was all about. Finally, my graduate sheepskins replete with advanced courses and seminars in hypnosis were going to pay off. From what I could fathom from the classified job ad in the newspaper, I'd be helping a slew of folks kick the nasty habit of smoking and all the while I'd be pumping up my bank account like an overinflated tire. Life is beautiful or so I thought for the moment!

Portions of this chapter are reprinted with permission of *Counselor, The Magazine for Addiction Professionals,* from the author's article "The Two Most Important Questions a Counselor Can Ever Ask," which appeared in March/April 2003.

Jed leaned forward across his 1940s' vintage desk that had seen better days and lowered the decibel level of his voice like a trusted friend who was going to reveal a coveted secret. "What do you pull in a year Rosenthal?"

I instinctively mimicked his behavior moving in closer to him. "Pull in sir?"

"Yeah. You know, how much money do you make in a year?"

"About fourteen thousand."

Jed's face was now contorted into a holier-than-thou smirk and he leaned over to such an extent he was now invading my space. "What if I told you, Rosenthal, that I have figured out a way that a hypno-therapist can rake in thirty grand a year?"

I must admit he had my attention. The prospect of helping people while all the while doubling my anemic, but somewhat typical salary at the time, was a very pleasant thought.

Jed whipped a worn sheet of yellow notebook paper out of his pocket with mathematical calculations taking up the better part of the page. He pointed at the paper, stabbing it again and again with his large right thumb. "Groups, Rosenthal, groups are the secret. Groups are the way to go." He donned a sinister smile. "Stick thirty or so chairs in a room and hit them all at the same time with the same hypnotic induction. And presto. Do the math. It's all in the numbers, Rosenthal. You, my friend, are going to be pocketing some very serious money."

"Does it work sir? I mean is the research there to support the group hypnotic approach to smoking cessation?"

"Stay there Rosenthal. I'll be right back."

There was no denying that this was the strangest job interview I had ever encountered. Jed was coming across more like the proverbial used car salesman your father warned you about than the director of a smoking cessation and therapy center. In fact, it began to occur to me that although I was the interviewee, the job candidate, or the future member of Jed's mega-buck practice . . . whatever I was . . . the tables were now turned and *I was conducting the interview.*

THE SMOKING GUN WAS A CIGARETTE!

Jed was gone for an extended period of time that seemed like eternity in the context of a job interview. Perhaps he was securing a journal article or two to support his notion of one induction fits all group hypnosis in the fight to ameliorate smoking. I periodically glanced at my watch.

Finally, the door swung open and Jed burst in huffing and puffing. His face was red as a beet. I looked up and quite frankly my mouth dropped open: Jed had a pack of cigarettes peeking out of the pocket in his faded dress shirt, and worse yet a cancer stick was dangling from the right side of his mouth. He whipped out his aluminum lighter and I detected a sigh of relief as he took a hearty puff. A cloud of white billowy smoke began to displace the clean air that had occupied the office.

He shrugged his shoulders and smiled. "Don't look so shocked Rosenthal. This is a luxury I don't have during the day."

Quite frankly, I was at a loss for words. "But, but . . ."

He cut me off. "Rosenthal, look, you don't really believe in this stuff do you?"

"Well, sir—." Again he interrupted.

"You've heard of Dr. X, Rosenthal?"

"Of course. I've read a number of his hypnosis books. In fact, I'm reading one of his books now."

Jed continued, using his cigarette in hand to drive home his conviction. "I worked with him, Rosenthal, for two years and he doesn't believe in hypnosis either. He also smokes, you know."

I attempted to interject my two cents when Jed cut me off again.

"Do you know how much Dr. X makes? With the books—hell you're reading one of them now—the seminars, the clients who come to see him from all over the nation; damn it, Rosenthal, the guy darn near has a license to print money. We can do it here, Rosenthal, the same thing. What do you say?"

What a sad comment on our field. Jed didn't believe in his product and he couldn't even manage his own tendency to smoke. I privately predicted that his money-making city on a hill group hypnosis center would be out of business in six months. Just for the record my prediction was generous. The center folded with an elapsed time of less than six weeks under its belt.

Would you want to work for Jed Wren? Would you refer your client to this man?

Finally, rest assured, you will not be perusing an interview with the famous or infamous Dr. X herein.

Was this an isolated incident? I think not. Please indulge me while I share another Svengali saga. Not long after the aforementioned interview, I interviewed for a job at a chain of hypnosis centers that was indeed very successful from a financial standpoint. I became a tad suspicious when the woman who owned the center, and was interviewing me, confided that new clients should always be instructed to throw their cigarettes away in the large trash receptacle in the waiting room prior to their initial session. She then explained that the building maintenance staff was given strict instructions never to empty that particular trash receptacle. Hence, when a new client came in to hear the pitch about treatment you would merely point to the can and tell him or her that "all these folks threw their cigarettes away during the first session of hypnosis."

While that statement hardly constitutes a lie, it certainly doesn't illuminate the cold, hard truth either. (Just interview the women at the convenience store next door about her cigarette sales.) After hearing this drivel, I asked the woman where she went to school.

She became somewhat irate and said, "Look, I went to the school of Hard Knox." She then glanced at my résumé for the first time in the interview. He voice took on an angry tone and she remarked, "Why would someone with all your credentials want to work for us anyway?"

An excellent question indeed! My answer: "I wouldn't!"

My point is not to malign hypnotists. A lot of reputable therapists are performing hypnosis out there, including yours truly. My point once again is that you can learn a lot from interviewing helpers!

IS IT THERAPY, OR IS IT AN INTERVIEW? ONLY THE CLIENT KNOWS FOR SURE

Lest the reader erroneously conclude that all interviews end in disaster I must point out that an interview with a helper can sometimes change your whole course of action for the better. Let me share an amazing saga that occurred in the life of one of my students.

I was teaching a fourth-year counseling class with a heavy emphasis on theories of psychotherapy and counseling. One of the assignments (if the student felt comfortable with it and had the financial means) was to interview or attend a counseling session with three therapists from three different theoretical persuasions.

Megan, a twenty-three-year-old senior, approached me. She explained that she had been severely sexually abused as a child and was making excellent progress with a local female therapist. Nevertheless, she wanted to perform the assignment. I insisted that she discuss the assignment with her current therapist since the last thing I wanted was for her course in counseling to get in the way of her mental health. Her therapist gave her a green light.

We picked out three markedly different therapists for Megan to visit. The first helper was a female hypnotist who advertised that her expertise was dealing with sex problems. Academic credentials related to our field: none. The second therapist was an accomplished female therapist who worked with one of the top sexual abuse treatment centers in the world. Finally, Megan would come face-to-face with a male therapist who espoused a strict behavior therapy stance.

Megan's first stop was at the female hypnotist's office. No surprises here. Megan timed the entire visit. It took just twelve minutes. When the hypnotist thought Megan was hypnotized she suggested to her that she would forget about her horrific sexual traumas of childhood (!) and return in two days and "pay another one hundred twenty dollars for another session." This woman was not only unethical, but a Freudian analyst's worst nightmare.

Megan's next stop: An interview with a top gun in the treatment of sexual abuse. Overall, she described her experience with this woman as very pleasant. Nevertheless, she confided that she still liked her own therapist a tad better.

Her last stop was an appointment with a cold, hard calculated behaviorist. Several class members pointed out to Megan that some of the literature noted that a male would not be as effective as a female for helping a sexually abused women. Much to everyone's chagrin, including mine, she felt unusually comfortable with the male behavior therapist and ended up telling him things in the first session she had never revealed to her own therapist (whom she liked) in over thirty sessions. She concluded that it was the most productive therapy session (interview?) she had ever attended.

TRICKS OF THE TA TRADE

As part of my graduate course in group practice, I was informed that I would need to attend four sessions of group therapy. My professor handed me a sheet with names of therapists from various persuasions (e.g., psychodynamic, gestalt, reality therapy, etc.) who had specifically expressed an interest in doing this. My eyes immediately came to a screeching halt when I spied the name of a TA (transactional analysis) therapist who had not only written books and achieved academic notoriety, but had a private practice with an income that seemed to rival a few divisions of General Motors. I would need to travel a rather substantial distance to attend his group sessions, but I deemed that it would be worth it.

I phoned his secretary, who was very kind. I told her about my assignment and she assured me that Mr. TA (not his real name, but I have a feeling you would have guessed that I have changed all the names in this chapter to protect the innocent or not so innocent parties) had plenty of similar requests.

Unlike Jed Wren's office, which was in dire need of a makeover, Mr. TA's office suite was so plush that I initially thought I had mistakenly wandered into a Hollywood producer's front office. The place was beautiful.

Mr. TA had a rosewood desk replete with polished brass handles that could indeed double as mirrors. Behind his desk was a large flip chart equipped with an array of colored markers.

I entered the room and reminded Mr. TA why I was there. He rose from his chair and grabbed a marker. He then launched into a lengthy explanation about the levels of TA proficiency, always tied to a stiff price tag (e.g., "For five thousand dollars I can make you a clinical member, for ten thousand a teaching member" etc.). My own self-talk told the whole story: For $15,000 I'm sure I could drive away in his new car and for a tad more I'm sure he could set me up in an elegant condo.

There I sat, dumbfounded. Throughout Mr. TA's *TA sales presentation,* I did not utter a single word. Not that there was a silence where I could have interjected anything. Finally, Mr. TA smartly popped the cap back on the marker and skillfully twirled it in his fingers like a miniature baton. "Well there you have it," he remarked. At that point in the interview he gave me a quick handshake and opened the door that led to the hallway in the office building. Hmm? Could it be that since his sales pitch was over and he was asking me to leave? Yes, Howard, very good, you are becoming unusually adept at reading people's nonverbal behavior. I would need to share this poignant example with the other students in my nonverbal proseminar later in the week. Just kidding . . . well, not really.

"Thank you, Mr. TA," I said, wondering if he would notice that I did possess speech capabilities. What came next clearly supports the old adage that truth is stranger than fiction.

"Okay, well it was nice meeting you. You'll be receiving a bill for eighty dollars for my time today and I look forward to training you."

Hello? This guy didn't hear one solitary word I was saying. Oh, that's right, I didn't really get to say anything.

I immediately contacted my empathic graduate professor who was seemingly as disappointed as I. He insisted that I stubbornly refuse to pay the bill. At that point in time a big grin spread across my face. Mr. TA couldn't bill me. Neither he nor his secretary had ever asked for my name. There really is a God.

MY FASCINATION WITH EXPERTS: SOME BRIEF COMMENTS ON THE PSYCHOLOGY OF THE '57 CHEVY

Initially, I was going to say that my inclination to interview experts began with the aforementioned sagas or perhaps with preparation of this book. Nevertheless, an armchair analysis of my own childhood reminded me that such a statement would be highly inaccurate.

My fascination with experts was evident during my teenage years when I would tinker with cars. My brother was driving a hand-me-down, aging 1957 Chevy Bel Air. My goal in life (like millions of other teens in America) was to make that baby faster. I had heard rumors from some of the guys in school that by rotating the distributor and advancing the timing I could increase the acceleration of the vehicle. Hell-bent on shaving a second off the car's zero-to-sixty time, and using superficial logic, I concluded that I could find the answers I needed by calling the best-trained mechanics—those working at Chevrolet dealers—and asking them.

The expert answers I received were both intriguing and perplexing.

Expert number 1: "Sure, it's totally safe. Go ahead and do it, but never raise the timing more than two degrees."

Expert number 2: "No, don't do it. It's not safe, causes pinging, and the engine will run hot."

Expert number 3: "Sure, it's totally safe. But if you don't raise the timing by at least six degrees, you won't notice any difference in performance."

Wait a minute. Weren't these guys all experts? Shouldn't they all be telling me the same thing?

My fascination, which bordered on obsession (though I probably didn't even know what the word meant at the time), piqued when a mechanic so wisely said, and I quote, "Hey, I just answered that question for you about two minutes ago."

As I worked my way down the phone book, I was so driven I had inadvertently called the same dealer and spoke with the same mechanic twice within a two-minute time period! Everything has a silver lining and that would become my most embarrassing moment if I needed one for a group activity or class exercise.

THE NEW CURE FOR BOWLING ALONE

History repeated itself on a number of occasions. I grew up in St. Louis, Missouri—a city that was dubbed the bowling capital of the world at that time. As a youngster you could walk into any bowling alley and easily obtain a tip on technique, or perhaps get a bowling ball drilled by a famous pro bowler—on occasion, even a hall-of-famer. But here again, it was the legend of the '57 Chevy timing all over again. The advice I received from the great and the greatest was all over the map:

"Always hold the bowling ball in the suitcase position."

"Wait a minute. I noticed that you are holding the bowling ball in the suitcase position. Never do that. Always get your hand under the ball and keep it there."

"Who in the world drilled that bowling ball for you? It's by far the worst drilling I've ever seen." (The pro that beat you in the final championship match last Saturday on national television, if you must know.)

THE FASCINATION BECOMES A REALITY

I graduated from '57 Chevy mechanics and legends of the lanes to therapists the moment my parents secured a copy of *How to Live with a Neurotic.* I snuck this book, written in 1950 by none other than Albert Ellis, into my room to read. On numerous occasions I interviewed Ellis in my mind. (Interestingly enough, my actual interview with him in this book is considerably more lively, honest, iconoclastic, and brutally frank than anything I could have ever imagined!)

For many years the notion of interviewing Ellis and other top therapists remained a figment of my imagination until I received a call from Lorna L. Hecker, Professor and Clinical Director of the Marriage and Family Therapy Center at Purdue University Calumet in Hammond, Indiana. Lorna also served as the founding editor of an exciting new publication, the *Journal of Clinical Activities, Assignments & Handouts in Psychotherapy Practice.* She asked if I would serve as an editorial board member for the journal, which, needless to say, I agreed to do.

Several months later Lorna contacted me to see if I would interview Jeffrey Kottler, author of over fifty books in the field. The interview focused primarily on creativity in psychotherapy. The interview was brutally honest. It was, I believe, a tribute to Jeffrey's willingness to share his true self, rather than trying to come across as an all-knowing holier-than-thou expert, who had written an endless string of successful books. Several people wrote me to say it was the most genuine, interesting, and compelling interview they had ever read in a journal. Lorna wisely suggested I follow up by conducting an interview with Dr. Sam Gladding, who is also an exceptionally creative therapist. I did.

The impetus was there and I wasn't about to let it slow down. With Lorna's blessing, I did an innovative husband/wife interview with marriage counseling scholars Ray and Dorothy Becvar. My next step: Contact Albert Ellis to fulfill that boyhood dream. I had been collecting questions in my mind for many years now and planned on hitting Ellis with some of the toughest in his career. Was his famous book *A Guide to Rational Living* initially a dud? Was the rumor floating around that Ellis created his theory after being turned down by 100 women for a date accurate?

I pulled out all the stops and so did Ellis, and the piece titled "The REBT Story You Haven't Heard: A No-Holds-Barred Interview with Dr. Albert Ellis" became a reality, and in my humble opinion, perhaps even a classic. Ellis also gave the interview very high marks. Even the off-color language, exactly as Ellis said it, has been unedited for your reading pleasure.

Both Lorna and I agreed that these lively interviews were providing a rare glimpse of these experts and their views on treatment that was sadly missing from their books or literature about them in other sources. The interviews revealed vital personal, theoretical, and clinical gems of wisdom that was heretofore unknown. I took the four aforementioned interviews, added fifteen more key experts, and this text was born.

RUBBING ELBOWS WITH THE BEST AND THE BRIGHTEST: INTERVIEWS WITH SOME OF THE MOST KNOWLEDGEABLE THERAPISTS IN THE WORLD

Let me forthrightly state that this book has a strong cast of characters. Together, these luminaries have enough degrees, awards, publications, accolades, and accomplishments to capsize a small battleship. For example:

Dr. Robert Alberti helped spawn the assertiveness training movement as well as the publication of serious bibliotherapeutic works. Any counselor who has ever seriously considered writing a book should read this interview.

Anybody who enrolls in a marriage and family therapy class will most likely encounter the names of doctors *Ray and Dorothy Becvar.* In fact, there is a high likelihood one of their texts will be required reading. You'll also get a rare glimpse of how marriage counseling experts handle stresses in their own marriage and how they met.

Dr. Bob Bertolino is not one of our seasoned pros, who was doing therapy when most readers were in diapers, but rather a rising star in the psychotherapeutic community. Bob is already the author of nearly ten books; several of them co-authored with Bill O'Hanlon, acknowledged as one of the true pioneers in the brief solution oriented therapy movement. Bob has worked extensively with O'Hanlon, and O'Hanlon as you may recall, trained with the great Milton H. Erickson and has been dubbed as Erickson's only work-study student. Bob's vita includes numerous lectures, publications, and clinical work that now fills twenty pages. Bob's interview illuminates what is new and hot in our profession.

Career and vocational counselors will not walk away disappointed, as an interview with *Richard Nelson Bolles,* the author of *What Color Is Your Parachute?,* graces the pages of this book. His book, I might add, is the best-selling job-hunting book in history . . . over eight million copies have been sold and counting. (Incidentally, as an added bonus, if you are personally seeking new or additional employment, this surprising interview is a must-read. I must warn you, however, that Bolles may overturn everything you *thought* you knew about getting a good job!)

Dr. Jon Carlson, who has not one, but two doctorates in the field, has penned 100 articles, 30 books, and has created 200 videos with hundreds of the finest therapists in the world. He served as president of the International Association of Marriage and Family Counselors (IAMFC) and was the founding editor of *The Family Journal.* His research into both "bad" and "good" therapy yields information that can help all of us.

Dr. Albert Ellis is the creator of rational emotive behavior therapy (REBT). Many, if not most therapists, would classify him as the world's leading clinical psychologist. He is the author of over 70 books and 800 articles on psychotherapy, sex, and marriage. Summarizing his interview I can only assert that you are in for a true treat: it doesn't get any more honest than this!

Dr. Robert Firestone is the innovator of an up-and-coming intervention known as voice therapy. Voice therapy can be used with myriad difficulties from depression and suicidal ideations, to child abuse, and relationships. In this work I share a unique father/daughter interview with his daughter *Dr. Lisa Firestone,* who is an accomplished therapist and mental health/suicide prevention trainer in her own right. You'll also get a sneak peak at what it was like for Lisa growing up with a father who was a noted psychotherapist.

It would be extremely difficult to find a psychologist, counselor, social worker, or even a K-12 teacher, for that matter, who is not familiar with the ardent work of psychiatrist, *Dr. William Glasser.* Dr. Glasser is the father of reality therapy, choice theory, and has written extensively on quality schools. When you read his interview you will immediately be struck at how Glasser's views differ from mainstream psychiatry.

As I was preparing this book, numerous colleagues and other contributors suggested that *Dr. Les Greenberg* be included in my lineup. Dr. Greenberg is the father of emotion focused therapy (EFT), a modality that challenges the belief that cognitive therapies or interventions that keep the emotions in check, are ideal for every client. Get ready to hear something creatively different when you read this thought-provoking interview.

We'll also catch up with *Muriel James* who over thirty years ago introduced many of us to transactional analysis and gestalt therapy with her book *Born to Win*—a hit with therapists, patients, and the general public—that has now sold over four million copies in twenty-two languages. Muriel, who has authored nineteen books and is currently branching out and writing history books, studied under Eric Berne, the father of transactional analysis. In my opinion, her practice what she preaches attitude personifies *Born to Win* as well as nearly anybody I have ever come in contact with. Get ready to lift your spirits.

Dr. Jeffrey Kottler has written over fifty books both in the academic and textbook arena. He has written (perhaps more extensively than any other practitioner) about the fact that even the world's finest counselors and therapists are fallible human beings just like the rest of us. As stated earlier, his interview goes a long way to help us all feel like more competent helpers. Several prepublication readers insisted that this was the most revealing interview with a counselor they had ever come across.

Dr. Lia Nower comes to the table with both a PhD in social work and a JD in law. She has researched gambling addiction from the luxurious roll-out-the-red carpet chrome laden slots in America to the smoke-filled tribal casinos that exist on the opposite side of the globe. Moreover, she is a clinical supervisor for the National Council on Problem Gambling in Washington, DC. The combination of her legal and mental health expertise gives her a unique perspective in understanding an issue that will concern more and more counselors in the coming years.

Dr. Al Mahrer of Canada is one of four recipients on the planet to snare the APA Division of Psychotherapy's Living Legends of Psychotherapy Award. Some experts believe that Dr. Mahrer's experiential therapy, a radically different approach to treatment, *is the future of psychotherapy,* but more on that later when you read his spellbinding interview.

Psychoanalysis, the psychotherapy, that truly started it all, is often conspicuously missing from modern books of this ilk. Not here. I shall interview *Dr. Nancy McWilliams,* a full-fledged psychoanalyst who teaches at Rutgers as well as several other universities. Her books are often required reading for the analyst in training. We'll discuss everything from whether Freud copped out and changed his theory to why things are looking up for nonmedical therapists who wish to practice psychoanalysis.

Most readers have used at least one textbook by *Dr. Samuel Gladding* or *Dr. Raymond Corsini.* As this book goes to press, multibook author, Dr. Gladding, a former president of the American Association of Specialists for Group Work (ASGW), will take over as the president of the American Counseling Association (ACA). In this interview he shares his roadmap for therapeutic creativity. Dr. Corsini, as you will discover when you read his interview, is listed as one of the 500 most significant psychologists since 1850. Many of us were weaned on his classic *Current Psychotherapies.* He also has a few psychotherapeutic war stories about Rogers and a truly little amazing anecdote about his initial meeting with Frankl. All I can say right now about the latter is: It's *not* what you think!

Dr. Francine Shapiro is the creator of one of the most controversial psychotherapeutic strategies of all time, eye movement desensitization and reprocessing or EMDR. This creatively different form of intervention has stimulated a wealth of research. Her interview is packed with resources and can help you decide if this is a form of therapy that you should be practicing.

Dr. Edwin S. Shneidman could arguably be called the most knowledgeable man in the world when it comes to the topic of self-destructive behavior, suicide, and the grief caused by taking one's own life. Dr. Shneidman even coined terms we use in the field such as "suicidology" and "postvention." You'll also hear what Shneidman has to say about the death and dying theory you most likely learned in school.

A BEVY OF UNCOMMON KNOWLEDGE

One very important caveat: Do not skim the interviews and foolishly assume that you will able to predict what are experts are going to say. The only predictable thing about these interviews is that our experts' answers are anything but predictable . . . which keeps the interviews lively, exciting, and extremely informative. You will experience a side of these people and their theories that cannot be gained from classes, workshops, journal articles, or books . . . even the books and articles they authored themselves! Moreover, accomplished therapists, like trained mechanics and professional keglers, seemingly disagree as often as they agree.

After you finish reading the interviews I'll be back to help you gather your thoughts about what insightful gems of wisdom we can learn from our experts. Enjoy the ride.

Chapter 2

Robert Alberti on Assertiveness: Rights and Writes

Robert E. Alberti, PhD, is a licensed psychologist, marriage and family therapist (MFT), Fellow of the American Psychological Association (psychotherapy and media psychology), clinical member of the American Association for Marriage and Family Therapy, and forty-year professional member of the American Counseling Association. Author/co-author of several books, including million-copy best seller *Your Perfect Right,* he is best known for his contributions to assertiveness and social skills training. As president and editor in chief of Impact Publishers, Inc., he has edited and published nearly 100 books by mental health professionals, and his work has received international recognition as the "gold standard" for psychological self-help. His current professional interest is in the field of emergency services and disaster mental health.

HR: *I first became acquainted with your work when I took some assertiveness training courses with Pat Jakubowski at the University of Missouri. In addition to the classroom course we were scheduled to run our own assertiveness training group and in both arenas Pat . . . who later wrote her own books . . . recommended your book . . . Your Perfect Right as the bible of assertiveness training. I have a rather antiquated cardboard cover edition that no doubt ought to be worth a serious chunk of change on ebay in the coming years. Is it accurate to say that this landmark work, co-authored with Michael Emmons, actually spawned the assertiveness training movement?*

Therapy's Best
© 2006 by The Haworth Press, Inc. All rights reserved.
doi:10.1300/5189_02

RA: It would be rather self-serving to say that our work "spawned a movement." Let's just say we were fortunate enough to have the right message at the right time. It is true that *Your Perfect Right* was the first book devoted entirely to assertiveness training, but we built on the works of several other important contributors, most notably Arnold Lazarus, Andrew Salter, and Joseph Wolpe. We studied their work, used it with our clients, and recognized the need for a more detailed discussion of the procedures. *Your Perfect Right* was built on that foundation.

HR: *Give us some history here. Was the book an instant success and did you self-publish the first few editions?*

RA: I could hardly claim "instant success" for *Your Perfect Right*! We did self-publish the book after learning that it would take a couple of years to get it out through established commercial publishers. The first edition was just a thousand copies. As that sold, we printed a couple of thousand more, then five thousand, and so on, as it caught on through the early 1970s. In 1974, with about ten thousand copies sold, we did a second edition, much revised and expanded. With help from a media-savvy friend, we found a publisher to distribute the new edition to the book trade. That really turned a corner for the book, because it got a great deal of exposure in the popular press. We also sold mass market paperback rights to a New York house, and got some good publicity for our work from them as well, although that was published under a different title.

HR: *I understand that the book has now sold well over a million copies and has been translated into fifteen languages. Why do you think the book was and still is so successful?*

RA: Timing had a lot to do with it, in several respects. As I said, we had the right message at the right time. Being the first book on assertiveness helped. Coinciding with the explosion of interest in individual rights throughout our society was a major factor as well. The women's rights movement was a huge social force in the 1970s, and the expansion of civil rights for a number of ethnic and social groups brought a lot of attention to *Your Per-*

fect Right. The title certainly didn't hurt!

Modesty aside, however, I believe that we gave readers a clear presentation of specific procedures for developing their skills in self-expression. And we have emphasized from the beginning that genuine assertiveness is aimed at equality in relationships—not getting your way at the expense of others.

HR: *Andrew Salter has been called the father of assertiveness training and at times the father of behavior therapy (although if I recall Arnold Lazarus actually coined the term behavior therapy). Did you know Salter personally and were you influenced by his work? I've been told he was very charismatic.*

RA: I had the great pleasure of working with Andrew Salter for a very short time in the mid-1970s. He was a charismatic person: "Andy, you're a dandy!" was one of his favorite expressions, referring to himself. Dr. Emmons and I owe much to his ideas. We published audio and videotapes of an extended conversation with a group of assertiveness training professionals we invited to meet with him for a day. The discussion covered a wide range of topics and applications of his ideas about self-expression, and we were all much enriched by that experience. The tapes were not hugely successful from a sales viewpoint, but I'm confident that those who saw and heard them became substantially better facilitators of assertiveness as a result.

HR: *I was fascinated by Salter's 1949 classic* Conditioned Reflex Therapy, *which in my mind bordered more on aggressive rather than assertive training. He had a very unique writing style that could really draw the reader in. I've heard some experts hypothesize that Salter never truly received the fanfare he had coming to him because he only had a bachelor's degree in psychology. Any thoughts on this?*

RA: There were parts of *Conditioned Reflex Therapy* that did border on aggressiveness, perhaps, but I believe that Salter was a strong advocate for the same sort of equal-relationship assertiveness that we have taught and written about. He wrote in a popular, self-help style that did receive professional criticism, and I'm convinced his lack of advanced training and formal credentials limited his acceptance among professionals. Yet his psychology was very sound—for the most part—and his ideas about "self-excitation" were highly influential to those of us who were helping clients to overcome social anxiety. It is noteworthy that his book is still in print—now in an online edition, I understand—after some fifty-five years! That's pretty good evidence of "fanfare" where it counts!

HR: *Are people more assertive now than when you first published the original edition of your book?*

RA: I don't know of any data that could prove that "people are more assertive now," but it seems that we have—as a society—reached a point of much greater openness and freedom of expression. That may not be all to the good, I might add! Some folks have used "assertiveness" as a pretext for all sorts of uncivil behavior—misinterpreting the concept as if it gave them license for rudeness, road rage, and boorishness. Fortunately that's not the rule, but I sometimes think we may have "created a monster," despite our best efforts to teach a self-expressive style that is respectful of others.

HR: *Does a therapist need to bend, fold, or mutilate the assertiveness training paradigm to use it when conducting multicultural counseling?*

RA: Dr. Don Cheek is an African-American psychologist who was a colleague of ours in the 1970s, and who taught us much about how to apply assertiveness training to clients of color. At the risk of overgeneralizing in the interest of space, I think it is always critical to take into account the unique circumstances of each individual when planning a behavior change intervention. Sensitivity to cultural background, age, gender, socio-economic circumstances, and a host of other variables (I'll be criticized for all those I don't mention explicitly, but there are too many) must be a part of a counselor's assessment and treatment plan under all circumstances.

HR: *How did you end up starting your own publishing company, Impact Publishers?*

RA: As we discussed earlier, *Your Perfect Right* was self-published. That was in 1970, and we did it because we wanted to get it out right away. We were still in full-time practice, and didn't intend to start a publishing company. A few years later however, when we were selling over 50,000 copies a year, we concluded that it made sense to begin to take on the work of other authors. We met Stanlee Phelps and Nancy Austin in 1974, and contracted to publish their book, *The Assertive Woman,* which we brought out in 1975. We incorporated Impact Publishers that year, and went on to publish four new books in 1976, and three to ten books a year since—over a hundred books now. A hallmark of the books Impact has produced has been that they are authored by well-qualified human service professionals.

We were fortunate to start with a couple of books that turned out to be extremely successful. *Your Perfect Right* has sold over 1.3 million copies in its eight editions. *The Assertive Woman,* now in its third edition, has over 400,000 copies sold, and is also still going strong.

HR: *I frequently talk with counselors who say something like "I want to write a self-improvement book." Most of these folks never get published. I tell them to read your other perfect right book, as I call it . . .* Your Perfect Write *that gives some great tips on how to get published. As a bonafide insider in the publishing business, can you share with us what these self-help wannabe authors are doing wrong?*

RA: As your question suggests, Howard, the answer is a book in itself! Let me suggest a key guideline: *Limit yourself!* That fundamental concept cuts at least three ways: *First,* think long and hard about your audience. Every writer wants to believe that the whole world will be interested in her or his book. Alas, "it ain't necessarily so." In fact, the chances are very slim. Your chances of success are much greater if you'll *focus on a specific audience. Second,* limit what you try to cover. Make it practical, and write it so your readers can use it alone—without you to guide them. *Third,* when you get ready to send your book to publishers, *limit yourself to those who actually publish the genre in which you're writing* (e.g., self-help). Nearly all publishers—except the very largest—specialize. Don't try to sell self-help to a cookbook publisher! That may sound obvious, but you'd be amazed how many poets and novelists come to Impact. Do your homework, and you'll save time and energy for yourself and the publishers you approach.

HR: *I know the top guns on the TV talk show circuit such as Oprah and Donahue have interviewed you. What was that like and do you have any feelings about the current crop of media therapists such as the Dr. Phil's and the Dr. Laura's of the world?*

RA: Let me answer the second part of your question first. According to the most recent information I have, Dr. Phil McGraw is a legimate professional psychologist, and a member of the American Psychological Association. He gets lots of press because of his TV work, but as far as I can tell, he has good credentials. Laura Schlesinger, as I understand it, has a master's degree in some mental health related field, and a doctorate in physiology. That's a recognized scientific discipline, but it's not a mental health field. I am an APA Fellow in media psychology, so I have a pretty strong identification with the ethics of that field. The most fundamental of those ethics is that when we're working with someone via the media—TV show or radio call in or advice column—it's important not to personalize the answers. That is, since we can't make an adequate diagnosis on the basis of very limited information about the individual, we must offer only general comments about the presenting problem. Too many popular media advice-givers ignore that ethic—at their "clients'" peril.

As far as my own appearances on *Oprah* and *Donahue,* they were very pleasant and interesting experiences. Both shows originated in Chicago at the time I appeared, and the on-air guests were treated royally. When Mike Emmons and I did his show in 1975, Phil Donahue was a friendly, involved host who made a real effort to bring out material that would benefit his audiences. Oprah's show was somewhat more "staged." The producers at that time (1990) brought in people who talked about a family problem, and I was asked to offer a helpful intervention. The show was taped on the day George H. W. Bush sent troops into Kuwait to repel Iraq's invasion, so it was hard for me to focus on the mundane issues presented on the show.

HR: *On the Impact Publishers Web site it mentions that you made a 2000 television appearance with Cybill Shepherd. That sounds exciting. What's the scoop?*

RA: Cybill had an afternoon talk show called *Men Are from Mars, Women Are from Venus* for about a year in early 2000. I appeared as her professional "co-host" with a panel of people who were working on divorce and relationship issues. It was a fun show, and I think the participants—and, we can hope, the audience—got something out of it. All of us in mental health disciplines recognize that we can't effect significant changes in people's lives in an hour of TV, but it is possible to open doors, or to help folks recognize that they can benefit from getting professional help. Cybill is a real media pro, and a sensitive person. I think she did a fine job "opening doors" for her guests on the short-lived show.

HR: *How do you feel about the path mental health treatment has been taking during the last few years . . . managed care doling out limited sessions . . . brief solution oriented therapies that cater to the managed care model . . . Prozac ads on prime time television . . . and psychologists gearing up to scribble on prescription pads in Guam, New Mexico, and the military?*

RA: I don't think you have room in your book for my answers to all those questions, so let me tackle two that I feel strongly about. I'm a believer in brief therapy. For better or for worse, in the twenty-first century we—and our clients—simply do not have the luxury of extended therapy sessions. And very little long-term therapy has been demonstrated effective in good research. The other issue I would comment on is prescription privileges for psychologists. Notwithstanding our society's demand for instant cures, it is my strong belief that we in psychology have legitimate interventions of our own to offer clients, methods that are proven effective. Why do we want to emulate physicians? Seems to me it all has to do with catering to the demands of insurance companies (read: getting paid), and of clients who come in asking for the latest designer drug they've seen advertised on TV. No way to run a profession, in my opinion.

HR: *You and the late Bruce Fisher have a popular book entitled* Rebuilding: When Your Relationship Ends. *My understanding is that about 50 percent of all marriages end in divorce in the United States. However, the figure for second marriages skyrockets to an alarming 65 percent. I realize that our readers need to read the book to secure the whole story, but can you tell us in a nutshell what usually goes awry in these second-time relationships?*

RA: Let me say first that Bruce was the real expert on divorce recovery. He had done good research, developed an assessment instrument—the *Fisher Divorce Adjustment Scale*—worked with thousands of clients and trained hundreds of professionals. I came along essentially as editor of his book, and—I hope—helped him to express his ideas more effectively. That said, to address the substantive question you ask: If there is a single key to successful second marriages, it is to do the work that's necessary to recover from the ending of the first relationship before getting involved again. Bruce's research suggests that two years is the average time required to go through the recovery process, and in *Rebuilding* we've identified nineteen specific "rebuilding blocks" along the way. Folks who do the difficult job of working their way through those steps before they commit to a new love relationship have a much greater chance of success "the second time around."

HR: *What final gem of wisdom would you like to impart to our readers that will allow them to become better helpers?*

RA: I've been a licensed psychologist and MFT for over thirty years, and during most of that time I've also owned and operated a small business (Impact Publishers). The single biggest shortcoming I see among counselors and psychotherapists is that they don't pay enough attention to the "real world" of their clients/patients. They focus too narrowly on "mental health" issues. Even so-called eclectic or holistic approaches to therapy tend to be limited to integrating methods from different schools of thought *within therapy.* I think it's just as important to consider the world that the patient lives in outside the therapy office. What are his or her living conditions? Friends? Family? Job? Neighborhood? Diet? Sleep habits? Financial needs? Future prospects? Political pressures? Lousy plumbing? A broken-down car? A nasty boss? A thoughtless neighbor with a noisy dog? A pile of unpaid bills?

The counseling and psychotherapy professions have tremendous resources to offer the world. We know that we can help relieve suffering, and we can help folks to live happier, more fulfilled lives. We do that better when we remember to consider client needs from the broadest perspective. I like Abe Maslow's advice: "If the only tool you have is a hammer, you will see every problem as a nail." I urge you to look beyond DSM, or family systems, or cognitive behavioral therapy, or unconditional positive regard, or defense mechanisms, or whatever your own orientation may be. Find out what really goes on in the lives of your patients/clients, and help them to discover or develop the tools they need to become the persons they want to be.

HR: *Thank you for taking the time to share your vast knowledge and expertise!*

Chapter 3

The Marriage Counseling Mystique:
A Candid Interview
with Dorothy and Ray Becvar

Dorothy S. Becvar is a Licensed Marital and Family Therapist and a Licensed Clinical Social Worker in private practice in St. Louis, Missouri. She is also President and CEO of The Haelan Centers, a not-for-profit corporation dedicated to promoting growth and wholeness in body, mind, and spirit. Dorothy has published extensively and is the author of the books, *In the Presence of Grief: Helping Family Members Resolve Death, Dying and Bereavement Issues* (Guilford Press, 2001) and *Soul Healing: A Spiritual Orientation in Counseling and Therapy* (Basic Books, 1997), as well as the editor of the book *The Family, Spirituality, and Social Work* (Haworth, 1997). She is co-editor, with William Nichols, Mary Anne Pace-Nichols, and Augustus Napier, of the *Handbook of Family Development and Intervention* (Wiley, 2000). Dorothy is also a well-respected teacher and trainer who has been a member of the faculties of the University of Missouri-St. Louis, St. Louis University, Texas Tech University, Washington University, and Radford University and has presented workshops and taught courses, both nationally and internationally, on a wide variety of topics.

Raphael J. Becvar is a Clinical Member and Approved Supervisor with the American Association for Marriage and Family Therapy (AAMFT). He is also a Licensed Psychologist, a Licensed Marital

This material first appeared in Rosenthal, Howard. 2002. "The Marriage Counseling Mystique: A Candid Interview with Dorothy and Ray Becvar." From *Journal of Clinical Activities, Assignments, & Handouts in Psychotherapy Practice,* 2(4), pp. 83-94. Reprinted with permission.

and Family Therapist and in 1986 was designated a Fellow of the AAMFT. He has been a member of the faculties at St. Louis University (1969-1987); Texas Tech University (1987-1989); Lindenwood College (1989-1991); and Northeast Louisiana University (1994-1997). He has also maintained a part-time private practice in St. Louis, Missouri, since 1975. At St. Louis University, Ray created the doctoral program in Marriage and Family Development and Therapy and was also Director of Counselor Education. At Texas Tech University he served as Director of the Accredited Program in Marriage and Family Therapy. While at Lindenwood College he was Director of Programs in Counseling and Psychology. At Northeast Louisiana University he was the first to hold the Hanna F. Spyker Eminent Scholars Endowed Chair of Marriage and Family Therapy. Ray has published many articles in professional journals and is the author of *Skills for Effective Communication: A Guide for Building Relationships* (Wiley, 1974).

Dorothy and Ray have co-authored four books: *Family Therapy: A Systemic Integration* (Allyn & Bacon, 1988, 1992, 1996, 2000, 2003); *Pragmatics of Human Relationships* (Geist & Russell, 1998); *Hot Chocolate for a Cold Winter's Night: Essays for Relationship Development* (Love Publishing, 1994); and *Systems Theory and Family Therapy: A Primer* (University Press of America, 1982, 1999).

HR: *Ray, I remember the first time I met you. I was a doctoral student at St. Louis University and you were coteaching my first course, a proseminar in doctoral education, with the eminent educational philosopher J. J. O'Brien. You told the class that you were a marriage and family counselor who wasn't married and that Yul Brynner looked like you. Obviously you weren't married to Dorothy at the time. How did you two meet and why were you compatible?*

RB: We met at an AAMFT conference in Philadelphia. Dorothy was co-facilitating a preconference workshop. A friend talked me into attending that workshop with her. I found Dorothy bright, attractive, and she showed the most engaging smile. How did we find out we were compatible? I think that took time. Initially we danced well together (literally and figuratively). Over a courtship of almost two years we continued to do so and added many new steps.

HR: *Dorothy, why did you agree to get hitched to this guy and what makes your marriage successful?*

DB: Ray was a bachelor—an unclaimed treasure—and we clicked almost immediately. However, it was tough for him to decide to marry, let alone take on the role of stepparent to two children, ages ten and thirteen. When it got to the point that he was convincing me that it could work, I agreed. And after twenty-four years, I can say it has been very successful despite some major challenges, including the death of my son and my subsequent experience of breast cancer. Our marriage works because we have never let the honeymoon end, meaning that we have remained aware of the importance of nurturing our relationship. What we share is mutual acceptance, respect, support, and unconditional love.

HR: *Your marriage and family textbooks are some of the best in the field; the benchmarks if you will. When you were a youngster (say in elementary school) did you have visions of being a great therapist and textbook author when you grew up?*

DB: As a young child I had a sense that someday I would like to somehow make a significant contribution. However, I had no idea what that meant or how it would happen. After graduating from college, I was quite content to be a housewife and stay-at-home mom and am very grateful for having had that opportunity. It wasn't until after my divorce that I became interested in therapy. In the process of leading family enrichment programs for my church I found that I loved working with and helping people. It was only then that I returned for graduate training. As far as being an author, I suppose it is logical given my passion for reading—I am a certified biblioholic. I also find great joy in both teaching and writing, which provide other important vehicles for working with and helping others.

RB: I had childhood visions of being a cowboy, aviator, and baseball player. I didn't know what a therapist or an author was. I was a somewhat above-average student who looked forward to playing ball, fishing, riding my bike, shooting my BB gun, and roller-skating. My childhood was in a much earlier era in a very small town of 250 people. In that context, one could get excited about very simple things.

HR: *What sold you on the marriage and family paradigm? In your case Ray, I thought I heard that at one time you were a behaviorist or a Rogerian and that you even wrote an early book with a nondirective or communications slant.*

RB: My doctorate was in counseling psychology from a university that was philosophically consistent with empiricism, or what I now call the Modernist philosophical tradition. Behaviorism was a natural in that context in that one dealt and could speak about only that which was observable and verifiable. I was socialized to think and practice professionally in that profession. However, the semester before I took my qualifying exams I read a book by Watzlawick, Beavin, and Jackson, *Pragmatics of Human Communication,* that moved me in the direction of systems theory and marriage and family therapy. Ideas from that book sneaked into my responses to my qualifying exam questions much to the chagrin of my professors. They gave me an extra year to try again when I could demonstrate that they had socialized me appropriately. After much formal study and reflection, the jump to systems theory (at the level of first-order cybernetics) came into my life about three years after I came to St. Louis. Also, shortly after I came to St. Louis, I met and worked with and learned from a colleague whose interest was phenomenology and philosophy of science. I began to ask fundamental epistemological questions about how we know what we know, what can we know, what does knowing mean?, etc., etc., etc. To me, systems theory was a significant leap, but conceptually was very easy and exciting. It came to full flower when I spent a sabbatical semester studying at Brigham Young University where they had a well-respected program in marriage and family therapy. The idea of context, or necessarily being a part of a system, was a no-brainer. That to which we necessarily belong has no outside for us. We and our clients are always a part of and evolve "problems" in context.

DB: Systems theory and family therapy made immediate sense to me, giving me concepts to describe beliefs and behaviors that I already espoused. Since my undergraduate work was in political science and history, and I had never previously taken a course in psychology, there was nothing that I had to "unlearn" as I entered this world that so often seemed strange to others. I began working toward a master's degree in social work just two weeks after Ray and I were married, knowing that I wanted to do family therapy. During my first semester I took as an elective a course in the philosophy of the behavioral sciences and was introduced to the work of Gregory Bateson. Despite the fact that I was often criticized by some of my other professors because of my interest in systems thinking, I was convinced that it would provide an effective way to help clients.

HR: *When you work together as cotherapists are there ever times when you are thinking, "Where in the heck is he (or she) going with this intervention?"*

DB: Whenever we have had the opportunity to do cotherapy it has been an enjoyable experience. We think very much alike but typically behave in very different ways. It is therefore always intriguing to me to watch Ray's interventions and compare them with what I might have chosen to do, recognizing that there are many paths up the same mountain.

RB: We rarely work together as cotherapists, but those few times when we have done so, it has been fun. I think we are both very flexible in our thinking and have a wide repertoire of ways we can interact with our clients. I also think we both are secure enough to allow the other to "take charge."

HR: *Dorothy, I know that you embrace some of the concepts espoused via the alternative health care movement. Paul Zane Pilzer, a Harvard-trained economist and advisor to two U.S.*

presidents, suggests that this movement is on a par with the advent of the automobile or perhaps the creation of the personal computer. Is this really the next big thing? Will our fast-food burgers of the future be fortified with St. John's wort or perhaps 5-HTP granules?

DB: As a holistic thinker, I think it is extremely important that everyone have the opportunity to make recourse to the best of both allopathic and alternative health care options in order to be whole in body, mind and spirit. I do agree that this movement ranks right up there with cars and personal computers. However, I believe that what is most significant about it is the change in consciousness it signals, with greater awareness of the ability of people to facilitate their own healing, with acknowledgment that the healing process involves a team effort, and with recognition of the importance of not relinquishing control to the professionals.

HR: *Psychologists in New Mexico and Louisiana have a green light to prescribe meds. Is this a good thing or are we truly becoming a Prozac nation?*

DB: I believe that the goodness or badness of having more professionals who are appropriately trained and licensed to prescribe medication is something that can be decided only relative to context. If it means that there will be greater access for those who need medication, and even more important the follow-up and monitoring of prescribed medications, then it may be a good thing. If it means that more people will be given medication without first considering or choosing other options that may be more appropriate, then it may not be so good. I believe that if medication were the answer, then we would no longer have so many questions that remain unresolved.

RB: Medicating clients (patients) seems to be the current zeitgeist in the mental health field. In my opinion, the fact that psychologists seek and, as you say, may soon get prescription writing privileges also reflects the economic issues in today's professional practice. I think it is a good thing in that sometimes clients need medications under some, very limited circumstances. That being said, I question whether we need more people prescribing medications. I question whether children in crowded classrooms need medications to control them. I also wonder about the contexts in which the chemical "imbalances" evolve. I wonder whether one can change his or her own chemistry by changing lifestyle, diet, relationships, and work. As we move toward medicating people more and more and this becomes a part of the ideology of our society, these questions will not be asked. Medicating is a way of changing without having to work at changing.

HR: *And speaking of the health movement, Ray, you always seem to be in terrific physical condition . . . more like a Mr. Olympia contestant than say a therapist and a graduate professor. This is no small feat. Are you in the back room performing supersets of biceps curls and triceps presses between clients? What's your secret?*

RB: You used the phrase "you always seem to be in terrific physical condition" in your question. The key word is "seem," for the rest is illusion. I do work out. Historically, my diet has been terrible. I try not to gain weight. But then, is not all life illusion from different perspectives?

HR: *Freud once commented that, "Psychoanalysis is the administrator of the estate left by hypnotism." What is the relationship between hypnosis and the marriage and family model?*

RB: In one sense, hypnosis is a procedure that can be used by any therapist. In another sense, one could say that people in relationship hypnotize one another to perform the recursive dance that is any relationship. This can also be said of therapy, including marriage and family therapy. In a third sense, the literature describes hypnosis as an altered state of consciousness—is not any state of consciousness an altered state from the point of view of a different state of consciousness? What is the state of consciousness we call "awake"?

DB: Gregory Bateson, one of the fathers of family therapy, was formally introduced to the world of hypnosis and the ideas of Milton Erickson at two conferences held in New York City, the first on December 7, 1941, and the second on May 11-15, 1942. The title of the latter conference was "Cerebral Inhibition," which according to Bateson was nothing more than "a respectable word for hypnosis." When Bateson's research team in Palo Alto, California, later began studying communication, with a particular focus on the role of the paradoxes of abstraction in communication, they focused on such areas as animal play, the language of schizophrenics, popular movies, humor, guide dog training, and the work of Erickson. Out of this work emerged the double-bind hypothesis, the first articulation of the importance of relationships and context for understanding human behavior.

HR: *I know you met the late great Milton H. Erickson. What was he like as a person and a clinician? And by the way, why was he so darn effective?*

RB: Yes, I spent three days with him on two different occasions and during the second time, Dorothy and I went together. Both were wonderful experiences. Erickson the person and Erickson the clinician seemed to flow together. He enjoyed people. He enjoyed himself being the teacher having fun with his students. I was aware of and somewhat in awe of the legend of Milton Erickson, and in this sense I was hypnotized by this legend. For me, it became impossible to try to be aware of and understand what he was doing with us. In a sense I had to go with the flow, and allow myself to experience his presence and his work rather than trying to understand it. He gave me permission to be creative, and to violate the mainstream paradigm of professional practice. I think he gave his clients permission to be creative and to violate mainstream ideas and ways of living.

HR: *In my interview with Albert Ellis, he implied that Erickson and some of his followers might have . . . shall we say . . . exaggerated their cure rate. Any thoughts?*

DB: I do not know about the cure rate claimed by Erickson and his followers. I do know that Erickson was fond of saying that people come in with problems they cannot solve and that what we would do was give them problems they could solve. I believe he did this and was thus effective in helping many people.

RB: I'm not sure what "cure" means in our field. The metaphor "cure" fits the medical model, and I don't think that way about people's problems in living their lives. I find it more useful to help people deal with the problems they present. In this sense I am consistent with the philosophy of MRI. After problem one is solved, lets move on to problem two. I don't believe we can help people live problem-free lives. I think we can help them live with some problems, solve some problems, and deconstruct problems. Further, I think that the best source for deciding whether I am effective as a therapist is to ask my clients. Their subjective experience brings them to therapy. Their subjective experience is the most valid source of information about the effectiveness of any therapy or therapist.

HR: *How do accomplished therapists like you handle managed care and insurance companies? Many won't even pay for marriage and family therapy much less give you enough sessions to perform it correctly.*

DB: I have only ever worked with third-party payers as an out-of-network provider in instances in which the clients have chosen to facilitate the process and the diagnosis has been related to serious physical illness. In general, I am very sensitive to the ethics of making an individual diagnosis for problems that I see as relational in order to receive compensation and of having the therapy process guided by anyone not directly involved. My clients pay me and if requested, I will prepare a statement and complete insurance forms which they may submit for reimbursement, being aware that reimbursement may or may not be forthcoming. This is all discussed at the outset so that clients have the opportunity to decide whether or not they wish to proceed with me.

RB: I don't do insurance. I don't work with managed care companies. My practice is a pay-as-you-go experience. I have trouble
with the concept of someone sitting in an office making economic decisions about my clinical work. I choose not to invite
them into the therapy room. I also have a problem with the pri-
vacy of communications with insurance and managed care organizations. These records may follow clients in ways that may
not be helpful to them later in their lives. My fee is on a sliding
scale which is negotiated with my clients in much the same way
as the course of their therapy is negotiated with them.

HR: *Okay, what is the biggest mistake that clinicians make when
performing marriage and family therapy?*

DB: I think perhaps the biggest mistake occurs when one assumes
that family therapy is automatically happening when the entire
family is in the room. In many cases, what is occurring is individual therapy in the context of the family. By contrast, family
therapy occurs as a function of the way the therapist thinks, regardless of the number of people in the room. Accordingly,
there is a recognition of interdependence and an emphasis on
process rather than content; mutual influence is assumed as
therapists perturb rather than treat; all behavior is understood as
logical in context and subjectivity is acknowledged as inevita-
ble; the therapy process is created in ways that fit and acknowledge the uniqueness of each client system; the focus is on the
ways in which problems are being maintained and a related
search for solutions; there is awareness of the storied nature of
reality and the participation of each person in its creation;
both/and complementarities are valued; and the goals for therapy are those articulated by clients.

RB: I'm not sure I would call it a "mistake," but some therapists
practice in a way that is inconsistent with the systemic paradigm (at the level of second-order cybernetics). That is, marriage and family therapists often see themselves as independent
of their clients. They think they can be objective observers
standing outside the system with which they are working. If clinicians saw themselves as participant observers, they would be

aware that both the client(s) and the therapist cannot not influence one another. Thus the therapy is coconstructed by the client and the therapist. Further, as a second-order cybernetician, the therapist would be aware she cannot know what is "really" going on or what the problem "really" is. All they can offer are stories which may be useful, but not true with a capital "T." Referring to clients as "resistant" or "not wanting to change" or "in denial" is evidence of the violation of the systemic paradigm. It is very difficult in therapy to get "resistance" unless one is pushing or pulling. It is a recursive dance—it cannot be otherwise from a systemic perspective.

HR: *I have always admired your creativity. How can a therapist improve his or her creativity?*

DB: I think creativity can be improved as we seek ideas and information from a variety of areas, or make recourse to what Bateson called "sources of the random." In addition to reading professional journals, for example, I think it is helpful to read good fiction. Our creativity also is encouraged as we go to the theater, listen to music, participate in physical exercise, watch movies, spend time with friends and family members, travel, and generally explore other worlds, either literally or figuratively.

RB: I like to think of "creativity" as something that is illogical to context. That which is illogical to context is something that makes no sense from the frame of reference one uses to call it illogical. However, that which is illogical is always logical from a different perspective. Erickson seemed to be aware of the boxes in which people lived their lives. Watzlawick, Weakland, and Fisch in their book *Change*, describe logic and illogic and frames of reference brilliantly. Thus, being creative is easy—if more of the same or its opposite is not working, something illogical or crazy (as it is often viewed) will work.

HR: *Very briefly, for therapists who are new to the field, can you explain the concepts of paradox and the therapeutic double bind? Give us one clinical example where you used it.*

DB: I think it important for therapists who are new to the field to recognize that a paradoxical injunction is not just a technique and
is always logical from some frame of reference. It only appears
paradoxical from another frame of reference. For example, to
tell someone who is depressed that it is appropriate to feel depressed may seem paradoxical. However, if one assumes that
all behavior makes sense in context, then there is a logic to the
depression. If one tells the depressed person to cheer up, she or
he may feel not only depressed but guilty or bad because she or
he doesn't feel cheerful. This is, in fact, a be spontaneous paradox, asking someone to control a feeling or a behavior that is
outside of their control, which only exacerbates the problem.
Given such a perspective, therefore, it makes sense (is not paradoxical) to tell someone who is depressed that it is appropriate
to feel depressed. In this instance, the person may feel validated
and understood, which may participate in alleviating the depression.

RB: By paradox I assume you mean paradoxical injunction. Paradoxical injunction and therapeutic double bind are different.
Erickson used what I understand to be a therapeutic double-
bind when he asked clients whether they would like to change
slowly or quickly. The issue here is not about changing or not,
but how and when. Thinking systemically and espousing the
belief that the therapist should be in charge of the therapy, Jay
Haley might say to a client, "I think that you will not like it very
much when your son changes." A client's response might be, "I
will be very pleased." Haley would maintain his skepticism,
and if the son changed and the parent was upset, Haley was
right. If the son changed and the parent was not upset, that is the
desired outcome. Haley's is another therapeutic double bind,
but it is also a paradoxical injunction in that he prescribed the
symptom of being upset if the son changed.

HR: *Dorothy, this is probably the question everybody wants to ask
you but they feel it is too tacky. I'm going to take a risk and ask it
anyway! Are there ever times when Ray's behavior is a tad out
of line and you decide to paradox him to get him back on track?*

DB: Like most couples, I am sure, we do occasionally have our struggles. What may be different is our shared awareness that whatever we create, we do it together. So, if Ray is a "tad out of line," I always must consider my part in the process and recognize that if I want him to change, I also must be willing to change. Fortunately, first-order change strategies tend to be sufficient so that using paradoxical injunctions (second-order change) has never been part of our behavioral repertoire.

HR: *Ray?*

RB: First, I'm never a tad out of line. If I'm out of line, I do it in grand style. I don't think we use paradoxical injunctions with each other. In my opinion, we can and do respond to direct requests for change and doing more of or less of some behavior.

HR: *Thanks for sharing your knowledge and expertise! The next time a managed care company doesn't give me as many sessions as I want I think I'll hit them with a double bind or perhaps a little Ericksonian hypnosis!*

Chapter 4

Schmoozing with Bob Bertolino: Solution-Oriented Brief Therapy Is Coming to a Treatment Center Near You

Bob Bertolino, PhD, is an innovator in the field of counseling and psychotherapy who is dedicated to creating and promoting respectful and effective approaches that encourage hope, happiness, healthiness, and change in the lives of people. A therapist, author, and trainer, Bob has been described as "genuine and compassionate" and a "lighthouse" for others in an era of pessimism and diminishing hope. Bob has taught over 200 workshops throughout the United States, Australia, Canada, Finland, France, Germany, and the United Kingdom. His workshops have consistently been highly rated, offering hope and rekindling the spirits of both professionals and the general public.

Bob has authored or co-authored eight books, including *Change-Oriented Therapy with Adolescents and Young Adults: A New Generation of Respectful and Effective Process and Practices, Therapy with Troubled Teenagers: Rewriting Young Lives in Progress, Even from a Broken Web: Brief, Respectful Solution-Oriented Therapy for Sexual Abuse and Trauma, Collaborative, Competency-Based Counseling and Therapy,* and *The Therapist's Notebook for Families: Solution-Oriented Exercises for Working with Parents, Children, and Adolescents.* He is senior clinical consultant at Youth In Need, Inc., founder of Therapeutic Collaborations Consultation and Training, a training associate at the Institute for the Study of Therapeutic Change, and an assistant adjunct professor in the departments of counseling/family therapy and social work at St. Louis University,

Therapy's Best
doi:10.1300/5189_04

and rehabilitation counseling at Maryville University. Bob is licensed as a marital and family therapist, professional counselor, and clinical social worker in the state of Missouri, a National Certified Counselor, and a clinical member of the American Association for Marriage and Family Therapy.

HR: *Bob why did you become a therapist? Can it be traced back to your childhood? Did you always want to help people even as a youngster?*

BB: I sometimes joke with people and say that my first two career choices didn't pan out. First, I wanted to be a professional baseball player and that was followed by my desire to be a successful musician. When neither worked out for me I had to figure out what I was going to do with my life. I'm from a big family and that has had an extraordinary influence on becoming a therapist. My family is full of amazing, compassionate people. I've always felt cared about, loved, and supported. So it's easy for me to point to my family of origin and acknowledge that they have had a lot to do with my passion for helping others. I wouldn't say that I wanted to be a therapist at a young age, however, as cliché as it may sound, I've always wanted to help others. I feel the same about that now as I did as a younger person.

HR: *I am proud to say that you are a graduate of the school where I work as professor and program coordinator of human services— St. Louis Community College at Florissant Valley. I must insert a plug here and say that I, too, am a graduate of this remarkable institution of higher learning. Why did you attend a community college for the first two years rather than some expensive state or private school?*

BB: This question really speaks to a significant period in my life. My family lived in Massachusetts and I graduated high school there. Following graduation I stayed with friends and moved back at the end of the summer, just a few days before I started college. I first attended the University of Missouri–Columbia and had little direction in terms of my studies. I was too busy being a teenager and having fun. After a year and a half I came home to St. Louis and transferred to St. Louis Community College. It was a significant transition for me because the community college atmosphere provided a relaxed, safe context where I could have the freedom to study many different disciplines. I took classes in film, communications, theatre, and of course, human development. I really enjoyed the courses that focused on human interactions and growth. Once I finished my degree, it was very clear to me that I wanted to be in the helping professions. I just wasn't sure in what capacity. So I would say that St. Louis Community College was a spark for me—it prompted me to pursue a career in human services. It wasn't until later that I went to an expensive private school!

HR: *We have a lot of readers who are probably struggling with that age-old decision of whether to major in social work or counseling. Your undergrad was in social work, yet your graduate programs were in counseling. Why did you switch disciplines and do you have any advice beyond flipping a coin or blindly accepting the guidance of school department reps for those who are currently ambivalent?*

BB: Great question! I'm often asked this question because I teach in graduate counseling, family therapy, and social work programs. For me, it was initially a choice between majoring in social work or psychology. I knew many people who had bachelor's degrees in psychology and struggled to find jobs. On the other hand, the social workers I knew were all employed. And not just employed, they were working as social workers! By the time I decided to pursue a master's degree, I had been working in the field for a few years and I could make some distinctions between social work and counseling degrees. Although there are similarities between these advanced degrees, I chose the counseling route because I knew I would get the clinical focus I was seeking. At the time, it was a risky decision as a master's degree in social work carried more clout. That is, because of the tradition of social workers in various contexts, the degree was considered to be "better" by many. I made the right choice for myself because I wanted an advanced degree that focused almost exclusively on therapy.

HR: *I know you've co-authored several books with solution-oriented brief therapy (SOBT) pioneer Bill O'Hanlon. How did you meet him and what is he like on a personal level?*

BB: Let me first say that Bill is one of the most genuine and compassionate people I know. It is a privilege to call him a colleague and more important, a great friend. When you meet Bill you can sense his immeasurable knowledge that is based on reading, studying, therapeutic work, and life experiences. I would say that Bill is a student of life. I met him in the early 1990s when I wrote letters to a number of people in the field whose work I admired. Bill was the only one who responded. This was in the days when e-mail wasn't as established as it is now and people actually had to pick up the phone and write and mail letters to each other. Bill took the time to write back to me. I them went on to meet him. He's been a mentor, a teacher, a confidant, a co-author, and a friend. He and his wife, Steffanie, also played a pivotal role in my dissertation research. Steffanie is a wonderful friend as well and has been a great support to me over the years.

HR: *The late, great Milton H. Erickson personally trained O'Hanlon. My understanding is that Bill worked as Erickson's gardener and only work-study student, so to speak. Has Bill ever given you any insight into what his training was like with Erickson and why so many people consider Erickson such a psychotherapeutic genius?*

BB: Bill has spoken with me on countless occasions about Erickson's therapeutic prowess and ways of teaching people. Bill, like many others who studied with him, often didn't know when Erickson was teaching or just having him do work, such as gardening. Ever the thinker, as he would work in Erickson's garden, Bill often wondered whether Erickson was speaking in metaphor to him or whether he really didn't him to weed the garden. Since Erickson was so indirect, Bill was often looking for embedded meanings and trying to make some kind of sense about whatever it was that Erickson had said. The fact is that sometimes Erickson was teaching and other times he just wanted the garden weeded! Bill and I have spoken at length as to why many consider Erickson a therapeutic genius. I agree with him on all accounts. I'll share just a couple of them here. First, Erickson was one of the first to believe and focus on patient strengths. Erickson believed that his patients had abilities both within themselves and their social system to resolve their problems. He worked to *evoke* those abilities and *utilize* them in the service of change. This was seminal as most clinicians focused on patient deficits. Erickson believed that people had within them what they needed to resolve their concerns. It can be said that he was strengths-focused.

HR: *In a few sentences or less can you explain how SOBT differs from traditional modalities?*

BB: SOBT certainly represents an outgrowth of other models; however, it also differs significantly from those models. For example, SOBT has ties to Erickson's work, behavioral therapy, cognitive therapy, person-centered therapy, and strategic family therapy, just to name a few. On the other hand, there are significant differences, many of which lie within the philosophy that accompanies SOBT. Whereas many traditional modalities focus on impairments and deficits, discovering pathology, viewing the therapist as the expert, and emphasize the past and past events, clinicians utilizing a SOBT approach focus on competencies, abilities, and strengths, search for differences, exceptions, and solutions to problems, emphasize the present and the future, and view therapists and *clients* as being coexperts and collaborators in all aspects of the therapeutic milieu. It can be said that a major difference between SOBT and many traditional approaches is that the former draws attention to what people are capable of as opposed to what they are incapable of.

HR: *Bill O'Hanlon refers to his new approach as possibility therapy. How does it differ from his original methodology and is it true that some strict Ericksonians are not pleased with the direction he has moved in?*

BB: Possibility therapy is an outgrowth of SOBT. I see it as addressing some of the larger concerns that have plagued approaches that claim to be "brief" or aimed at "solutions." For example, oftentimes clinicians who are employing solution-based approaches tend to be too "positive." That is, they minimize problems or in some cases are even "problem phobic." This can be quite invalidating to clients who are suffering or in pain. A second concern that I see as leading to the development of possibility therapy is the lack of attention that is sometimes given the importance of the therapeutic relationship and alliance in solution-based therapies. Until recently there has been a distinct absence of literature discussing the importance of the therapist-client connection in solution-based approaches. Finally, possibility therapy is less formulaic. Instead of focusing on cookbook type questions, it is much more reliant on questions arising from therapeutic interactions. Possibility therapy, then, is much more of a collaborative approach. I do think it's important to say here that because therapists practice differently, it's unfair of me to stereotype therapists whose work is situated in briefer or solution-based approaches as being this way or that way. The overarching concern, I believe, is in some cases therapists can be "solution-forced" which is as concerning as being only problem-focused. Possibility therapy addresses this by offering an orientation that helps therapists to work with clients to acknowledge and validate their internal experience, understand their concerns and problems, identify strengths and solutions, and remain present to future-focused without downplaying the past.

In terms of Ericksonians' response to possibility therapy, there will always be those who agree or disagree with new directions that are taken. My concern is that we have allegiances with our clients, not our models. Allegiances to models only create boundaries, dissention, and unrest. If as clinicians we are committed to helping our clients then battle lines should not be drawn. There's a nice credo that I like to keep in mind whenever a new theory is developed: "Therapists buy theories, not clients." I think that says it all.

HR: *A lot of workshops and books in the field talk about using the miracle question when using solution-focused brief therapy with clients. Can you give us an actual example of how you used it and how you worded your question to make certain the rest of us are on the right track?*

BB: I'm glad you asked this question because it's an excellent opportunity to discuss the relevance of the "miracle question," how it is used, and some concerns I have with it. Let me start by saying that large-scale meta-analytic studies have demonstrated that a future-focus can be very helpful with clients (Duncan, Miller, & Sparks, 2004; Miller, Duncan, & Hubble, 1997; Wampold, 2001). By working with clients to create or rehabilitate a sense of the future we can learn what they want different in their lives. The miracle question is but one way of helping to gain a future focus. The concern I have with the miracle question is that clinicians can become so enamored with the actual technique that they begin to become formulaic in their approaches. While a future focus is important, we have to keep in mind that model and technique factors contribute very little to therapeutic outcomes (Duncan, Miller, & Sparks, 2004; Lambert, 1992; Wampold, 2001). I encourage therapists to be creative in working with clients to gain a future focus and not get so hung up on any technique, method, question, or other "intervention." So there are many possibilities for gaining a future focus. One is the miracle question. Others include "The Question," which was developed by Alfred Adler, "The Crystal Ball," which is derived from Milton Erickson's pseudo-orientation in time, or simply using future-orienting questions such as: "Let's say that as a result of us meeting together, the problem that brought you here was resolved. How would you know?" or, "How will you know when the problem is no longer a problem? What specifically will be better?" or "How will you know when you no longer need to come to therapy? What will be different?" (Bertolino, 2003; Bertolino & O'Hanlon, 2002). Let me give a brief example of how a future focus can be developed with a client.

A parent brought her son to see me because he was receiving failing grades in school. I asked the mother, "Let's say that a few weeks or months down the road your son has shown improvement in school. What kind of improvement would you need to see from him that would indicate to you that he was doing better and perhaps, no longer needed therapy?" The mother responded, "He would have better grades." "Better grades," I inquired. "What specifically do you mean by that?" I followed. The parent stated, "Well, he would be passing his classes. You know, at least receiving Ds."

For this particular parent, the future she was hoping for with her son was based on improved grades. Whether the miracle question or some other approach is used depends on the relationships we have with clients. What we want to do is keep in mind the importance of helping clients to determine what they want different in their lives and then figure out how to make the visions come to fruition. And while the miracle question is used frequently, it is just a technique and can alienate clients when it is overused or misused. I actually had a client, who had seen another therapist who frequently asked the miracle question, say to me: "Is that question in a book or something?"

HR: *Thanks! Okay, the other thing we hear a lot about in this approach is using so-called exception questions. Here again, do you have a good example to make this come alive for us?*

BB: Exception questions are designed to orient clients to times when their concerns or problems are less dominating or absent altogether from their lives. It's based on the idea that problems do not exist twenty-four hours a day. There are times when they are more or less dominating or severe. Our aim, then, is to explore with clients times when then they have had influence over their problems as opposed to their problems have influence over them. Examples of exception questions include: "Tell me about a time when the problem would typically occur, but it didn't." or "How far back would you have to go to find a time when the problem didn't affect you the way it has recently? What was different?" In many instances it's better to inquire about small differences, which are more palatable to clients. If we ask, "When doesn't the problem happen?" we're more likely to hear something like, "Never! It's always happening!"

To counter this we make sure we acknowledge and validate our client's internal experience (i.e., feelings) and ask about smaller exceptions. For example, I might say, "It seems like you've really been struggling with your concern. And as I sit here, I wonder how you've managed to make it to work on time everyday this week. How have you done it?"

Exception-oriented questions are crucial because they create a context where clients convince clinicians (not vice-versa) of their strengths, abilities, resources, and coping skills through actions they have already taken. Therapists merely ask questions that reorient clients to times when things have gone differently. Then clients are able to offer examples as to how they got the upper hand, to any degree, with their concerns. This makes clients experts on change.

HR: *Brief therapists often talk about performing Ericksonian hypnosis. How does this differ from the hocus-pocus, you're getting very sleepy and will never smoke another cigarette again, traditional version?*

BB: Another great question. I could write a volume or two on this. Traditional approaches to hypnosis are based on the idea that some people are hypnotizable and some are not. From an Ericksonian perspective, all persons have the ability to go into trance. Examples might include driving a car and spacing out, not hearing someone calling your name, or *forgetting* you have to go to the bathroom during an intense scene in a movie. All of these involve intense focusing on some particular thing while other aspects of a person's surroundings are dropped out of his or her experience. So instead of having an actual *induction*, most Ericksonians begin trance with stories, metaphor, or by reorienting people to previous trance-like experiences or familiar situations. This allows clients to become experientially immersed and absorbed.

Second, with traditional approaches to hypnosis there tends to be much more on direct suggestion (e.g., "You *will* go into trance," "You *are* experiencing a lifting of the hand."). Those working within the Ericksonian tradition tend to be more permissive with language by saying, "You can," "You might," or

"You could," for example. This gives clients choices to do what is right for them.

A third distinction I would like to highlight here is that therapists practicing within the Ericksonian tradition hold the general belief that clients have most of the answers they need within themselves to resolve their concerns. This means that Ericksonians *evoke* client strengths, abilities, and resources, and, *utilize* whatever clients bring to therapy as fodder for change. Clients are truly seen as the primary agents of change.

HR: *SFBT is often presented in textbook chapters along with narrative therapy and other so-called postmodern or constructivist approaches. For those of us . . . me included . . . who have been out of school for eons of time, can you briefly explain what these approaches are and if, in indeed, you feel they are truly second cousins to SFBT?*

BB: Many of the so-called "newer" approaches to therapy, what Bill and I sometimes refer to as "third-wave" approaches (Bertolino & O'Hanlon, 2002), are often lumped together in texts. They do fall under a postmodern umbrella in that they share the premise that there are multiple realities and ways of viewing and understanding the world. In addition, there is a common thread that links these approaches together—it's social constructionism. This is a philosophical terms that relates to how people create meaning through language and interaction. Both problems and solutions, therefore, are embedded in social discourse. Because language and interaction are primary means by which we facilitate change, it makes sense to work as anthropologists to learn the impact of context (i.e., culture, family background, religious/spiritual beliefs, etc.) on our clients' lives. By understanding that problems can be created in language and interaction, we help clients to "restory" or "reauthor" new narratives of hope and change.

A downside is that there are distinct differences between these models which are sometimes lost when these models are lumped together. For example, narrative therapists tend to emphasize how problems are the result of oppression, whether it's cultural, societal, economic, familial, religious, or some other influence. The idea is that the person is never the problem. The problem is the problem. So focus is on separating people from there problems by helping them to form relationships with their problems. For example, a narrative therapist might say, "How has anger managed to sneak into your life?" This is a very different way of talking with people.

Some of the other models that are typically considered post-modern, such as solution-oriented and solution-focused therapies, are not based on the same philosophical tenets as say narrative therapy or the collaborative language systems approach. We are certainly talking about a paradigm that continues to emerge; however, I believe we are still in its infancy stages. As we do more research and gather more anecdotal information I think we will see more and more written about these models in texts. I also think there will be further comparative analysis in terms of how these models are both different and similar from one another.

HR: *Is SOBT always the treatment of choice? You know . . . you hear the criticisms that it doesn't really focus on one's childhood, it's over before the client's chair gets warm, or it doesn't target the underlying cause of the behavior, or it is based on a limited number of clever techniques.*

BB: No model works with every client all the time. In fact, I think the rigidity of how models are taught and utilized is quite a problem. What Bill and I have tried to do in our clinical, teaching, and writing is emphasize the human element in therapy. It is important to have a good understanding of the client's story, what his or her concerns are, what there ideas are as to how change has occurred in the past and how it might occur in the future, and what strengths, abilities, and resources the client brings into the therapeutic milieu that we can help him or her to utilize in the service of change. In my mind, a therapist who is working respectfully with a client will pay close attention to what the client wants. This sometimes means searching for an explanation to a problem. A major distinction, however, would be that I would not enter a session believing that I must find *the* underlying cause for the client to improve. In so many cases we will never know what the cause of a problem is. As I mentioned earlier, there are multiple influences in people's lives. What I'm interested in finding out is what clients see as influences on their problems and them working with them in ways that match those perspectives. I believe this is what effective therapists, not just those working within a SOBT philosophy do.

The other thing I would add here is there is a risk with any approach that techniques can become too large of a focus in therapy. SOBT is similar to other approaches in that there are certain techniques that have gained notoriety (e.g., the miracle question, scaling questions, the first session task, etc.). I believe (and this is what studies have continued to demonstrate) that methods, models, and techniques must fit with our clients' worldviews and ideas about change. I think that is the respectful route and very different from the assembly-line, medical model approach that all clinicians must be wary of.

HR: *Is SOBT a successful form of multicultural counseling and does it work well when counseling gays and lesbians?*

BB: This question speaks to how SOBT is taught and practiced. If it is taught and practiced in a way that flowcharts and techniques are the main focus then I think there is a risk that cultural sensitivity can be lost. This is because the human element is minimized by leaving the most significant contributor to change, clients, out of the therapeutic process. Bill and I emphasize several important points that we believe makes SOBT an excellent form of multicultural counseling (Bertolino & O'Hanlon, 2002). For example, we take great care to understand each and every client's story. We ask ourselves, "Who is this person?" If you've ever seen the movie *Amistad,* directed by Steven Spielberg, this idea is illustrated very well. As mentioned previously, we also pay close attention to what clients see as influence on their concerns and problems. We don't assume. We ask. We ask clients to teach us about their lives, their traditions, their rituals, and so on. Clients are our best teachers. We then work with clients in ways that are respectful of how they live and breathe in the world. Because of this close attention to client worldviews and an utmost respect for people, I believe SOBT offers an excel-

lent way of working with gays, lesbians, bisexual, and trans-
gendered individuals.

HR: *What's the biggest myth that counselors who practice other
modalities have about brief therapy?*

BB: Wow, this is a difficult question to answer briefly—one that's
worthy of a dissertation! But let me focus in on one specific
myth. I think the biggest myth that counselors who practice
other modalities is that brief therapists are shallow in their work
with clients. I think this is a belief that counselors are not getting to the "underlying issue" and are being "superficial." I actually find the term "brief" misleading. In my opinion it's irrelevant. Therapy takes as long as it does. What makes therapy
briefer is a focus on working with clients on specific goals and
not aiming for personality transformation or believing that we
must help people to have problem-free lives. Who has a problem-free life? Brief therapists are not shallow in their work,
they are merely working with clients on their concerns as opposed to letting our theories tell us what is wrong and what to
do about it. This is consistent with the general practitioner
model that is used by medical doctors. MDs want to learn from
you what you are concerned about and then they explore treatment alternatives for the presenting problem. For example, if
you go to your doctor and tell him or her you have a sore throat,
he or she does not ask you about your left foot. Yet this is precisely what we often do in therapy. A client comes in and says,
"I think I'm depressed. I have these negative thoughts that I
know aren't true about me, but I still keep having·them." The
therapist then says, "Tell me about your family. What are they
like?" This is therapy that is theory-driven. Why should a therapist let his or her theory guide the session? What I am suggesting is that we take the time to learn from clients what their concerns are and then continue this collaborative process by creating
and offering ways of addressing their concerns that fit with
their views. This is respecting clients as the engineers of change.
    I'd like to mention one other thing about brief therapy that is
often misunderstood. If we are going to work in ways that are
considered briefer, I think we have to be very good at strength-

ening the therapeutic relationship and alliance. Studies continue to demonstrate that client ratings of the therapeutic relationship and alliance are the most consistent and best predictors
of outcome (Gurman, 1977; Horvath & Symonds, 1991; Duncan & Miller, 2000; Duncan, Miller, & Sparks, 2004; Kopp,
Akhtarullah, Niazi, Duncan, & Sparks, 2001; Lafferty, Beutler,
& Crago, 1989; Lambert & Bergin, 1994). In addition, the
strength of the therapeutic bond is not highly correlated with
the length of treatment (Horvath & Luborksy, 1993). In other
words, although it takes longer for some clients to feel connected with us, many will feel connected right away. And as an
analogy, most people trust their medical doctors even though
they may only see them once in a while. In working briefer with
people, we need to develop strong connections, otherwise we
will not have the rapport needed to help them to take action to
change their lives.

HR: *Most of the experts included in this work take a dim view of
managed care and the way that insurance companies handle
payment for treatment. Is SOBT the exception since it is very
time-limited . . . not a lot of sessions . . . precisely the thing these
folks seemingly want to keep their costs down?*

BB: Managed care has certainly had a significant impact on the field
as a whole. SOBT does offer a very nice fit because it focuses
on immediate concerns that clients have. I would add that SOBT
also fits nicely in a managed care climate because what I refer
to as a "revolving door" philosophy. Specifically, there are many
brief therapists who see clients for a handful of sessions, or until a problem is no longer a problem. Then, as with medical doctors, they leave the door open for clients to return in the future if
the problem reoccurs or if they experience a different ailment.
This is precisely what we do with our medical doctors. Although there is no stigma about returning to see your medical
doctor, there does seem to be one when it comes to returning to
see a counselor once you've terminated services. That makes
little sense to me. I think we should provide services to people
when they first request them and extend an invitation to return
in the future if they need to. Although SOBT is about as man-

aged-care friendly of an approach that we have, it is client-driven. Clients are transitioned out of services when both the therapist and client agree that therapy is no longer necessary.

HR: *How many sessions do you think the average client actually comes to you for therapy?*

BB: Most studies indicate that regardless of the model employed, clients only attend a handful of sessions—usually six to ten (Garfield, 1989; Koss & Butcher, 1986; Levitt, 1966; Miller, 1994). In my experience the average with SOBT is between four and eight sessions. Having said that, I've seen clients both long- and short-term. It is not the length of therapy that is the issue, but whether clients are benefiting from the services provided.

HR: *Just curious: Are you for or against nonmedical therapists prescribing meds?*

BB: This is issue has been raised in several different states with psychologists, in particular. For me, this issue of medication looms large in North America. In other parts of the world we don't medicate so much. I have to say that I don't feel I'm informed enough about the arguments on both sides to take a stance on the issue. At the heart of the matter, however, is what we are promoting as psychologists, counselors, therapists, social workers, and as a profession that advocates for treatment approaches that are likely to produce the best results with the least side effects. I think that the more we advocate for professionals other than medical doctors to prescribe psychotropic medications the more we get away from our mission of promoting psychotherapy, which we know has far less side effects and is much more cost-effective than medication therapy.

HR: *By the way, a lot of counselors have embraced coaching. Are you involved with this and how does it differ from mainstream counseling and psychotherapy?*

BB: Coaching is certainly an in vogue movement these days. I see it as a cousin to counseling and psychotherapy. My work with clients can involve coaching as many people are not necessarily seeking to resolve problems, they are exploring new life or career directions. I am concerned that anyone can call himself or herself a coach with little or no training or educational background in mental health. The fact remains that even when coaching clients there is the possibility of other "stuff" coming up that a coach may or not be prepared to deal with. I have the same concern about people other than psychotherapists using hypnosis. At core we are working with human beings who can and do respond in a myriad of ways to both traditional and non-traditional approaches. This, I believe, necessitates appropriate training and supervision.

HR: *Okay, let's switch gears here. I often joke with my college students and tell them that "most of you think you want to work with adolescents or clients who have addictions but most of you will discover you want to work with neither." You have written extensively about working with adolescents. Just why are adolescents so darn hard to help?*

BB: Great question, Howard. To me adolescents are very exciting to work with. Oftentimes we think that because we've been one (an adolescent) we know what kids need. Then when they don't respond as well as we would have liked we sometimes become frustrated. Adolescents are challenging for so many reasons. They are still developing individually, they are in families that are evolving, and there are outside influences such as peers, drugs, and society (just to name a few) that all can influence their lives. When we begin to understand that the problems adolescents and families experience are typically multilayered therapy becomes more challenging. And of course, how many adolescents do we know who want to attend counseling? Still, I believe that when we are able to establish strong relationships with adolescents, the opportunities and possibilities for positive change increase dramatically. So my advice to those who may be changing their minds about working with adolescents is to stay with it! These teenagers need us and sometimes change is three steps forward and two steps backward.

HR: *If you could give every counselor and therapist just one secret you've discovered to help troubled teens in treatment, what would it be?*

BB: Always believe that the possibility of positive change exists. When you have a philosophy that change is possible, there are so many more options. The minute we start seeing adolescents as "defiant," "oppositional," "unmotivated," or through some other lens of negativity, it's the minute we become just another person who is giving up or already has given up on him or her. Philosophy is everything.

HR: *What's the dumbest thing parents do with their adolescents who misbehave?*

BB: This is a tough question because I think most parents have good intentions and are doing the best they can. Nonetheless, myself included, we can find ourselves repeating patterns that just don't work and may even make things worse. There's the old saying, "Insanity is doing the same thing over and over and expecting different results." So I would have to say that parents who recognize what isn't working and change things through creative thinking and action are less likely to become frustrated and give up.

    If I could, I would like to add one other comment here. I think consistency is a big issue in parenting. Many parents give a consequence then back down from it. Or, they change the rules to make their lives easier. Parenting can be challenging. But we often complicate things when we aren't consistent with adolescents and make idle threats. Consistency is a must!

HR: *What do you do when one of a therapist's greatest nightmares becomes a reality? . . . I'm referring to that unfortunate situation when the teen and the parent get into a stealth bomber*

powered argument right in front of you during the therapy ses-
sion and the screaming is so loud it wakes the newborn baby
three blocks away.

BB: In situation such as this, it's important to remember that we
have an ethical obligation to protect our clients. Just because a
certain behavior happens at home, doesn't make it okay. So
when I have adolescents and parents arguing to the point of being disrespectful and possibly even abusive, I first work to interrupt the pattern. I do this by acknowledging and validating
the feelings (internal experience) of each person involved and
simultaneously hold each responsible for his or her actions. For
example, I might say to an adolescent, "It's okay to be so angry
at your mom that you'd like to yell at her and it's not okay to
yell at her." I give permission for internal experience but not
permission for actions that may be harmful to self or others. In
situations where the arguing continues, I separate adolescents
and parents/caregivers. I have to say that more often than not,
the acknowledgment of internal experience works well. It's fairly
rare that I have to separate people.

HR: *What constitutes bad therapy when working with teens?*

BB: This is a hard question to answer. I think there are three risks we
face as counselors working with adolescents. First, when what
we are doing isn't working we do more of it. As I mentioned before, we do more of the same and expect adolescents to respond
to our methods. I think it's a mistake on the part of counselors to
keep repeating unhelpful methods. Next, when we're stuck
with adolescents we start creating explanations such as, "He
has to get worse before he gets better." That's a dangerous idea
and completely unfounded. It's an excuse coming from the
mouth of a frustrated therapist. Last, we tend to give more severe diagnosis when adolescents aren't changing as we had
hoped. We start doling out personality disorders, for example.
Again, I think this is representative of counselors' frustrations
with adolescents. Each of the pathways to impossibility I think
could potentially represent "bad therapy" and are things we
need to guard against.

HR: *You are obviously a rising star in the psychotherapeutic community. What is the mind-set that makes Bob Bertolino so successful?*

BB: That is very kind of you to say, Howard. I really think that philosophy is the driving force behind what I do and what I try to teach. We can teach methods, models, and techniques. There are over 400 models of psychotherapy available to us. Conversely, it's much more challenging to teach philosophy. My mind-set is that positive change is always possible. I'm not talking about being "positive" here. I'm talking about being hopeful and realistic. I always keep in mind an acronym that I came up with a while back. It's H.O.P.E. "H" stands for humanism. We need to have a human connection with our clients. It's those core conditions that Carl Rogers spoke of. The "O" is for optimism. We need to be optimistic that change can occur even in the most challenging of situations. When we have a healthy sense of optimism there are more possibilities for change, which is the "P." And finally, there's the "E," which stands for expectancy. We should expect change to occur with our clients. Hope is not the only condition necessary for change, it's a catalyst. The presence or absence of hope can have enormous effects on change. And let me add here that it's not enough to have a philosophy about change. As counselors we must "walk the talk." We need to first believe in what we are doing and then put it into action with our clients.

HR: *I know I'm asking you to reveal a trade secret, but here goes: Every time I turn around I see you are teaching part-time at another institution of higher learning. Do you wait until the college or university runs an employment ad in the newspaper? Do you approach them even when no job opening is evident? Do you blow them away with your credentials in the interview? Do you have a special curriculum vita that baits them? What's your secret? Perhaps we need to share it with Richard Bolles (also interviewed in this book) so he can include it in his next edition of his well-known job-hunting guide* What Color Is Your Parachute?

BB: I have been very fortunate in this area. Usually universities contact me and ask me if I am interested in teaching a course and if I am available, I typically do it. I love teaching and I love being part of helping students to evolve both personally and professionally. I don't think you can affect one without affecting the other. I wish I could say that I have some sort of formula, but I really don't. I continue to write, teach, and see clients and hopefully my work in these areas will continue to speak for itself!

HR: *Bob, it would be an understatement to say that you have done a lot of lectures and presentations. Can you give our readers a few tips for becoming a good speaker? Do you attempt to project a certain image of yourself? Also, a lot of neophyte counselors and therapists are squeamish about accepting money for their presentations. Any thoughts?*

BB: This is something that I've really had to learn. I must admit, I am my own worst critic. I always want to improve as a speaker. I want to connect with people and offer them useful and practical information. I've watched hundreds of speakers and have learned a lot from them. There are many things I've learned that have been very helpful. First, always be respectful of the audience. Acknowledge other's points of view. Don't embarrass them if they ask a question that seems out of context, in appropriate, or something you've already answered. Always treat people with respect and be genuine. I think that is the most important advice I can offer. Next, you can't be an expert on everything. There are topics I speak on and others I won't. When someone approaches me about speaking about something that I feel is out of my area of expertise, I refer that person to someone who knows more about the subject matter. Another thing I've learned is to use multiple ways of engaging people. Because some people are more visual, or auditory, or kinesthetic, I think it's important to enhance the information offered through lecture by using visual aids (e.g., PowerPoint, video, etc.) and/ or experiential exercises. You won't please everyone all the time, but read evaluations and learn from them.

HR: *Let's say a counselor wants to write his or her first book. Is there any advice you would give him or her?*

BB: I think there are so many people who have great ideas but never muster up the courage or strength to share them with others. I always encourage people to write their ideas down. I have literally a dozen notebooks and journals with ideas in them. At some point they become books. It reminds me of a story I heard about Ray Bradbury. During a lecture, he was once asked by an audience member, "How do I get in the mood to write?" Bradbury responded, "Sit down and start writing young man. It will get rid of all those moods!" So the first thing is to sit down and start writing. It will help one to improve as a writer and develop his or her own voice. I think it's also important to choose an audience for your book, develop a strong outline, a couple of sample chapters, and a proposal that will hook in editors at publishing houses. Then research book companies to find one that will provide the best fit for your proposal. There are hundreds of book companies that are looking for great ideas and writers. It's common to have proposals rejected. I met Peter Vegso, the owner of Health Communications (HCI), the company that has made the "Chicken Soup" books a publishing phenomenon. He told me that over 200 publishing houses turned down Jack Canfield before HCI published the first chicken soup book. The same can be said about Scott Peck and *The Road Less Traveled.* Be persistent, and as you would with your clients, don't give up!

HR: *Assume you are personally having the ultimate day from hell. Do you have a pet self-help strategy you employ?*

BB: Self-care. I go for a walk, listen to music, talk with colleagues or friends, and listen to my internal dialogue. We all have rough days and we can only be helpful to our clients when are in tune with and feeling okay about ourselves. Once again, I would encourage counselors to walk the talk.

HR: *All right, time for a few rapid-fire questions. They (whoever the heck they are, in my case I believe it was a couple graduate professors) say that you can tell a lot about a person based on the*

vehicle that he or she drives. What type of wheels are you get-
ting around in and what type of house, condo, or townhouse do
you live in?

BB: I have a 1999 Isuzu Rodeo, which will get me through any type
of weather conditions. I also live in a townhouse.

HR: *What would I find in the tape or CD player of your vehicle right*
now?

BB: U2. I've first heard U2 in high school and their music absolutely speaks to my soul. I think Bono is an amazing person.
He is not only a gifted artist but an influential social activist. He
continues to advocate for human rights and issues related to
AIDS in Africa and debt in third-world countries. I would love
to meet him!

HR: *Favorite movie with a psychological plot and why?*

BB: There are so many I could list. But I would have to say that
Good Will Hunting is my favorite. I think there are so many
themes that occur throughout the movie and it is one of the few
films that actually portrays a counselor (Sean, Robin Williams'
character) in a favorable way. It's a very touching film.

HR: *Best counseling and therapy book ever written, excluding your*
own?

BB: *The Heroic Client* by Barry Duncan, Scott Miller, and J. A.
Sparks. All are terrific writers and innovators in our field.

HR: *If Bob Bertolino had decided not to go into the field of psycho-*
therapy and mental health treatment, what would he be doing
today?

BB: Playing professional baseball or working as a musician.

HR: *The year is 2050. What type of counseling and psychotherapy*
will be in vogue?

BB: I see the field as moving toward more client-informed, collaborative, and outcome-oriented approaches. Services are more likely to be driven by outcomes than models in the future. That is, regardless of the model employed, we will be asking if our clients are achieving specific outcomes. And when they are benefiting from services, what are the factors that are contributing to that change? This is already happening in our field and is something I write about and teach about.

We are also learning a lot from neurological studies that tell us what happens to the brain and how that affects the body when people are exposed to trauma, abuse, stress, and so on. Practitioners and researchers such as Bessel van der Kolk are making significant strides in this area. This can only help us to refine our approaches. I find this particularly important given the world we live in and will likely continue to experience in the year 2050.

Finally, there is quite a movement toward nontraditional approaches (e.g., EMDR, TFT, EFT, etc.) in our field that I think will continue to evolve and gain notoriety. These approaches blend Eastern and Western philosophies and challenge many of the long-held traditional assumptions we have about people and change. We will need more much more research on these approaches, which are primarily sensory-based, but they are very intriguing and have shown promise.

HR: *Bob, thanks. You are a wealth of information and an inspiration to all of us!*

BB: Thank you, Howard! The pleasure has been all mine!

Chapter 5

Flying High with the World's Best-Known Job-Hunting Counselor: Richard Nelson Bolles

HR: *Was there any foreshadowing in your childhood that would have predicted you would grow up to become an icon in the job-hunting and career counseling field?*

RB: "An icon," huh? Well, no. Absolutely nothing foreshadowed it. First of all, I was painfully shy—and I mean "painfully." After high school, and a short term in the U.S. Navy, I was aiming at a career in chemical engineering—working primarily with "data" and "things," rather than "people." No one sifting through the "tea leaves" of my young life at that point would ever have predicted where it would end up. I came from a journalistic family: my grandfather was editor of the *Janesville Daily Gazette,* in Wisconsin; my father was an editor for the Associated Press in New York City; my brother, Don, was a reporter for the *Arizona Republic* in Phoenix. Today, one might claim in hindsight that I have become a kind of investigative reporter myself, focusing on the job hunt and career-change. But who would have guessed that?

HR: *My understanding is that you self-published the first edition of* What Color Is Your Parachute? *using a local San Francisco copy shop. What was the deal? Were agents and editors clueless that your manuscript would later sell more than eight million copies? Were they unable to see that you had written what would become the best selling job-hunting book of all-time?*

Therapy's Best
© 2006 by The Haworth Press, Inc. All rights reserved.
doi:10.1300/5189_05

And just for the record, did you ever in your wildest dreams think that the book would sell 20,000 copies per month for the next thirty years?

RB: To answer the latter question first, "Did I ever dream . . ." the answer is "Of course not! Not in a million years!" To answer the question about why I self-published it, some four years prior to *Parachute* I had a bad experience with a publisher. They had asked me to write a book about a particular subject (turning a community from one that only met their own needs, to one that was outwardly focussed on helping others in need). I slaved over this book in my spare time for a year, and then when I had it done, they declined to publish the work they had commissioned, claiming "interest in this subject has passed." So, when I was inspired to write *Parachute* four years later (in 1970) I didn't even think of taking it to a publisher. I self-published it— took it to a local copy shop, as you mentioned. However, after self-publication three advocates/friends of mine sent the book off, without my knowledge, to three different publishers, and all three turned it down. Time moved on, and then, in 1972, out of the blue, a small publisher in Berkeley, California (Ten Speed Press) approached me and asked permission to publish it commercially. I instinctively trusted the man I met, Phil Wood, who was and is the owner of Ten Speed Press, and it is with him and only him that I have published for the last thirty-two years, even though other publishers (upon seeing the tremendous success of *Parachute*) have tried, over the years, to win me away from Ten Speed.

HR: *Has your work been influenced by any of the major career theorists such as Anne Roe, John Holland, or Donald Super?*

RB: In order to answer that, I need to sketch some background. That is, the whole field of career or vocational experts divides broadly into two camps. The one camp contains the theorists about the why and wherefore of career choice—usually psychologists, by background—a group that historically includes the people you just named, plus John Crites, and others. The other camp contains the practitioners, who deal with the nitty-gritty, step-by-step business of the job hunt—usually job counselors by background—a group that historically includes John Mills of General Electric, Sidney and Mary Edlund, Bernard Haldane, Richard Lathrop, John Crystal, and myself.

Often, these two camps do not communicate with each other, are not really familiar with the thoughts of the other, and so on. Standing in that tradition, I am familiar with the work of the "major career theorists" but it is only John Holland and Sidney Fine that have really influenced my own thinking and outlook.

HR: *Do you put much stock in the Freudian notion of sublimation (i.e., that the job is a socially acceptable way of fulfilling an unconscious impulse)? You know, a person who likes to cut people might become a surgeon rather than a Jeffrey Dahmer to satisfy his needs and make his Mercedes payment.*

RB: As a practitioner, this notion is of no interest to me. Plus it strikes me as nuts. On the other hand, were I a theorist, I would of course contemplate it long and hard, inasmuch as a theorist is anxious to speculate about all the motivations that drive people, in the work sphere. I am not. I just want to help them find an appropriate job—one that matches their favorite portable skills, their major interests, and most-desired people environment.

HR: *What about career counseling tests? Any preferences?*

RB: Don't much care for tests, sad to say. A "test," or more accurately, "an assessment instrument," is simply a comparison—and often a faulty and misleading one, at that. Every "assessment" is simply saying, at its heart, "Here's what we know about other people who chose the same answers as you did. This may or may not give you some ideas about your own choices." That is not, of course, how the results are usually interpreted by either test taker or administrator. "According to this, you should be . . ." is the usual way test administrators interpret the results.

HR: *What's the dumbest thing people do when they draft a résumé?*

RB: Expect it to get them a job. All a résumé should ever have as its purpose, is to get them an interview. Smart people know:

résumé gets interview (maybe); interview gets job (and again, maybe). Hence they put in their résumé only that which will get them an invitation to come in for an interview.

HR: *When individuals write a résumé should they use a specific job objective (e.g., Seeking a position as a chemical dependency counselor in an outpatient setting) or a generic or general objective (e.g., Seeking a position in the counseling field)? It seems that either approach would have its pros and its cons.*

RB: This depends entirely on the preference of the interviewer you are trying to get in to see. If he or she prefers that your résumé have a specific job objective, then obviously you should use a specific job objective. On the other hand, if he or she prefers a generic or general objective, then you should use a generic or general objective. The problem, of course, is that you don't know which the interviewer prefers. And in a blanket mailing or "posting" of your résumé, you're trying to cover many employers—a group that includes both preferences. This is why a résumé is not the best way to approach employers, and never has been . . . Period. Instead, choose which employers you'd like to work for (whether or not they are known to have a vacancy) and then ask all your contacts (everyone you know) if they know someone who works there. If they put in a good word for you with the person there who has the actual power to hire, you can get an interview on their say-so, rather than because of your résumé. (This works best, of course, with small organizations—not the ones that occupy four city blocks.) Don't drop the idea that your résumé may be useful to you further down the line. Committees are often involved in the decision to hire, so your interviewer needs to be able to later bring the others "up-to-speed." Hence, the old, wise adage: "A résumé is something you should never send ahead, but always leave behind (after the interview)." After the interview, if it goes well and this place interests you, you should (truthfully) tell the employer that you didn't bring your résumé with you (don't!) but will send it over as soon as you get home. Once home, that evening, rewrite your résumé for that employer, and that job, putting into your résumé the exact job-objective you learned in the interview that the employer wants. That's *the employer.* And you. Send it by overnight mail, or by e-mail *and* overnight mail.

HR: *Assume I'm seeing a client for career counseling. He's a male, he's job-hunting, and wants to approach a particular place through a résumé and cover letter. Is there something I can suggest to him that will make his cover letter stand out as clearly superior to the rest of the pack?*

RB: Yes. Tell your client to research the place every which-way he can (Internet, library, present or past employees he may know, picking up that place's literature, etc.) and then in the cover letter mention some things that he particularly likes or admires about that place. (Places love to be loved, just as people do.) That will make him stand out.

HR: *Now that same client is set to go to a job interview. There's what . . . maybe a 98 percent chance that the interviewer will ask about his strengths and weaknesses? Discussing his strengths shouldn't be a problem . . . but what does he say when questioned about his weaknesses? Should he rely on the old ploy: "Gee I tend to work too hard" or whatever, in order to mention a faux weakness which is really a strength?*

RB: There's a popular approach to preparing for the interview, which suggests your client should memorize the 100 or so most common questions that he is likely to be asked; and then be ready with a "canned" answer to each. The question you just posed belongs to that "school" of thought. Experienced interviewers have heard every one of these canned answers. I prefer, instead, an entirely different approach that consists of teaching your client to memorize only three simple rules for any interview. First, *try to let the interviewer speak half the time; while you speak the other half.* In other words, a fifty-fifty conversation, timewise. The second rule is: *when you are asked a question by the interviewer, your answer to each question should last between twenty seconds to two minutes.* No more. If you need more time for that question, say, "I could amplify this if you wish." If the interviewer nods affirmatively, then continue, but for no more than two minutes more. Third rule: *put yourself in the chair, and mind-set, of the interviewer.* As the interviewer asks each question, ask yourself "Were I the interviewer, why would I ask a question like this?" Hint: the interviewer often asks questions about your past, in order to try to predict your future—with them, should they hire you. This moment of thought should give you useful guidance in deciding how to answer.

HR: *Is the old rumor that interviewers focus more on shoes than any article of clothing true? Should we be cracking open our old tins of parade wax and finish up with a spit shine?*

RB: In preparing for interviews, "generalizations" like this should be avoided *like the plague!* To begin with, there is no such thing as "interviewers." They are not a "group," of one mind and one body. They are a whole bunch of separate individuals, each of whom has a different opinion about almost anything you can name. Some interviewers will never even notice your feet; others may focus on them. So, the advice of the best experts is: "Play it safe. Go to any interview with your hair cut, washed, and neatly combed, teeth brushed and breath sweet, clothes newly washed or dry-cleaned, and shoes neatly shined."

HR: *Persons A and B are equally qualified for the position. However, person B gets the job. What generally makes person B superior in the interview?*

RB: Person B approaches the interview not as "a job beggar" (to quote Daniel Porot) but as "a resource to help the employer." Person B is thinking primarily of what he or she can do for the employer, not primarily about what the employer can do for him or her. And, Person B sends a thank-you note after the interview.

HR: *On your Internet site, www.jobhuntersbible.com, you suggest that the 9/11 terrorist attacks changed the face of job-hunting. What impact did this monumental tragedy have?*

RB: Whenever events like September 11th occur, they cause the equivalent of an earthquake in the job market. Hence, I call this "a workquake." The characteristic of a "workquake" is that the market changes in dramatic ways. Whole industries go on "life support" and are not fruitful places for the jobhunter to look. But at the same time, whole industries come off "life support" and flourish. The other characteristic, from a jobhunter's point of view, is that all the things that used to work, don't any more. For example, sending out résumés, etc. You have to rethink your whole job-hunting strategy. Plus the imperative to think about changing careers grows stronger. It's time to notice what industries are flourishing. If you are out of work, you do well to pay huge attention to which stocks are flourishing, and which are languishing. That often is a clue as to who is hiring. You also do well to pay huge attention in the newspapers and the news on TV, radio, or the Internet, to notice which products or services are suddenly feeling a groundswell of demand. They also offer clues as to who is likely hiring.

Go to the job-posting sites on the Internet, not just to look for particular jobs, but—as a part of your research—to notice which industries are now appearing on the job boards again and again. All of this presumes you know a simple fact: that you have basic skills, like advising, budgeting, developing, illustrating, auditing, coordinating, diagnosing, fixing, lecturing, driving, negotiating, painting, planning, recruiting, selling, singing, typing, troubleshooting, writing, etc., that are transferable from one industry to another. If this concept of transferable skills, is unfamiliar to you, then run, not walk, to get your hands on a copy of my book *What Color Is Your Parachute?* updated annually. (In the 2003 edition, this material is explained on pages 159 to 175; it's on the same pages in the current 2002 edition.) Read, mark, learn, and inwardly digest it. This concept is your key to transferring from one industry to another—from the industry that downsized to an industry that is expanding.

Throughout your job hunt in this new world pay constant attention to your emotions. In the wake of September 11 such emotions as fear, depression, insomnia, anxiety, grief, despair, listlessness, decreased energy, feelings of estrangement from one's loved ones, have multiplied to a worrisome level. If you do not have a health care professional to assist you with such emotions, there are many Web sites that can help you with useful perspectives and helpful advice; just type one of those words—e.g., "listlessness"—into your favorite search engine (e.g., http://www.google.com), and see what it turns up.

If you are a person of faith, now is the time to take those "Sunday-go-to-meeting clothes" out of the mothballs, and put them on.

HR: *Will the World Wide Web change everything and eventually replace the newspaper as the number one source for job listings?*

RB: I doubt it. Currently of those job hunters who go to the Internet searching for job listings, only one out of ten actually find a job as a result. The Internet is not a very effective technology, much as we would all like to believe technology could or should change the face of job hunting.

HR: *If you had to give just one piece of advice to the career and vocational counselors of the world what would it be?*

RB: It is not your "techniques" that are most helpful to your clients. It is your empathy and your compassion. For example, it is your ties to the internal world of spirit, not your knowledge of salaries in the workplace, which makes you the most helpful. From the Internet, information is easily found. For anything more than that, the job hunter needs a person, a hug, kindness in the eyes, and compassion from the heart.

HR: *Let's say an administrator or board member at the college where I teach reads this interview and decides to fire me on the spot . . . which I assume is a realistic possibility after he or she reads my question to you about surgeons and sublimation. What one gem of wisdom could you give me about finding another job?*

RB: Go out with the mind-set that you are a "resource" for any new employer, not "a job beggar." You are doing them a favor; not vice-versa.

Chapter 6

The Mummy at the Dining Room Table and Beyond: An Insightful Interview with Jon Carlson

Jon Carlson, PsyD, EdD, ABPP, is distinguished professor in the division of psychology and counseling at Governors State University, University Park, Illinois, and psychologist at the Wellness Clinic in Lake Geneva, Wisconsin. He has written thirty books, over 100 professional articles, and developed 200 professional videotapes.

HR: *Let me begin with a humorous little story. I was selling books of mine at a conference and I had my personal copy of the fascinating book you and Jeffrey Kottler just completed,* The Mummy at the Dining Room Table: Eminent Therapists Reveal Their Most Unusual Cases and What They Teach Us About Human Behavior. *A woman lifted your book off the table and began thumbing through it. I mentioned that the book was my personal copy and it wasn't for sale. She told me she would pay a bonus to get it and I reiterated that it wasn't for sale. "I must have this book," she said. After I helped another customer I turned around and the woman had taken the copy of the book and had left a sum of money on the table! Can you share with our readers where the* Mummy at the Dining Room Table *portion of the captivating title came from?*

JC: I see a lot of clients; between fifty and seventy per week. The mummy at the dining room table was a true story of one of my client families. The story involved a family that mummified their beloved mother and kept her in their daily life after she had passed away. Mom would sleep with Dad. They would get her up, and set her in front of the TV so that she could watch her favorite programs while Dad went to work and the kids went to school. In the evening they would have their evening meal and start the cycle over again.

HR: *I know this is a tall task, but can you summarize what the book taught you personally about human behavior?*

JC: That the truth can often be harder to believe than fiction. Some of the stories were just so amazing. I learned the depth of compassion by hearing the stories told by the various therapists. I learned that we are not alone with our own bizarre or unusual behavior. Some just take a different form. I am also reminded of the saying of Rudolf Dreikurs that one needs to develop the courage to be imperfect.

HR: *Was there any theme in terms of the way that the eminent therapists in the book handled these strange situations?*

JC: One of the themes I noticed is that they all established a safe relationship. They had faith in their clients and showed compassion and respect regardless of the bizarre nature of the story.

HR: *Just curious, how did you end up becoming a therapist? Was it related to anything in your childhood?*

JC: Probably. I was raised in a privileged suburb of Chicago. All my friends were high achievers in academics and athletics. I was good enough at both but even better socially. I think I knew most of the 2,000 people in my public high school. We had a summer home as well in Lake Geneva, Wisconsin. I clearly remember the high level of wealth as well as level of unhappiness in the community. I think having an interest in people and seeing unhappiness among the wealthy posed a challenge that I still wrestle with today.

HR: *You must be a superachiever. My understanding is that you have a doctorate in clinical psychology and a doctorate in counseling. Tell us about that.*

JC: I would keep going to school today if my wife, Laura, would allow. I would probably study anthropology and/or world religion. I do have the two doctorate degrees. I guess it is even worse than that because I also have yet another doctoral equivalent which is called a Certificate of Psychotherapy, which is Adlerian equivalent of being an analyst.

HR: *A number of readers are no doubt struggling with the issue of whether to pick a graduate program in psychology or counseling. Can you give us some insight from your unique perspective? How was your PsyD in clinical psychology different than your EdD in counseling?*

JC: I wish I could be more helpful. I think people can benefit from both programs. The counseling degree taught me about theory, research, education, and prevention while the clinical degree offered advanced clinical work with a wide variety of clients.

HR: *Okay, say that the same reader who is struggling with which graduate program to take aspires to become the president of a professional organization or the founding editor of a journal as you have (i.e., you served as president for the International Association of Marriage and Family Counselor or IAMFC and the founding editor of* The Family Journal*). What steps does a person take to end up in these key roles?*

JC: I became interested in professional journals in my mid-twenties when my mentor, Don Dinkmeyer, allowed me to guest edit a special issue of the *Elementary School Guidance and Counseling Journal* on consulting. I served on the editorial boards of *The School Counselor, Counselor Education and Supervision,* and *Elementary School Guidance and Counseling.* I also was the associate editor of *The Journal of Humanistic Education and Development* and for eighteen years was the editor of the *Journal of Individual Psychology* (Adlerian Journal). I also was the editor of *The International Journal of Individual Psychology* and *The Family Psychologist* before beginning *The Family Journal.* It is fair to say that I worked hard over a twenty-year plus period of time before forming *The Family Journal. The*

Family Journal is now in its thirteenth year. I urge readers to get started by becoming ad hoc reviewers, review books, apply for editorial positions, and learn the ropes of the publishing business. As far as being president of a professional association that is a somewhat different matter. Fortunately I had a lot of organizational experience in high school and college as well as holding elected municipal public office before becoming president of IAMFC. I guess that my message here is similar. Get some experience before taking a leadership role in a professional association. It will make your life as well as the life of others less miserable. One can get experience by volunteering, as there are often calls for help in the professional newsletters.

HR: *I know that you have made a numerous training videos using master therapists. How did you initially get involved in such interesting work?*

JC: I was fortunate that I did a book promotion tour in the mid-1980s and underwent media training from Random House publishers. I also did a national teleclass that taught me the importance of learning a different medium.

HR: *What were these therapists like on an individual basis?*

JC: They were wonderful. All were very helpful and cooperative and a joy to work with. It is interesting to note however that most had some fear and worry as to whether or not they would do a good enough job.

HR: *Did you walk away from the filmed sessions with any gems of wisdom about performing counseling and psychotherapy?*

JC: I guess I walked away with too many gems. I have learned so much from doing this and my therapy skills have increased. I guess I have learned the importance of the relationship, caring for our clients and having faith in them to resolve their own issues.

HR: *Have you observed any gender differences? Are female different than males in terms of their therapeutic interactions?*

JC: I have not really observed gender differences. I find that good therapists are just good therapists.

HR: *As counselors and therapists, many of us were weaned on Everett L. Shostrom's landmark 1965 Gloria movie* actually titled* Three Approaches to Psychotherapy *with Rogers, Perls, and Ellis. At the end of the movie, Gloria, the client, is asked which therapist she felt helped her the most. She chose Perls. As young pups in training most of us were shocked. Perls was aggressive, if not downright abusive with Gloria. Nevertheless, many of us tried to become clones of Perls. Rogers later reported that he ran into Gloria a year or so later at a Western Behavioral Sciences Institute weekend conference he was leading. Gloria told Rogers she was enraged by the power she had given Perls. Were we duped? Did Perls really do good Gestalt therapy with Gloria or was he merely practicing mental judo on her?*

JC: *Three Approaches to Psychotherapy* was clearly an important part of all of our professional development. Gloria was a very savvy client and seemed to be able to find benefit in her work with Rogers, Perls, and Ellis. I am not sure whether Perls did good Gestalt therapy with Gloria because I really don't know what good Gestalt therapy is. I did feel, however, that he had her engaged and being able to engage a client and create collaboration is a very important part of the treatment process. When I watched the session I thought that Perls really would have gotten through a lot of my early defensiveness and felt that he impacted Gloria as well.

HR: *You and Jeffrey Kottler (also interviewed in this book) edited the book* Bad Therapy. *If you had to encapsulate your findings: What is the anatomy of a bad therapy session and any key strategies for avoiding these therapeutic sessions from hell?*

---

*The so-called Gloria film actually refers to a landmark movie titled *Three Approaches to Psychotherapy,* made by therapist Everett Shostrom. In 1964 a client of Shostrom's, Gloria, was filmed receiving therapy from three of the greatest therapists of all-time: Carl R. Rogers, Albert Ellis, and Fritz Perls. After it was released, the movie became one of the most popular training aids ever created for counselors and therapists.

JC: Jeffrey and I learned that all therapists have had some bad therapy. The important aspect of bad therapy is that we learn from it
and we don't continue to repeat our bad performances over and
over and over again. I think through practice and good supervision we learn to identify our strengths and weaknesses and we
learn to work in areas that we feel most effective.

HR: *Do practitioners who perform therapy day in and day out become stale after a while and, if so, is there a way to avoid this
malady?*

JC: I think a lot of therapists and practitioners do become stale because that is all they do. I think it is important to have a wide variety of interests and activities. It is important to read, exercise,
meditate and take time for friends. Herbert Benson at Harvard
University suggested that we use what he called "the breakthrough principle." That is to take time out from what we do
and get involved in some other activities, which will increase
creativity.

HR: *You have obviously studied all the major schools of helping but
seemingly prefer Adlerian therapy. What is it about these modalities, which makes them so valuable? Some texts don't mention Adler theory at all or just gloss over it as being a second
cousin to Ellis's REBT.*

JC: Adler was a genius and a man way ahead of his time. He was
the first theorist to talk about the importance of the social environment and culture. I like his ideas because they were easy to
understand. They involved working with the entire system and
viewed mental health as involving caring and concern for others or social interest. Adler's theory was called individual therapy. By this Adler meant that individuals were indivisible.
They could not be divided as the Freudians and others were attempting to do. He saw people as being holistic . . . as whole. I
am not sure whether or not Adler's really is a second cousin to
Ellis's REBT. When I talk to Al, he believes that much of what
he does is very similar to Adler's work.

HR: *You also have done a wealth of work in marriage and family counseling. Why do 50 percent of all marriages in this country end in divorce?*

JC: I don't know if there is an easy answer to this question. Some of us wonder why it might not be more. We live in a society that is largely controlled by corporate values. As Vance Packard said many years ago "We have become a throwaway society. We buy a car and use it for a few years and throw it away or trade it in on a new one. We do the same thing with our relationships." Nothing is permanent or forever. I am less concerned with the notion that 50 percent of all marriages end in divorce than with my guess that only 5 percent of the marriages are truly satisfying. Satisfaction is something that we can learn and many of us involved with the Smart Marriages organization meet yearly to develop new ways to change policy, legislature, and develop training materials to increase more satisfying marriages. Some people believe that we have a tendency to be drawn toward people who are different from us. Anthropologists say that this occurs so we will meet, mate, and procreate and our offspring will have the best immune system. The problem is that most of us have never been taught how to deal with differences and therefore we deal with differences just as poorly as our parents did.

HR: *What is the biggest misconception clients harbor about therapy? And what about therapists themselves?*

JC: The biggest misconception that client's tend to harbor about therapy is that therapists are all a bunch of kooks, fruits, flakes, or nuts. Therapy has gotten a lot of bad press in recent years. They also fear therapy is forever. Therapists tend to believe that their clients love to talk with them and would like to spend as much time as possible with them. The truth is that clients are a lot like us when we go to a doctor. We want to get in and get out and get our help and get on with our life. We don't want to talk on and on to the physicians that we see.

HR: *Let's say I could wave a magic wand so that you could meet for ten or fifteen minutes with every therapist who finishes grad school. What advice would you give each person?*

JC: Be patient with yourself. Becoming a good therapist takes time. Practice. Get supervision. Read books. Learn different ways to work with people, as you will encounter many different types of people. (Whether or not you acknowledge this is a different matter.)

HR: *What is the number one therapeutic blunder therapists make?*

JC: I don't know if there is just one. I think that there are many and in our book, *Bad Therapy,* we came out with several. One that jumps out to me though is that the therapist makes the same mistake over and over again and is not aware of what it is that he or she is doing. Another would be not listening to the client and following his or her own agenda as if the therapist knows what is best for someone else.

HR: *I know that you have done a lot with grief work. Are there major differences in dealing with different types of grief? For example, let's say you are working with a mother who has lost a young son versus a woman who has lost her husband. Would your approach be markedly different due to the nature of the loss?*

JC: Loss is so very different for different people. It is important to understand how one formulates the loss and whether or not he or she is really having a difficult time. Many people around the world do not have such a difficult time dealing with loss because of their spiritual beliefs. For example, Buddhists detach themselves from such situations, and other religious traditions see death as a normal occurrence.

HR: *When I was running grief groups, clients were somewhat obsessed with what stage of grief they should be in. Seemingly this has been the result of the popular press sharing the works of folks like Elisabeth Kübler Ross. When I interviewed Ed Shneidman, the noted suicidologist and thanatologist, for this text, he went as far as saying that he had never seen a client whose grief fell neatly into these categories. I'm just curious, what is your take on this phenomenon?*

JC: I, like Ed Shneidman, have had a difficult time finding the Kübler Ross stages appropriate. Some people do well by talking about grief and others do well by keeping it to themselves. More and more research is coming out that tends to support the wide range of differences in the way that we grieve.

HR: *Let's play word association. I say managed care and you say . . .*

JC: Outrage. How can it be that we have developed a health care system that provides fewer services for more money and call it managed care when it is really mismanaged noncare.

HR: *As of late, classes, books, and workshops have emphasized multicultural diversity and more stringent professional ethics. I remember using textbooks when I was in graduate school that literally never mentioned either topic. Has this movement strengthened our field?*

JC: I believe the multicultural diversity emphasis has been very helpful, although it has created great complexity within our field. It is very important to realize that we cannot be effective without taking into account the culture of our clients. Therefore we have really strengthened our profession and our field through this emphasis. I am not so positive about the more stringent professional ethics. Professional ethics codes have taken on a life of their own and are not quite so black and white in practice as they appear on paper. I do believe that policing ourselves with ethics has strengthened our field however I think we have gone a little overboard.

HR: *Psychologists will be giving meds soon. Is this a benefit or a health hazard?*

JC: Psychologists have already started to prescribe medications. Over the years I have become a lot more like William Glasser, who does not prescribe medication for behavioral problems. I think to start prescribing medicine is to buy into the fact that problems are biological and not psychosocial. Once we start to do this, our approach will be a totally chemical one. An important link will be lost if we start to approach all problems as though they are biological. My colleague, Len Sperry, has both a PhD and an MD. He went to a recent APA convention and urged that psychologists do not get involved with prescription privileges. He finds that all they will do is spend their time doing med check all day and will lose the opportunity to do counseling and therapy.

HR: *The three-minute cure has gone primetime with the* Dr. Phil *television show. In fact, a writer from the American Counseling Association's publication* Counseling Today *just contacted me because she is doing an article on the new Dr. Phil certification for therapists. After I pinched myself to make certain I wasn't dreaming . . . and I wasn't . . . I discovered that the certification really does exist. What are your feelings about this type of phenomenon?*

JC: When I have watched Dr. Phil on television I have been impressed with his ability to entertain, but there does not appear to be a strong theoretical base for the kinds of suggestions that he makes other than to help himself become popular. If he is teaching others to do this kind of work, I worry. My friend, John Gray, set up a similar program of Mars and Venus counselors. This didn't work and my hunch is that Dr. Phil's instant career will also bomb.

HR: *Just curious, do you have a favorite self-help strategy you use on yourself when you are feeling a bit depressed or stressed out?*

JC: Actually I have two. Meditation and exercise. I have been meditating for many years and I find myself going within and getting my batteries recharged. I have been a long-distance runner for thirty years and find that this is another way to help me decrease stress and increase clarity.

HR: *When you look into your crystal ball twenty or even fifty years from now, what do you see for the future of psychotherapy?*

JC: As I look into my crystal ball and see twenty-five years out I see some big changes occurring especially in the area of genetics. This will be an area in which we will have a much better understanding of the biological impact upon human thought and action. Another area of growth will continue to be the work of counselors and psychologists in the health care field in helping to assist physicians in providing biopsychosocial interventions. I also see technology using computers and video connections to see a lot of our clients from our own homes.

HR: *Thanks for sharing your knowledge and expertise!*

Chapter 7

Psychotherapy Is a Strange Field: An In-Depth Chat with a Seasoned Professional, Raymond J. Corsini

RC: I was born in Rutland, Vermont, to an Italian immigrant family. We then lived in Colorado, and then in Georgia, and at about my age five, the family went to New York City where I finished elementary and high school and then received a BS and MA in educational psychology at the City College of New York (CCNY) and then started work as a psychologist in Auburn Prison, then Elmira Reformatory, then became the chief psychologist at San Quentin Prison, and then was the supervising psychologist of the Department of Correction of Wisconsin. While at Auburn I studied for the PhD at Syracuse University and when at San Quentin, I studied for the PhD at Berkeley at the University of California, and was flunked out each time. I finally quit my job at Wisconsin at age thirty-nine to try for the PhD with Carl Rogers at the University of Chicago and finished at age forty-one with the desired degree. I then changed to industrial organization and became the managing partner of a commercial firm and later I moved to Hawaii, started a private practice, and ran it until I was seventy-five.

HR: *First, congratulations are in order. I understand that you were cited as one of the 500 most significant psychologists since 1850 in the* Biographical Dictionary of Psychology. *When you were a young child did you ever think you would become a famous psychologist?*

Therapy's Best
doi:10.1300/5189_07

RC: After graduating from elementary school, I refused to go to high school against my widowed mother's wishes. I worked as an errand boy for a year and finally, I entered high school, graduated, and then entered CCNY because in 1933 there was a depression and I could not find work I was offered a full scholarship to CCNY and then took a master's in education because I wanted to become a teacher, but I failed the speaking test necessary to taking a final course and the only other option for me was to change to psychology—and so I was forced by circumstances to be a psychologist and I had no prior intention of entering this field. About my being famous, I see that Albert Ellis, who is real famous, will also be in this book. He is a year older than me and has published more books than anyone, more than my sixty plus under some forty titles. He usually writes about his system while I tend to scatter my efforts in various directions.

HR: *I know you are critical of the standard educational system and thus created a model called the Corsini 4R system of education. Tell us briefly about your model and what you personally found distasteful about traditional education.*

RC: I love education and hate the educational system because it is based on the same concepts as prisons—and I have always been a failure in schools. For example, when I entered CCNY I took a series of academic tests with 2,000 other students. I was one of the top twenty and the dean called us together and told us we were the best of the best since CCNY always was first on these tests and we would all be successful. When I graduated from CCNY, I got a C-minus average in the lowest decile re: grades also for the master's. This was my usual history: doing well on tests and poor in grades, more about this later. The system I developed is called Individual Education (IE) or 4R System and is based on logic and democracy. It has three main teaching goals: academics, creativity, sociability. Students never need to go to classes, are not graded by teachers, have complete freedom to be in any or no classes. They can study anything else they want besides academics and the school will try to help them learn. There are weekly objective evaluations of students re: academics and students can take these tests if they wish, but there are compulsory annual proctored academic examinations that will go to the parents directly. There are no rewards and no punishments in IE, only natural and logical consequences. No homework and no report cards. Parents and teachers can only communicate with each other only if the child is present. The result: a school where everyone is happy and busy. Academics are learned in less time for students and teachers. There are only three school rules and logical consequences for violations that lead to counseling and eventual dismissal. These rules are 1— Do not do anything that is dangerous for you or others or harmful to materials; 2—Always be under supervision except when going from one room to another; 3—Obey the GO and STOP signals. This last rule demonstrates the difference between IE and the traditional system. If a teacher sees any student as disturbing her or him or any of the other students, the teacher will call his or her name, point to the student and he or she must leave the room immediately in silence. This is the GO signal. The STOP signal does the same to a student entering a classroom whom the teacher does not want in her or his class. So in a traditional school a student must go to assigned classes, and in an IE school not only is this optional, but a teacher can keep out any child that she or he wishes. The four Rs are the development of responsibility, respect, and resourcefulness. Once the first three are obtained they lead to the goal of responsiveness that means the same as the German word *Gemeinschaftsgeful* that means, "feeling for community" or love of all people.

HR: *May I ask how old you are?*

RC: I was born in 1914 and as time of writing this, am eighty-nine.

HR: *Correct me if I'm wrong, but I believe the last time I spoke with you, you were writing something like eleven books concurrently. Where in the heck do you get ten times the energy, the drive, and the motivation of a twenty year old? Is it diet, exercise, your writing . . . what is your secret? You seem to have truly stumbled onto the fountain of youth.*

RC: During the time I worked on my dictionary, which took ten years to do, at the same time I worked on four other books. So, in a sense I did five books at time. That is the most I ever did at one time. For me this is easy to do.

HR: *Do you do all your own research for your books or do you use graduate students to help you?*

RC: I am not a professor and no one else helps me, except collaborators and co-authors and co-editors and my wife who knows computers. For the dictionary, I depended on a clerk who worked for me for seven years and over one hundred collaborators. I never enjoyed either going to school as a student or being a professor. But I taught at several schools including Berkeley which, had flunked me some ten years earlier.

HR: *Even though this book is packed with experts, I have this uncanny feeling you can answer this question better than anybody since you've rubbed elbows with so many of the immortals in this field. Who was the greatest therapist of all time and why?*

RC: I can only answer this question relative to people I had known, and with whom I have worked. The greatest therapist I have ever met was Dr. Rudolf Dreikurs, an Adlerian and later I became one of his therapists in his office. He had an amazing knowledge of people, and he selected me to work with him, a non-Jew while all others in his office were Jewish: five other therapists, a social worker, and two clerks. There may be thousands of therapists who are better than me and Dr. Dreikurs but I have no way of knowing how good either of us was. I would rate Carl Rogers as no better or worse than other therapists that use his system.

HR: *Just for the record, I know that you believe that counseling is different than psychotherapy. What is the basic difference?*

RC: The basic difference is that good counselors know the right answer to the question of what to do re: their client's problems, while the same persons would probably not know what to advice or suggest in therapy. For example if a parent tells me her child is a bedwetter, I know what to advise the parent to do. This also goes even for more complex problems such as for marriage counseling. One can learn what to advise from experience or from another counselor or a book. The situation is different for a therapist. He or she is presented with a problem for which the therapist has no answer. Example, I will now state my problem as I presented it to Carl Rogers when I asked for personal therapy after I resigned my position at Wisconsin at age thirty-nine.

"Dr. Rogers, I have come to the University of Chicago because I think I need your help. I have been a success in my life re: my profession of prison psychologist starting as a library clerk and then became a prison psychologist at four prisons, each time going up in salary and finally I hit the top of this strange field, becoming the supervising psychologist of the Department of Correction of Wisconsin, the best paying position in this field. I have also done well re: publications, and have about twenty articles published. I have always done well in doing objective tests, usually being in the top 1 percent. What I have been a failure at is getting good grades from professors. This is a puzzle that began from the first grade and I never did better than average in any school. I have been flunked out from two universities and at age thirty-nine am I trying again. I know there must be something wrong with me, but what is it?"

Think this over Dr. Rosenthal, how would you answer me or how would you go about solving my problem, and it was solved by Rogers method by a graduate student and how it is told is in a book co-edited by Frank Dumont and myself called *Six Therapists and One Client.*

HR: *You told me once that Rogers mentioned to you and that he could teach anyone to perform client-centered (now person-centered) therapy in two weeks. Give me the scoop on this.*

RC: I would be able to teach someone to be a Rogerian counselor in one sentence. For example, if some otherwise qualified, asked me how to be a Rogerian, I would say "Do what I did: read Rogers' books and follow his directions."

HR: *What was Carl Rogers like as a person and was he really as nondirective as the textbooks made him out to be? For example, did he ever give clients direct advice?*

RC: When I first met him in his office, I told him about myself as previously discussed. He then told me he would like to see me but his schedule was full, but he would put me on a list. Then he *suggested* that I might want to enter a therapy group that one of his students was running. I accepted his offer and had therapy with the student—and had then had the grandmother of all abreactions and it changed my life and I got my degree. About six months later I saw Rogers as a client. During that period at one time I said something such as the following: "You know, Carl, I can predict everything you are going to say and I get the impression that you are like the statue that is in the Disney theater of Abraham Lincoln that says a speech." He replied: "So, you can predict what I am going to say." I thought that he might take umbrage by my remarks but he did not seem at all surprised. Yes, he was very nondirective as a therapist. Later I ran a psychodrama group and he was in it. I asked him to play the role of a mean son of a bitch professor—Carl was known as a kind of a saint at Chicago—but he played the role so well that I wondered about the depth of feelings that he had shown and when later I heard that he had suffered some kind of mental breakdown I assumed that the role he had taken was really another part of himself. He was a complex person.

HR: *Do you agree with Rogers that the relationship with the client is extremely important or do you feel he overemphasized empathy, congruence, and genuineness in the psychotherapeutic puzzle?*

RC: I think he was right. This is a whole and complete system. There is nothing wrong with it. Everything is part of the system.

HR: *I know that Perls was included in your* Current Psychotherapies *... the textbook many of us grew up on and used as the gospel. When one reads his autobiography,* In and Out of the Garbage

Pail, Perls seems . . . well a little wild, to say the least. Do you have a favorite story about Perls?

RC: I met Perls only once while I was president of a group therapy organization and have these three memories of him. He was talking in a small group at one time and they were seated on the floor and he talked while lying face down. Then later, he took a role in psychodrama, which I conducted and he acted as the father of a young man but he did nothing special. Later, in doing a demonstration I used the empty chair technique that I had seen Rosemary Lippitt use and then Perls stated that he had learned it from me but actually I believe it was first developed by J. L. Moreno as claimed by Adam Blatner. So there was nothing noteworthy in my contact with Perls.

However, I was at a convention somewhere and a man decided to sit next to me and I noted that he was writing something and when the speaker finished, this unknown man showed me the paper he had been writing on. It was a sketch of a woman stretched on a couch and a man on a chair. And from the woman's mouth was a bubble and in it were these words: DR. CORSINI, WILL YOU KISS ME? I asked who he was, and he replied Viktor Frankl. Surprised that he was in the United States and that he had found me, he informed me that he had asked someone where I was and had sat next to me and then had drawn the sketch, and then he thanked me for introducing him to the American public by including him in *Critical Incidents in Psychotherapy.*

HR: *You were instrumental in Albert Ellis changing the name of his theory from rational emotive therapy (RET) to rational emotive behavior therapy (REBT). Give us some insight into your theoretical rationale and what transpired between you and Dr. Ellis. I heard it wasn't an easy sell.*

RC: I first heard Al Ellis speak about fifty years ago and his topic was Carl Rogers. He attacked Rogers' ideas. This had a strong effect on me and even though I had liked Rogers and his therapy had changed me for the better, Ellis had the effect of my moving from Rogerian to Adlerian concepts. I have met Ellis about a dozen times including once at my home and once sleeping in his home office, but not once have we really met and discussed counseling and psychotherapy. There will be a "roast" for me during the 2004 APA conference in Hawaii, and I hope you and he can make it, although he is one year older than me and maybe I finally can have a conversation with him.

J. L. Moreno used to tell a joke that is appropriate here re Ellis. He referred to a player of a musical instrument that had only one string. When asked why? He replied: "Other people can't make up their minds but I always know what string to hit." What I mean about that, I see Ellis's system more like counseling than psychotherapy, I suggested that he add behavior to his system. He demurred several times and finally agreed to make change. I remember well his story about how he felt inferior relative to women and then decided to talk to X number of women and then found that they were easy to talk to. And I meant by "behavior" not the stupid business of bribing people but rather of people actually "doing" something that they fear.

HR: *You probably know as much about psychotherapeutic orientations as any man or woman on the face of the planet. How would you describe yourself now? Are you eclectic, integrative, REBT, marriage and family, strict Alderian, etc., and why?*

RC: I am an Adlerian and this means that I am eclectic, which is what Adler was and Dreikurs and Harold Mosak. My theory is Adlerian but the process is general for example, when I was doing psychotherapy I used Rogers' technique of listening and Moreno's technique of psychodrama and when I edited the first edition of the *Handbook of Innovative Therapies* I tried almost every system at that time. So my theory is Adlerian which is really common sense.

HR: *I know you are famous for your creativity. Give us an example or two of the most creative ploys you ever used in a psychotherapeutic session.*

RC: I was the managing director of a private I/O organization, and I got a call from a man who said he wanted to know if I did vocational counseling. I said "yes" and he came immediately. He was a man of about forty, wore glasses, seemed overweight, and when I asked for his education he told me that he had graduated elementary, high school, college, medical school, and then law school and then stated he had specialized in ophthalmology and he did not like that profession and that he had recently taken and passed the bar exam but did not like being a lawyer. I asked this doctor-lawyer one question: Did he live with his parents? He answered in the positive. I knew now that he was a *yeshivabucher* and so I recommended that he study to be a rabbi. He thanked me and gave me one hundred dollars for my vocational advice.

A woman came to see me and she never stopped talking for a full fifty minutes and told me over and over again that she had a husband and three small children who were each going to school, two to one school and one to a different school. Her routine was to be up by 6:00 a.m. to make her husband's breakfast who then departed at about 7:00, and she would go upstairs and downstairs from 7:00 a.m. to 8:45 a.m. to make the marital bed, to wake up each of the children, to make breakfast for them, since each wanted a special breakfast, one wanted eggs every morning and one did not want any. And she had to help some with their homework and some with their clothes and sometime to drive them to school. At 9:00 she was wiped out. She went on and on and on. I never tried to stop her. When time was over I made only the following statement: "Tell your family that your doctor has ordered you not to get out of bed until 9:00 a.m. every weekday." I then told her to go. She appeared in a week and she was a new woman and told me how the children had fought to get her out of the bed, but she refused. In a month the husband and the children were doing fine taking care of themselves and she now was relieved of her concept that a wife and mother should be a slave to the family.

And a final item in which was the only time I was threatened with being sued. I had a business client, a self-made man who ran a printing shop and he stopped in my office and the talk turned on his son, Roger, his only child. The son was about twenty-one, and was a failure in everything he tried. He had flunked college, could not keep a job and seemed to be a worthless individual but was the delight of his mother's eyes. The one thing the son valued more than anything else was his motorcycle, which was currently not operating and he had a mess of unpaid bills to pay including four traffic violations. The last exploit of this young man was to go with several friends to have a cup of coffee in a restaurant in Milwaukee—from Chicago. He got back to Chicago about three in the morning and slept past his working time. He thus lost his job in a postal office. I also learned that his mother was content that the motorcycle was out of commission. The father then asked me what he should do. I told him—and then the father did exactly what I told him to do.

On getting home the father called Roger and said that he would pay all the money for the motorcycle repairs including the bills for traffic violations and then he would give him one hundred dollars (I specified it should be in one dollar bills) but that Roger should not let his mother know that he was going to go on his own (as he had often said he would do).

Several days later I got an angry phone call from Roger's mother who accused me of violating his and her rights and threatened to have my license to practice nullified and to sue me. I listened to all this and said nothing and she finally hung up.

About three months later I saw the father again and he told me that his son had returned. Roger had gone as far as Louisiana and had gotten a job on an oil well. He had been beaten several times, had taken to drink, had his motorcycle stolen once and it was damaged and finally he had come home. The father said that the son had been a boy when he left and came back a man. The son put his mother in her proper place, he had grown a beard and now he wanted to work in his father's shop (which he had turned down before) and the son was now living outside of the home and the father called him a good worker.

HR: *So many therapists these days are forced to see mandated clients who don't want to be in therapy. You know: You'll lose your kids or if you don't see Dr. Freudianhouser for five sessions or whatever. Do you have any creative tricks up your sleeve for dealing with clients of this ilk?*

RC: No. And I would rather give up psychology than go along with that kind of shit. I have had several cases of mandated clients, one of them in the first week of my private practice. The client was referred to me by a psychiatrist, who had never seen patients in private practice. The father called me and I told him that I wanted to see both him and his son first. He was reluctant but then agreed. When the two came in I learned that the son had threatened suicide and this was the reason for the referral. I then turned to the son and asked how he planned to kill himself, and he replied that he had not yet decided how to do it. I immediately decided that this was most probably a ruse and I began to suggest various ways to kill himself. The father grimaced to stop me, but I continued suggesting poisoning, hanging, jumping off buildings, while his father kept signaling with face and hands and finally his son stopped me by saying: "I was only trying to get my father to give me more money. He spends more on cigars than on me."

And that closed the case.

In other such cases, I explained that I did not want to see them unless they were willing to participate. All were below the age of twenty-one and none wanted to see me. I then had a problem. I could refuse to see them but then had to explain why to the referring agents. Or I could tell my "clients" that they could come and read a book or play some kind of game or talk about anything. Or I told them to say that I refused to see them unless they participated. Whatever I suggested they did not like but they took one or the other of my various suggestions, and some finally participated in this rape of the human mind. Counseling, psychotherapy and education must always be free and have people who want to be treated or to be educated.

HR: *Psychotherapeutic homework is becoming increasingly popular. Nevertheless, resistant clients often do not follow through when given such assignments. Any pipelines to heaven on how to handle such clients?*

RC: I never give assignments. I regard this in the same sense as mandatory homework. But if in the course of discussion the client will bring up something, say excessive anger, I will try to use psychodrama to enrage the client—but only if the client will agree. My object is to work with the client and not like a torturer to struggle against him or her to try to force him or her to do what he or she does not want to do. Sometimes I will suggest changing roles but never as an assignment, such as trying to be kind to people.

HR: *If you were faced with a mediocre therapist and instructed to give him or her just one or two tricks of the trade to improve his or her efficacy, what would you suggest?*

RC: It would depend on many things. First, the therapist himself or herself: if I feel that the therapists are flawed (such as not being intelligent enough) then I would have nothing to do with them. I ran into one of this type while working as the chief psychologist of San Quentin and this man had been brought in by the chief psychiatrist without consulting me. His "therapy" consisted of telling the clients that whatever they had done, he had done something worse. I maintained a good relation with him, but refused to try to show him his errors because in my opinion he was not qualified. After several weeks he disappeared. If I am asked to help someone who I view as professionally trained and capable, I would recommend that he or she become a Rogerian since in this way he or she cannot hurt others. I would not want to go further. I have had some calls from other psychologists who asked for assistance for specific problems such as for a man who could not climax in sex and had to go to a bathroom to masturbate. I had no idea how to handle that problem. And one wanted therapy from me to learn about my method of operating.

HR: *There has been a tremendous emphasis on multicultural counseling and beefed up ethical guidelines in the last several years. Are these two changes for better or for worse?*

RC: I personally pay no attention to such changes. I have my own ethical standing and know well the APA standards. Therapists should be smart enough to know what to do and what not to do. Relative to multicultural counseling I once had this experience. I was teaching for a summer at a university in California and the head of the department referred a male student to me who he said had shown signs of serious maladjustments and would I see the student. I said "yes" and the student came in and after some discussion he told me that he masturbated. On hearing this, I told him that practically all males masturbated, and told him that in a research in a divinity college all male students admitted that they masturbated and then I told him that in a United States federal document on child care that masturbation at one time was considered harmful and dangerous and then was considered safe and natural. On hearing this, my client who had come from Central America, got into a rage and accused me of being a pervert and then stated that all Americans were perverts and told of how from the age of thirteen on he had had sex with women and in this environment there were no women and he had to engage in this terrible disgusting practice.

I then reported all this to the head of the department and that was the end of the situation as far as I was concerned. Paul Pedersen recommends in such cases, the therapist in such cases should have a third person who is of the same cultural group and who is also conversant with current concepts, to lessen the possibilities of conflict between people of two cultures.

HR: *Recently, I had a graduate assistant who was helping me teach a course. I explained that she did not need to attend all of my sessions since she might find it boring. She told me that she was getting a lot out of my lectures because in the graduate program she was attending there was no "emphasis put on the classics." For example, she had never heard of Joseph Wolpe's systematic desensitization or Arnold Lazarus. Everything was focused on brief strategic therapy; even one-session cures. I was recounting this saga to a colleague of mine who teaches in a graduate program of counseling who remarked that it didn't surprise her. She was admonished by her department chair to focus exclusively, if possible, on works and research conducted in the last seven or eight years. Assuming this is becoming more typical, do you feel this a healthy trend for our profession?*

RC: Psychotherapy is a strange field. No one is smart enough to decide what is proper training. I would say that the more that we learn the more we are likely to do well, but if one has the proper attitudes and skills one needs little or no training to learn any single system. I started with Rogers' nondirective method and at that time I knew nothing about other methods except psychoanalysis. It might be better for someone to know only one method and stick to it than learn a lot of methods, which would only confuse him or her. But I believe all therapists should know as much about other systems. In my case I was first a Rogerian and then I used psychodrama and then become an Adlerian and used whatever I wished, but that is what Adlerian therapy is to me.

HR: *Are you for or against psychologists giving prescription medicines?*

RC: Against! Psychology should be about psychology and physiological treatments should be by physicians or druggists. I believe if psychologists can prescribe, then another group, such as sociologists and social workers will become the therapists of choice, not psychologists. Many of the people who came to see me did so because they were afraid that physicians would give them pills rather than trying to find the source of problems.

HR: *I've been asking almost every expert whether he or she is enamored with managed care and insurance companies. Just checking. Didn't you tell me you only saw one client under the watchful eye of insurance and found it too restrictive to conduct prudent treatment?*

RC: I am still owed money by some insurance companies because I refused to tell them something that they wanted to know. I believe that insurance companies force psychologists to lie in order to get paid. This is not good for therapists or the public.

HR: *Okay, here's a tough one. Can you sum up what you learned as a prison psychologist? What makes one person end up in the slammer while the other ends up sunning and funning as a CEO?*

RC: Your question is too tough for me to answer. Each person had a different reason for getting into trouble. And I could not come to any conclusion except that various cultural factors lead into crime. Why more black men end up in prison than white women should be obvious to anyone with any sense.

HR: *How will psychotherapy change in the next fifty years or so? Will there be a violent reaction against the brief strategic therapy movement with a renaissance of long-term psychodynamic Freudian-laden psychodynamic therapy, or are those days gone forever? Will therapists for the most part become life-coaches? What's your best guess?*

RC: I guess over time that new and better systems will evolve and that Freudian therapy will retain its hold on perhaps 5 percent of people. For example, no one now knows of Alvin Mahrer's *Experiential Psychotherapy* that I expect will take over the field eventually.

HR: *We have a lot of readers who will be performing counseling and therapy hanging onto every word. Any gems of wisdom you'd like to leave them with?*

RC: Read my books on counseling and psychotherapy.

HR: *Do you wish to say anything special?*

RC: I am not a conventional religious person but when I do counseling or psychotherapy, I feel that I am a God or an instrument of God and at the time I realize that I have the power to change people. I have this feeling more for counseling than for psychotherapy, because perhaps I can see immediate changes. Let me tell of a recent one that I participated in to illustrate the point.

The family consisted of a father, an attorney, his wife, who worked as a flight attendant, and they had a three-year-old daughter, Peggy. Then the wife's sister was killed by her husband, who was sentenced to life imprisonment, and their five-year-old son, Bobby, was adopted by the parents of Peggy. When they came to see me this was their problem: Bobby, the five-year-old spoke thus to the parents if they ever reproved him: "You cunt. If you don't leave me alone I will cut your daughter's head off and kick it around." The parents, a babysitter, and an aunt combined to tell him not to talk that way and all sharp knives were locked up and unavailable to him. The family was at their wits end what to do. Now I ask you and the readers what you would recommend for these adults? I had no problem and no hesitation in telling them to: (1) *About his threats.* Listen to him quietly and then ask him to repeat them. When he is engaged in something that interests him, interrupt him and ask him what he intends to do to Peggy. The aunt had to agree or else she was not invited to visit the family. Never criticize him. (2) *About the knives.* Allow one knife and keep a watchful eye on it and see if he ever has any intention of going for it.

Results: Bobby soon stopped that familiar threat and showed no interest in killing Peggy. Now, how did I know exactly what to recommend?

1. I assumed that he had learned that language from his father, who eventually killed his wife, Bobby's mother.
2. I assumed that he used this language and the threats to get attention and the more attention that he got the more likely he was to use it.
3. I assumed that if people would annoy him by asking for the same language and interrupt him when he was playing to ask him for this language, he would refuse.
4. How many five-year-olds kill other children by stabbing them to death and kicking their heads?
5. And they were thinking of warehousing him in a foundling's home, a perfectly normal child.

HR: *Thank you for taking this time to help all of us become better helpers!*

RC: You are most welcome.

Chapter 8

The REBT Story You Haven't Heard: A No-Holds-Barred Interview with Albert Ellis

Albert Ellis, PhD is the president of the Albert Ellis Institute and the father of rational emotive behavior therapy (REBT). He is the author of over 70 books and over 800 articles on psychotherapy, sex, and marriage.

HR: *I understand you still see an incredible number of clients a week and hit the lecture circuit. You are more active than the nineteen-year-olds I'm teaching in my college classes. What is the secret of your remarkable longevity? Have you spiked the water at the Albert Ellis Institute with vitamin E or something? Are you into herbs, cranking out crunches on an ab blaster while your clients are telling their tales of woe, or is it the REBT rational thinking that is keeping you young?*

AE: First of all I have good heredity. My mother and her whole family lived into their nineties. My father died at eighty, but he was one of the youngest in his family to die. So I haven't used any special thing except working on my emotional problems and not upsetting myself about various things. And I have the motives of learning new things and helping more people and of listening to and composing music and that keeps me going.

This material first appeared in Rosenthal, Howard. 2002. "The REBT Story You Haven't Heard: A No-Holds-Barred Interview with Dr. Albert Ellis." From *Journal of Clinical Activities, Assignments, & Handouts in Psychotherapy Practice*, 2(3), pp. 49-61. Reprinted with permission.

HR: *When you were a child did you ever think that you were des-*
tined to become the leading clinical psychologist in the United
States? If I recall you mentioned in Arthur Burton's Twelve
Therapists *that your "mother was not eligible for any prizes of*
mental health" and that your parents were divorced by the time
you were twelve. On the surface, that doesn't exactly sound like
the perfect breeding grounds for a stellar career. On the other
hand, I heard a story that early in your career you were riding
in a New York cab with Judy Wallerstein, the eminent divorce
researcher, and you predicted that one day you and your ideas
would be famous. Did your confidence manifest itself after you
began practicing therapy?

AE: Yes, I really thought to a certain degree that I would be famous
. . . that I would be a writer of great Nobel Prize-winning novels.
It wasn't until I got into graduate school and started studying
psychotherapy that I thought I would become a great psychologist. I don't remember riding in a cab with Judy Wallerstein
though I did know her husband and so it is possible that I did
tell her that one day my ideas would be famous.

HR: *At one time you were a psychoanalyst. What was wrong with psy-*
choanalysis as a treatment modality? Salter began his 1949 clas-
sic Conditioned Reflex Therapy *with, "It is high time that psy-*
choanalysis, like the elephant of fable, dragged itself to some
distant graveyard and died. Every literate non-Freudian in our
day knows these accusations to be true." Was Salter on target?
And by the way, about twenty years ago Jeffrey Masson suppos-
edly made this landmark discovery that Freud copped out and
changed his theory (i.e., that patients really were abused, and not
just fantasizing about it as postulated in his Oedipus/lectra com-
plex theories). Does that supposed monumental finding really
change everything or is analysis still an insipid form of treat-
ment?

AE: Yes, analysis is one of the most ineffectual forms of treatment
in that it takes long and reveals all types of irrelevant material. It
is pseudo-deep. I discovered this after getting trained in analysis and practicing it in a classical manner for about six years.

Jeffrey Masson was probably correct about Freud, but that finding is relatively unimportant. Freud made innumerable errors and stuck rigidly to them and hated everybody who disagreed with him. But again, I found out that psychoanalysis is very inefficient especially since it doesn't recommend that clients engage in psychotherapeutic homework. So it is very cognitive and very emotive, but it is not very behavioral. Freud snuck in a few behavioral homework assignments but he and most analysts didn't use them on a regular basis. I snuck them in with a little guilt or regret when I was an analyst but then I discovered that it was desirable to have many more of them and to check up on them and to push people into doing things.

HR: *Okay, know this sounds like an "E Biography" but I cannot forego asking you this question. I heard or read that as a young man you went through a phase where you were afraid of women so you went to a park and asked 100 women out to combat your fear. Moreover, the saga suggested that most of them turned you down and thus between changing your irrational beliefs and confronting your fear you ameliorated this problem. True or false?*

AE: Definitely true. At the age of nineteen I was scared shitless of public speaking and of approaching new women. If I was introduced to a woman that was fine but I couldn't approach, though, I went to the Bronx Botanical Garden 200 days a year and flirted with many women. But even when they seemed receptive, I never talked to them. I read John B. Watson and Mary Cover Jones and his other assistants, and found that he desensitized little children to animals by in vivo desensitization. So I said to myself, fuck it! If it's good enough for the kiddies, it is good enough for me. So I gave myself a famous homework assignment in August when I was off from college. Every day when it didn't rain (and it didn't rain at all that August) whenever I saw a woman sitting on a park bench alone I would sit next to her, not a bench away, and I gave myself one minute, one lousy minute, to talk to her. "If I die, fuck it, I die." So I did that. I sat next to all 130 women I saw on the park benches. Thirty immediately got up and walked away. But that left me with an even sample of 100, good for research purposes. So I spoke immediately to the 100 about the birds, the bees, the flowers, the trees, their knitting, reading, etc. If Fred Skinner would have known about my antics (he was teaching psychology at the time at Indiana University) he would have thought that my conversational attempts would have been extinguished. Because out of all the women I talked to only one made a date and she didn't show up! I had prepared myself through my hobby, studying the philosophy of happiness. I saw that nobody could take out a stiletto and cut my balls off (they only do that these days). Nobody vomited and called the cops; nobody did anything bad. I had pleasant conversations. I then continued to approach the next hundred women and I made a few dates. So that is a very true story. In a sense that homework assignment started REBT, although I didn't even know I was going to be a therapist at that time.

HR: *You also had to contend with professional rejection. In my mind RET was the Tucker automobile of psychotherapies. Your 1965 book* Suppressed: Seven Key Essays Publishers Dared Not Print, *contained a bevy of powerful ideas, but not everybody was ready to listen. The book contained lectures that organizations forbid you to present. How did you cope with this, "We won't allow you to say this" mentality? Tell us about your own self-talk in this respect.*

AE: Well yes, especially *Reason and Emotion in Psychotherapy* that came out in 1962 was hated by practically all psychologists; especially the outstanding therapists like Fritz Perls and Carl Rogers. But I still persisted with REBT, nonetheless, because I gave myself unconditional self-acceptance (USA) and got through it in spite of the criticism. And the few people that contacted me, such as Rudolph Dreikurs, who corresponded with me in 1956 after my first talk on REBT, I appreciated. But the vast majority of psychologists, psychiatrists, and social workers were against me and did everything they could to stop me from speaking and even writing. Nobody killed me, however, and nobody harmed me in any way. I thus decided to use my own philosophy of REBT to not put myself down or put them down because they disapproved of me. I used REBT largely on myself and was able to take their criticism of me, which was often very vile, not too seriously.

HR: *I remember reading your stuff and must admit that you became my role model as a therapist. In addition, your books and articles were always lively and interesting. Quite frankly, many of the works by other theorists could and should have doubled as sleep therapy. Was this the novelist portion of your personality manifesting itself and did you have any heroes or heroines who influenced your career?*

AE: Yes, again my hobby was philosophy. From sixteen onward, before I became interested in psychology, I translated Immanuel Kant's *Critique of Pure Reason* into simple English; and that affected me very much. I read hundreds of books on philosophy, especially the ones on the philosophy of happiness, and learned very much from them. This wasn't the novelist portion of my personality manifesting itself but the writing and the propagandist portion. I had previously been a revolutionary in the political movement against the Communist Party and against the Republican, Democratic, and Capitalist parties. I prepared myself by not caring too much what any of them thought of me. But my modern influences were John Dewey, Bertrand Russell, as well as the ancient Asian, Greek, and Roman philosophers; especially Epictetus.

HR: *Let's talk about multicultural counseling. Are the irrational ideas postulated via REBT valid for working with clients who are culturally or racially different?*

AE: Yes, for the most part they are, because as I say in a new edition of *Overcoming Resistance,* which is going to press soon, REBT doesn't interfere with the desires, preferences, and goals of people, which are largely multicultural. When individuals dogmatically adhere to their goals and say "I absolutely must do what other cultures say," then REBT tries to get them to try to change their dogma but not their originally culturally imbued notions. So REBT I think has always done well with multicul-

tural clients. It gives them UOA or unconditional other acceptance. It tries to get them to see that only when their rigid belief
system harms them and other humans should they change their
dogmatism and absolutism. It suggests that they don't have to
change, but they preferably better change. So I think REBT is
an improvement over most cultural counseling systems that
don't distinguish their flexible preferences from their rigid demands. REBT looks for views where people contradict their
own philosophy, in theory and practice, and beat themselves
over the head and blame themselves and people in other cultures. It gets them to stop damning (or minimizes damning) of
others and the world. REBT, therefore, allows them to be as
multicultural as they can feasibly be.

HR: *In my humble opinion your* Guide to Rational Living *stands
alone as the best bibliotherapeutic work ever written (though to
be sure* Help Yourself to Positive Mental Health *written by myself and Joseph Hollis runs a very close second!). How did you
meet your co-author Robert Harper and why do you think this
book was so influential?*

AE: Well, I met Bob Harper several years before we wrote the book,
in New York at an American Association of Marriage and Family Therapists conference. He was a well-known therapist and
family counselor in Detroit at the Merrill Palmer School at that
time. So we both agreed that Carl Rogers, who we both listened
to at one of the meetings at the AAMFT, was a very nice person
and unconditionally accepting, but very passive and wouldn't
get very far especially with marriage and family clients. So we
kept in contact over the years. I think we met in 1955 and he became one of the first converts to REBT. I kept in touch with him
and we wrote two books, *A Guide to Rational Living* and what
was later called *A Guide to Successful Marriage* presenting the
REBT point of view in fairly simple language and still including profound ideas about its therapy.

HR: *Was* A Guide to Rational Living *an overnight success or did it
take some marketing to catch on? I know that Melvin Powers,
the lay hypnotist and mail order genius of Wilshire Publishing*

Company, took the book on and he had a track record for pro-
ducing winners such as Psychocybernetics. *I have a vintage*
1975 edition and I'm fairly sure that his mug is gracing the
Guide*'s cover.*

AE: The book was very influential, but not in its original form. The
main editor at Prentice Hall left and they neglected to push it in
hardcover form. But then a few years later, you correctly note
that the book was picked up by Wilshire Books of North Hollywood, California, and Melvin Powers, the publisher, wrote a
preface praising the book and pushed it, pushed it, and pushed
it. You are indeed correct that various editions did include pic-
tures of Melvin, his wife, or children on the cover. The book has
now sold about two million copies and has been translated into
many languages throughout the world.

HR: *Indulge me for just a moment while I speculate about the suc-*
cess of REBT books as well as the therapy itself. Students and
supervisees routinely come to me and outline a client's difficul-
ties. Then they'll say something like, "Okay, what would such
and such theory say about this problem?" My position is often
that I'm clueless, with the exception of REBT, which is the only
theory that is universally applicable to almost any situation.

AE: Yes I think that is right. As I tell people, including clients, all
the time : "If you give me your goals and then give me A the activating event that blocks them and C the consequence, such as
depression and rage, I can tell you in all probability what B,
your irrational belief is, so we can fit practically all disturbance
into the ABC network. And even when you are endogenously
disturbed, as in endogenous depression, you almost always dis-
turb yourself *about* the depression and that can be put into the
ABC network, we can and go on to D, disputing, and E an effective new philosophy. So we can very quickly show you that
you have musts, shoulds, and oughts, that produce disturbed results and are not factual. Other therapies can do this in an existential form or complicated manner that often helps screw people up more. Most REBT clients are able to see that they have a
choice of ideas and feelings and that they can change their basic
philosophies, feelings, and behaviors.

HR: *In the St. Louis, Missouri, area where I practice the disease model of addictive behavior is the gospel. You know . . . you have a disease . . . you need to attend a twelve-step group and work your program . . . you must admit you are powerless and need a higher power, etc. Briefly, what is your take on this model of addictions?*

AE: Well that is the AA model and it has some truths in it since you may have OCD (an obsessive compulsive disorder) and have little control over your problem. But in REBT we don't call it a disease like tuberculosis. It might do some good to have a higher power to help you overcome your addiction, even if it doesn't exist. But you don't *need* a higher power, you can do it by yourself. A lot of evidence shows that people who give up drinking and smoking do it by themselves. And you certainly don't need to attend a twelve-step program for years and years and years to become unaddicted. So AA has some good things in it. For example the concept of "stinking thinking," which they may have gotten from me: and *The Serenity Prayer* that says "give me the courage to change the things I can, and the wisdom to know the difference." AA, however, has exaggerations in it and only 5 percent of people continue in AA groups. So it has advantages but it also has distinct disadvantages and even when it works it probably works (laughs) because people have faith in a higher power that may well not exit and they think that they cannot help themselves. AA encourages them to think like this. AA does a great deal of good but also a great deal of harm.

HR: *Are we as a society getting away from therapy and relying too heavily on psychiatric medicinals? I cringe when preschool teachers tell me that nearly half of their class is on Ritalin and Prozac for ADHD. I know that a lot of therapists such as Peter Breggin and William Glasser have taken a strong stand against this medical model.*

AE: Yes, these therapists, especially Glasser, have some points but they exaggerate. And although it is sad that so many children are on Ritalin, and now they even give it to adults, it does do a lot of good as well as some harm. Prozac may also keep people from using REBT and applying it. It is both and rather than either/or. In REBT we preferably try to help people minimize their anxiety, depression, and rage without medication. But in the case of severe personality disorders, where people have a biological as well as a social learning disability, it is often best to try the medication, to see if it has any bad side effects, and to try it for a while with very high frustration tolerance to see if it does more good than harm. Probably in most cases it does more good than harm.

HR: *Lately, grad schools really seem to be pushing the family therapy model to the hilt. A lot of the training seems focused on general systems theory. As a pioneer in marital and sex counseling, do you view this as productive or counterproductive?*

AE: Well it is productive in the sense that just as REBT says that emotion, behavior, and thinking are all interrelated and affect each other. General systems theory says that practically everything such as your heredity and environment affect you. It explains things, but often in too much detail. When you use it for therapy and it includes REBT it is all right. But if you use it only for exploration and don't show clients how to act then general systems theory may do harm as well as good. It has value and therapists had better be aware of general systems theory, but not use it exclusively or to the hilt.

HR: *What about the tremendous focus on Milton H. Erickson? Was he a therapeutic genius and did his strategies actually work because the clients changed their internal verbalizations? Quite frankly, some of his techniques seemed, well, a tad mystical to say the least.*

AE: Right. I believe that Erickson believed in his techniques and because he believed in his techniques and told people some dubious things, such that they absolutely would get better under hypnosis, his therapy often worked. He had faith largely unfounded on fact. He also believed that humans are able to constructively change if they push themselves to do so. But Jay Haley and others have made a cult out of Erickson. If you use some Ericksonian techniques with REBT that would be okay.

But don't go to extremes and give your clients unrealistic polly-annaish views, which may or may not help them. As I frequently say, if you devoutly believe in the devil and think that he is on your side and will help you, then you may actually help yourself. But that doesn't mean that the devil exists. Now Milton Erickson of course did exist and was very influential. But several reputable scientific people in the field of hypnosis think that he fabricated some of his case histories. Milton Erickson was a remarkable therapist but very little scientific study of the Ericksonian position has been done.

HR: *As a consummate professional are you ever critical of your own psychotherapeutic style? For example, someone told me that you didn't think you did that great of a job on the* Gloria *film. I couldn't see it. To me you were hitting all the right keys on the Carkhuff . . . no make that . . . the REBT scale.*

AE: No, I definitely was below par, my own par, on the *Gloria* film because we only had twenty minutes and I tried to get too much into the twenty minutes. So if I had focused on one or two things it would have been better. I think I do quite well on what I do most of the time. But because of my own low frustration tolerance, I don't do things that would bore me or bore the client but might be effective. So I can easily criticize my own psychotherapeutic style and am often skeptical of that. And so I have changed somewhat over the years but not as much as I had better change.

HR: *How do you know when you had a good therapy session with a client?*

AE: Well, sometimes right during the session the client experiences a quite profound change. A client might have a great many "musts" that are screwing him or her up. So I may get indications that I have had a very good session with a client and then he or she just doesn't *use* our session to change later. Thus, there is no absolute way of knowing. But if the client seems to be following REBT theories and if she or he seems to be working his or her ass off to follow them, I believe, but still don't absolutely know, that our sessions are good.

HR: *What is the number one therapeutic blunder that a typical therapist makes?*

AE: Well, there are so many possible blunders that I am not sure. Most therapists gather too much irrelevant information, especially about early their client's early childhood. This may do some good but compared to the time it takes and the fact that it may turn the clients off may be too sidetracking. Most therapists are motivated by several rational philosophies but they don't show the clients their own philosophies and how to dispute them. The cognitive-behavior therapies until recently were not emotive, emotional, or forceful enough but now therapists like Judy Beck have changed. Some therapists, like Leslie Greenberg, focus on emotions but then do it too much and dispute irrational beliefs too little. So I think that most therapists, if they really follow REBT, do some good disputing but they don't call it that and the don't teach their client how to effectively do it. Others sadly neglect encouraging clients to do homework.

HR: *Your therapy sessions always seem so innovative despite the fact that you are working out of the same ABC theory of personality. How does one become a creative therapist?*

AE: Mainly by not being dogmatic even about REBT and exploring and using its cognitive, emotive, and behavioral methods flexibly and looking for other methods of helping unique individual clients. Steven Hayes, for example, who really is a cognitive behavior therapist, but calls himself a radical behavior therapist, ignores regular disputing but often disputes with metaphors. Now we use the regular REBT disputing and also make frequent use of creative metaphors. And again, therapists had better have about thirty or more potential cognitive, thirty emotional, and thirty behavior techniques and experimentally see which work best with this particular client under which conditions right now. In the beginning they can start with the most popular techniques of REBT. But creative means that you go beyond that and experiment and see whether they work out and possibly devise new or fairly new techniques in the process.

HR: *Can you give our readers four or five tips for improving their therapy sessions?*

AE: Well the main things that we look for in REBT are, first, we see that disturbed people are probably doubting themselves and thinking "I must do well and be approved of by other people" so we emphasize USA (unconditional self-acceptance) over and over, very actively. At the same time, we give (unconditional other-acceptance). Very often we show clients that they are doing stupid, dumb, and even immoral things but they are still okay as persons. We accept them and we teach them to accept themselves and others.

Our third major thrust is to show people that very often they have low frustration tolerance and had better change it to high frustration tolerance or what I now call unconditional life-acceptance (ULA) that is—to accept life when it is bad and may not change. They can have the serenity to accept life, but still strive to improve it. As therapists, we tackle these three main goals, while using other tenets of REBT. But again, we try to apply REBT to every client *individually.* Therapists had better be flexible, open, and give the client unconditional other-acceptance while pushing them into action. Willpower comes from the decision and the determination to change and then acting, acting, acting on this decision and determination. Without *action,* will has very little *power.*

HR: *Recently RET became REBT. Tell us about the change. Ray Corsini told me he was instrumental in convincing you to add the "B." Also, did you receive any flak after changing the name of your therapy?*

AE: Yes. Ray almost twenty years ago said RET should be REBT and I said it was. But at that time the name RET and rational emotive therapy were fairly famous and I resisted changing it. But I finally admitted that I was wrong, so I changed it in 1993. After I changed it, I had very little flak. But some therapists insisted that it really wasn't as behavioral as I said it was, despite the fact that I showed in my first paper regarding the new name that it was exceptionally behavioral.

HR: *Is managed care the savior of psychotherapy or mental health's worst nightmare?*

AE: As far as I can see from my own practice, it has been something of a nightmare since it stops many people from getting my therapy, because they don't have the right managed care company. And our nonprofit institute is only accredited by a few managed care companies. Also they require all kinds of data and paper work that interfere and waste the therapist's and the client's time. As far as I know, nationally, many good therapists are unable to practice and therefore go into forensic psychology or something else. So I think that in all probability it has done much more harm than good but I can't substantiate that completely.

HR: *What will the psychotherapy pundits say about REBT in the year 2050?*

AE: Well they may say little because it may not be mentioned as REBT. It may be called cognitive-behavior therapy (CBT), and I think that it will flourish. REBT, I think, is the most comprehensive form of CBT. Almost certainly it will be practiced, practiced, and practiced, in 2050, whatever name it is called. Moreover, REBT has integrated, especially in my recent writing, some of the other schools of therapy, such as some psychoanalytic and some Rogerain methods. So therapy is becoming much more integrated and maybe all the names we now give it may be changed to integrated therapy. But included in integrated therapy will be a great deal of REBT, more than will be included from other kinds of therapy.

HR: *Thanks for taking time out of your busy schedule to share your vast knowledge and expertise.*

AE: I think you had very good questions and you certainly understand REBT and probably are one of the main people in the country who thoroughly understand it. A good interview! Thank you!

Chapter 9

Voice Therapy: An Interview with Robert and Lisa Firestone

Robert W. Firestone, PhD, noted psychologist and author, pioneered an innovative methodology known as voice therapy. Dr. Firestone worked as a clinical psychologist engaged in the practice of psychotherapy from 1959 to 1978. His major works include *The Fantasy Bond, Voice Therapy, Combating Destructive Thought Processes,* and *Compassionate Child Rearing.* He is well known for creating the Firestone Assessment of Self-Destructive Thoughts (FAST), a scale that assesses suicide potential. His daughter, Lisa Firestone, PhD, is the Glendon Association's (located in Santa Barbara, California) Director of Research and Education. Since 1987 she has been involved with clinical training and applied research related to suicide and violence. She has published numerous professional articles, several books, and her studies helped create the aforementioned FAST assessment tool.

HR: *Why did you pick psychology as a career?*

RF: It sounds trite in this day and age of cynicism, but I really wanted to help people. I had compassion for people, and I knew early on that I was going to work either in medicine or psychology. I always felt for people who were hurt, for the underdog, for people who were disadvantaged. As an adolescent, I was especially sensitive to people who were injured, crippled, or deformed.

As to the choice between medicine and psychology, when I started actually taking courses I found the psychology curricu-

Therapy's Best
© 2006 by The Haworth Press, Inc. All rights reserved.
doi:10.1300/5189_09

lum much more interesting and it gave me a broader perspective. I thought that if I pursued a career as a medical specialist, I'd have a very narrow focus in terms of an overview on life. But the field of psychology is open-ended and appeared to offer the widest horizons of any profession. It applied to every aspect of the human condition.

I disliked the scholastic regimen in general but read extensively in psychology. Basically I hated school from kindergarten through the PhD, but my desire to become a clinical psychologist and to practice psychotherapy kept me going.

My father was a medical doctor, and my values were much like his in regard to working with people. He was very compassionate toward his patients, and very concerned about their overall well-being, and I think he set a good example.

In terms of my intellectual development; at first I studied philosophy because I was interested in the world of ideas. But philosophy didn't get at the essence of what I was really concerned with. I was really interested in what made people tick, why people felt the way they did.

Early on I was aware that most people were living a defensive type of existence, that they weren't telling the truth. They were acting as though real issues, like the meaning of life and death, were unimportant. I saw there was a huge amount of fantasy, dishonesty, and outright phoniness. People focused on everything but the most important and relevant concerns. I sensed that most individuals lived in a state of denial.

As an adolescent I was searching for meaning and wanted to get at the root of things. Probably on an unconscious level I was curious about what made me the way I was, what contributed to me being the sort of person I turned out to be, and what caused me pain in life.

I saw psychology as a means of helping human beings in distress. I thought that people who suffered from mental illness were people who came by it honestly. In other words, I realized that some tragic circumstances must have contributed to the way they became. These were not just those people who were seriously disturbed, but people in general. I felt that, to a considerable extent, human suffering is a result of ignorant, immature, emotionally inadequate, or even hostile child-rearing patterns. We are all products of our emotional experiences with other people and the earliest years are the most formative.

In summarizing my motives for becoming a psychotherapist and theorist, I wanted to make a meaningful and important contribution to the welfare of other human beings. I felt that it would be an exciting, compelling, and personally rewarding endeavor and my career has fulfilled that promise.

HR: *Were any theories pushed during your formal training such as analysis or behaviorism?*

RF: When I first became involved in psychotherapy, psychoanalysis was still in its prime and most clinical psychologists followed that discipline in relation to both theory and, to some extent, practice. Generally, clinical practice was psychoanalytically based, although most often not in a strictly orthodox manner. I was trained in psychoanalytic theory and experienced several years of personal analysis with a traditional psychoanalyst. I was impressed with Freud's courageous work and inspired by his unique insights and understanding. His concepts immediately resonated with my own thinking. I felt at home with the concepts of unconscious motivation, defense mechanisms, transference, and resistance. Although I was drawn to psychoanalytic thought, I did not accept either Freudian theory or methodology uncritically and early on began to formulate my own theoretical ideas.

In my opinion, the most valuable contribution of psychoanalytic methodology has been its focus on identifying and working through resistance and transference distortions in the analytic sessions. This painstaking process enables individuals to reshape their personal relationships through genuine emotional insights.

However, I approach the subject of resistance and transference from a somewhat different angle than the traditional analyst. For one thing, I consider much of what traditional psychoanalysts consider to be transference and countertransference to be erroneous. A good deal of personal feelings and reactions toward one another on the part of both therapist and patient are simply human emotional responses to the here and now interaction and do not necessarily relate significantly to figures from the past. The fact that an analysand comes to love his or her therapist is an appropriate response to being with someone who is kind, unusually attentive, generally supportive, and wishes the best for the person. On the other hand, it is natural for an analysand to respond with critical feelings and anger to a cold, unsympathetic person, who may well be bored or hostile. Indeed, there is a core problem for a noncommittal therapist acting as a blank screen because this detached posture often replicates the patient's treatment by his or her own parents and may exacerbate his or her problems. Often sincere and well-meaning therapists' deviations from the blank screen approach have inadvertently been of significant benefit to their clientele.

I feel that the free association methodology in psychoanalysis is a valuable technique and have found it especially useful in any type of creative process. To do free association, to free your mind to just flow, to recognize every nuance of thought, is of tremendous value in any creative project, problem-solving issue, or even in business or other realms. By breaking free of the usual structure, you can come up with ideas that are surprisingly unique.

There are problems inherent in using free association in psychotherapy to get at core issues. It takes time for a client to learn to use this technique effectively and many people are resistant to the method. I believe that there are better techniques for getting to relevant material, particularly those involving deep feeling release. Sessions utilizing deep breathing and encouraging the release of intense feelings reveal the secrets of the past more directly and powerfully. Patients form their own insights and make their own connections.

HR: *Lisa, what was it like growing up with an accomplished psychologist for a father?*

LF: I don't know if this would be true for children of other accomplished psychologists or not, because my father is an unusual person. Growing up with him and the intellectual and emotional atmosphere surrounding him was really an amazing experience. He related to my brothers and sisters and me as very separate people, more than anyone else that I've observed with their children. He was helpful any way he could be because he really cared about us.

HR: *Were there times when your dad seemed to be treating you more like a patient or client than a daughter? Any incidents where you yelled, "Dad, I'm not your patient!" or something like it?*

LF: I never felt like I was being treated like a patient in any way. It's interesting that in his writing, he has made an analogy between psychotherapy and parenting. He noted that many of the traits that a good therapist would have in treating a patient are also qualities of a good parent: to treat the other person with respect for his or her boundaries, to be compassionate, and to not intrude on his or her uniqueness. I think those principles apply to both arenas, and my father exemplified those qualities.

HR: *Lisa, did your dad want you to follow in his footsteps and become a psychologist?*

LF: No, but I was very interested in the conversations he had with his friends and colleagues about philosophical and psychological ideas. I wanted to understand people, how they worked, how they felt, what motivated them. So I began reading books about psychology in my early teens. I was really fascinated by the subject and that's what got me into the field.

RF: I never encouraged her to go into psychology. I had no investment in my children's choice of career, or in Lisa's choice of career. My two sons went into business, but it was interesting that she did choose psychology. Lisa grew up in an unconventional environment where people were always talking about ideas and nuances of feeling. They were very concerned about the quality of life and were proactive in creating a warm and sympathetic lifestyle. It's been exciting that she did choose to go into psychology and I personally have benefitted from the collaboration.

LF: It was an exciting and stimulating environment for thinking about people, because there was always a feeling of adventure, of learning something new or trying new things.

RF: My interest in psychology was not limited to the office. It was part of every aspect of my daily life, and the majority of my friends had similar interests. Lisa grew up in a unique environment.

LF: Very unique. I was exposed to trying new things. For example, when Bob first started dealing with deep feeling therapy, I was really interested in the project and the results. It was fascinating and everything was shared openly with me. In fact, I found that what I was learning at home about psychology was much more interesting than what I was learning at school initially. By the time I went to college, the focus there was more on behaviorism. Freud wasn't very well regarded in my undergraduate program. However, in graduate school, I did learn more about psychoanalysis.

    I didn't feel that my father had any stake in my choice of career. But it's been really important to me to get his ideas out and available to the field of psychology, conducting workshops, presenting ideas, and discussing them with people. I love doing that. I was pursuing my own interest in ideas and beliefs, not just following in his footsteps.

RF: Speaking, lecturing, and teaching have never been my interests. I like developing ideas, theorizing, and writing about our clinical findings. So I was surprised when Lisa went into lecturing and teaching. I felt good that she did and I think it's had a big impact.

    There's something about respecting the independence of your children that left me not ego-involved in their choice of careers. I had no plan for them. I just wanted to see them develop their own feelings and make their own choices. It was never an issue what they chose. There were never any problems with them. If things had been negative, I would have interfered, but there was never a need. They all chose things that interested them. My life was active and full, and I had no need to live through my children in any way or for them to follow in my footsteps.

I think there was pressure on me to follow in my father's footsteps, to do what he did. I shied away from ever wanting to have that impact on Lisa. In my case, there was always pressure to perform but I never expected that of my children. And I admired my kids, I liked the kind of people they were and are and I like the way they approach life. I like their values. And we're a close family, a very close family.

HR: *Lisa, I understand that the environment that you grew up in wasn't the usual family structure. It was an environment that included a lot of people. Did that have any effect on your career choice?*

LF: I think it had a significant effect; it really stimulated my interest in people. Our house never felt like it had rigid boundaries. There were always people in and out. There was an open, welcoming attitude toward people. I remember the other kids in the neighborhood being drawn to being there. I have always lived in an extended-family atmosphere that has now grown to include a large number of people who share many aspects of life including work and travel.

I believe that the way I grew up taught me an attitude toward people that was nonjudgmental, not putting people into categories, and seeing all people as being essentially the same. Understanding that we're all hurt in some way or another, the hurt just manifests itself in different ways in different people. But the basic humanity of people is what is more important than any differences. I feel like I grew up in a very honest, open, and compassionate environment, very unusual.

When we were growing up, people who weren't part of our immediate family were important to us as role models. We still have personal feelings toward these people. We are a very close family, but it's not an exclusive family.

HR: *Okay, let's talk about voice therapy. Is voice therapy a complete system of psychotherapy like psychoanalysis, reality therapy, or cognitive therapy, or is it a powerful adjunct to use along with an existing psychotherapeutic modality?*

RF: I feel that voice therapy and separation theory are basically a complete system but the specialized techniques can be used by therapists from different schools.

As I described the methodology in my book *Voice Therapy,* the technique is made up of several segments. The part that most people have come to know as voice therapy, is the part where people express their self-attacks in the second person in a dialogue format, and react emotionally. Voice therapy per se involves three segments: verbalizing the self-critical inner voices and releasing the accompanying feelings; developing insights regarding their sources; and formulating corrective suggestions for important changes in life. In current practice, we have found it valuable in many cases to have deep feeling sessions prior to the voice sessions because it opens up relevant material, builds rapport, and helps clients to integrate material from the voice therapy dialogues.

These feeling release sessions are akin to primal therapy where people are simply encouraged to let out their deepest emotions. This expression of feeling relieves tension, revives painful childhood feelings and the traumatic events that caused them, and leads to important personal insights. In previous work with deep feeling release therapy, we placed a strong emphasis on confining immature emotions to the sessions and not acting them out in one's daily life.

Therefore, in the first stage of voice therapy (it doesn't always occur in this sequence) clients access their voices and are encouraged to let out their feelings. In the second stage, they come to understand the sources of their self-attacks thereby recognizing the enemy within, where it comes from, how it developed, and how it impacts their present-day lives. Negative introjects are revealed through verbalizing self-attacks in the second person in the dialogue. Becoming aware of these alien attitudes and prescriptions leads into the third sequence whereby patients and therapists collude in formulating life-altering suggestions that counter the faulty programming and limitations that are mediated by the underlying voice process.

As noted, the third part of voice therapy involves corrective suggestions; methods of countering inappropriate defensive behaviors, breaking with addictive processes, and risking new alternatives in life. Addictive behaviors include substance abuse, food addictions, compulsive habit patterns, withdrawal of affects in an inward posture that reduces the emotional exchange of give and take, fantasy preoccupation, and imagined connectedness or fusion with another in place of genuine relating (the fantasy bond). Accepting and acting on these suggestions demands significant resolve and courage on the part of the patient as there is always accompanying anxiety experienced when a person challenges core defenses. Nevertheless, the patient who faces the challenge and triumphs over his or her character defenses, has a maximum opportunity for personal growth and successful relationships.

In some cases, clients may feel motivated to "answer back" to their voice attacks spontaneously. They sense a need to affirm their own point of view after verbalizing hostile attitudes and thoughts towards themselves. However, expressing the process of answering back to the voice represents an attack on parental introjects and can arouse considerable guilt and anxiety in clients. Therefore, this particular method should be applied with considerable care and by a skilled and experienced therapist.

In conclusion, if you think of all three stages mentioned previously, voice therapy is a broadly based system of psychotherapy complete with an underlying theoretical basis. In what I and my colleagues have termed separation theory and therapy, a person challenges psychological defenses arising from separation anxiety and early trauma, confronts the fantasy bond with parents and family and eventually one's mate and children, moves toward individuality and independence, and faces his or her existential aloneness and death issues.

The theory unites psychoanalytic thinking and existential thinking because it not only deals with psychosexual trauma (particularly the oral level) and defense formation dynamically, but also emphasizes the importance of aloneness and death anxiety in solidifying the defensive apparatus throughout life. Death anxiety is conceptualized as the extreme form of separation anxiety and abandonment fears. When children become aware of death they first fear for their parents' lives and then for their own. The dawning realization affects children in different ways that support previous defenses formed in relation to traumatic interpersonal events. Many hurt children become cynical and hopeless, thinking and feeling, "What does my life or anyone else's matter, if you only die in the end?" Others who are more fortunate remain close to their feelings and place value on their personal ties and ambitions.

Separation theory explains how a person compensates for psychological pain, feelings of aloneness, and death concerns by forming intense fantasy bonds to alleviate anxiety. It goes on to demonstrate how these fantasy bonds interfere with personal relationships, career success, and overall life satisfaction. The concepts of the fantasy bond and the voice process explain the intergenerational perpetuation of debilitating psychological defenses and negative child-rearing practices, the emotional investment in religious dogmatism and other isms, and offer insight into the tragic problem of ethnic strife.

When fantasy bonds are established as a primary defense, people feel threatened to have their fantasies exposed or challenged and they experience considerable anger and an uncomfortable feeling of disequilibrium. This plays a strong part in negative interpersonal interactions. On a social or societal level, when other people's core beliefs disagree with their own, people feel threatened and most often manifest aggression. This intense aggression can be seen in racial and religious prejudice, religious crusades, ethnic cleansing, terrorism, and the like.

HR: *What is the basic difference between voice therapy and primal therapy?*

RF: What I call deep-feeling release therapy is akin to primal therapy; both tend to recover traumatic memories and feelings that people suffered as children. In the cathartic emotional release, they achieve insight into these hurtful experiences and realize the effect of these events on their present day lives. It's not a historical method of digging back into the past, yet it reveals the past in very direct, emotional terms, and leads to a kind of automatic insight, much as Arthur Janov described in primal therapy. However we feel that the release of feeling and accompanying insight is not a complete therapy.

In voice therapy sessions, as people verbalize their self attacks, and talk to themselves in the second person, intense emotions are released. Whereas primal therapy exposes the trauma of childhood from the child's point of view, voice therapy illuminates the parents' negative attitudes, feelings and critical points of view toward the developing child. These negative introjects (incorporated as inner voices and prescriptions) are a serious barrier to each person's fulfillment in life and play a significant part in self-destructive thought and action.

When people express their self-attacks in sessions, their voices often take on the tone and intonation of their actual family members. I have always been amazed at the intense negative affect and depth of sadness exhibited by patients during this procedure. These sessions recreate the family atmosphere and the original conditions that caused the emotional distress, bringing them to the foreground where they can be dealt with.

But insight, even insight combined with feeling, isn't enough to facilitate significant behavioral changes because ultimately a person must put into action the things that he or she has learned. In order to change on a character level, people must have the courage to challenge core defenses, particularly addictive behaviors that are limiting to their fulfillment. In our work we realize that defenses generally pose a limitation, but we respect a person's right as to how much he or she wants to challenge his or her defensive patterns. We understand that corrective suggestions to break with defenses are very anxiety-provoking. Patients may or may not decide to formulate the suggestions and following them but basically the therapy affords them the opportunity to go as far as they want to go.

HR: *Voice therapy seems to be conspicuously missing from the theories and techniques depicted in traditional counseling textbooks. When I interviewed Glasser for this book I mentioned that reality therapy was in this same predicament. Have mainstream counselor educators embraced voice therapy, or is it too new to tell?*

LF: I think more and more people are becoming interested in voice therapy as well as the theory on which the method is based. Last year, my colleagues and I conducted our first training workshop in voice therapy for clinicians. So I believe that people are becoming more informed about the method and its applications to various areas of clinical practice. We've also been invited to contribute chapters to a number of edited volumes on a wide range of subjects, including in a book about suicide intervention and prevention and a handbook on intimacy and closeness. However, I do think clinicians, as well as clients and people in general, have strong resistance to therapies that involve deep feeling and that challenge defenses in so direct a way as voice therapy does.

RF: In the beginning, teaching voice therapy techniques as such to psychotherapists or in workshops was not our focus. At first we viewed voice therapy primarily as a laboratory procedure which might advance our theoretical knowledge. Since we did not influence or interpret the material from our patients and volunteer subjects, the process yielded information that was both valuable and unique. In voice therapy sessions we simply described the technique, taught the patients to say their voices in a dialogue form, and encouraged them to express their feelings as they went through the process by saying such things as "Say it louder," "Let it out," "Don't hold back." As we assimilated the raw data from these sessions, our focus was to communicate the results of our work to the profession at large in the form of documentary films, theoretical papers, and books. In an empirical research project, we found that there was a close connection between voices and self-destructive behavior and developed a scale to assess suicide potential. Later we extended our work to assess an individual's potential for violence and had similar findings. Violent behavior was closely associated with negative voices toward self and others, particularly voices associated with victimization.

I think that the main reason voice therapy and theory has had only limited acceptance is largely because it represents a direct threat to psychological defenses. Our theory and methodology directly expose the abuses children experience in family life and the debilitating consequences of the internalized negative thought process once it is established. The method causes a great deal of discomfort for many practitioners because it elicits exceptionally strong affect, challenges fantasy bonds, and deals with core issues of separation and death anxiety. In a sense, there is no safety in this theory.

Psychoanalytic therapies tend to ignore the death issue or re-interpret it to a considerable extent, but they do focus on the "down and dirty psychodynamics" of childhood trauma and psychosexual issues. On the other hand, existential therapists focus on aloneness and death anxiety but don't deal sufficiently with developmental abuses and defense formation. So there's an element of safety in focusing on one or the other. Voice therapy and its overall approach to defenses is threatening to most individuals because is focuses on both issues and involves intense feelings. Our methodology is basically a depth therapy and people nowadays are shying away from deep feelings and depth therapy in general; they favor short-term solutions.

Furthermore, in spite of their wish to be objective, most professionals seek safety in their psychological theories. In our presentations, we have found that people in the field are drawn to the ideas until the basic issue of challenging core defenses becomes apparent to them on a personal level. Their interest is not in dealing with this issue in their own lives. For me, using this method of therapy is more challenging and threatening to defenses than any approach that I can imagine.

In summary, our work exposes the fantasy bond and other illusions that offer comfort and security, involves breaking with addictions and addictive routine habit patterns, copes directly with death and aloneness, and involves powerful emotions. In a day and age when many people are alarmingly conservative, defensively protective of families, moving away from close personal feelings, seeking short-term therapies, quick cures and designer drugs, it is unlikely that voice therapy will become integrated into the mainstream of psychological thought. Perhaps the future will offer a resurgence of interest in the truth of human experience. That is our hope.

HR: *I'm wondering, from what you just said, if you'd still want to become a therapist today, if you were a young person, and if so, whether you'd enter with the same sense of enthusiasm and excitement?*

RF: I think that I still would but I would realize that I was working against a strong negative trend in the field. If I had gone into practice in this more conservative, reactionary type of era, rather than the sixties, I probably never would have made the discoveries that I did or the overall contribution. I would have felt more restricted in every regard.

I would say that there's been a real backlash against freedom of thought and against delving into interpersonal issues, and even into existential issues for that matter. Voice therapy and the theory behind it would have been more popular in the liberal atmosphere of the sixties. People today are much more frightened and moving away from feeling. With the computer and increased mechanization, it's probably less likely that they'll move in a direction that allows for deep feelings and a focus on exposing painful issues of family life.

I was very idealistic when I entered the field and impressed with the courage of my predecessors. I wanted to get at the core of what caused the suffering and grief of my patients and make a contribution. I got into more than I intended because my investigations not only exposed the depth of damage within the families of my patients, but as I branched out I realized that these patterns extended to so-called "normal" families as well. Indeed, the normative dynamics of life in the nuclear family have become increasingly pathogenic. Current family practices are turning out more and more disturbed individuals and it shows up in every type of statistic, whether it's alcoholism, mental illness, drugs use, or suicide rates.

I am not opposed to family life; indeed, my life with my wife and children is my highest priority. Nevertheless, we must not hold the family sacred in a manner that protects it from being scrutinized and improved. Instead, I favor an extended-family view over the exclusiveness and seclusiveness of the nuclear family.

HR: *A lot of what passes for scientific psychotherapy is merely an expression of the founder's personality. For example, some psychotherapy historians believe that Freud's admission that he couldn't stand to be stared at for eight hours per day prompted him to practice his craft from a physical setting where the client*

*could not see his face (although Freud claimed this setup en-
hanced free association). My understanding is that voice therapy is the exception to the rule . . . well researched . . . and that
voice therapy was originally a laboratory procedure validated
with well over 1,000 clients. Tell us a little about the evolution
of voice therapy.*

RF: Voice therapy started as a psychoanalytically based system. As
I began working with John Rosen applying methods of direct
analysis in treating schizophrenic patients, I became aware of
the importance of the fantasy bond, and the incredibly debilitating effect of fantasy as a defense mechanism. When I studied
hallucinations and other schizophrenic productions, I began to
understand the concept of voices and their source. The period
when I was developing, understanding, and elaborating the
concept of the fantasy bond and exploring its relationship to
psychopathology, couple and family relationships, social issues, prejudice, nationalism, and religious phenomena was the
most exhilarating time of discovery that I have ever experienced. Afterward, when I was engaged as a psychotherapist in
private practice, I applied the knowledge about the fantasy
bond and internalized voices to a wide range of disorders. I
learned that the nonhallucinated voices of the normal, borderline, or neurotic individual paralleled those of the psychotic.
But at that time it was only a preliminary understanding.

At one point in my practice, my associates and I became interested in group work and marathons and in those situations,
our patients got into deep feelings. We found that there was unusual therapeutic value in getting into that depth of feeling. Ultimately we utilized methods, in part suggested by Arthur
Janov, to help people get into deeper, more primal feelings and
integrated the program into our clinical practice. In sessions
that involved over two hundred individuals, participants relived
painful childhood episodes with powerful insights that confirmed and expanded our theoretical views.

Years later, I began an observational study of family life in an
unusual environment made up of friends and families, a sort
of experimental laboratory, spanning twenty-five years and
involving three generations of "normal individuals." Because

these people lived in close proximity and spoke openly about their personal lives it offered a unique window into both their innermost thought processes and their interpersonal interactions. We were able to observe the intergenerational effect of these connections.

The marathons and the historical study of families tended to support our theory of the fantasy bond as a core defense. In each situation, people, with unusual honesty and courage, offered their personal experience and insights. In addition, they collaborated with the psychologists in the group in the development of theory.

HR: *How did you come up with the particular technique of saying voices in the second person?*

RF: On a personal level, I've always been pretty objective about criticism, but I noticed that certain attacks hurt my feelings and caused a great deal of pain. Upon analysis, I realized that these attacks didn't appear to be objectively true. I began to wonder why the attacks bothered me so much if they weren't valid. I came to the conclusion that it's not necessarily the truth that hurts us but rather the criticisms that coincide with negative attitudes and feelings we hold about ourselves. In other words, any experience that supports negative introjects caused by painful childhood experiences will tend to trigger self-attacking thought processes.

So I began to reveal my own self-attacks and bring them out into the open and it provided some relief. Later when people were struggling and were stuck in certain ways, I talked to them about revealing their self-attacks more openly and directly. I suggested to one of these people, "Why don't you just say those negative thoughts to yourself as though you were talking to yourself?" This immediately had a very powerful effect. As the man said his negative thoughts in the dialogue form, hateful, venomous, even savage thoughts toward himself came out. The intense degree of his rage and sadness surprised him. The people who witnessed this first voice session recognized its significance and concluded that further research into the dynamics of what we came to call the "voice"was essential. Soon, numerous patients and volunteers were exposed to the technique.

Amazing things happened when people said their voice attacks in that dialogue format. Instead of saying "I'm a bastard," "I'm tight," "I'm not nice," the minute they said, "You're bad," "You're not nice" etc., as though talking to themselves in the voice sessions, subjects exhibited deep feelings of rage toward self as well as incredible sadness. The intensity of the self-attacks was shocking. I had no idea, even knowing these people well, that they harbored such strong negative affects. None of them had exhibited any sign of the kinds of emotional reactions that came out when they started to say their voices in the new format. Along with the emotional release, subjects had clear insights and understanding. Noting the therapeutic progress of the first participants, we formalized the voice therapy technique and applied it with continuing success to a variety of individuals. It proved to help many people get past difficult barriers in their development.

HR: *Several therapies emphasize self-talk or internal verbalizations such as Aaron T. Beck's cognitive therapy or REBT as set forth by Albert Ellis. Specifically, how does voice therapy differ from modalities of this ilk?*

RF: I believe that our overall therapeutic approach is more comprehensive than cognitive or rational emotive therapy because it is a cognitive/affective/behavioral methodology. More important, it is based upon a theoretical system that explains the core defense of the fantasy bond and self-parenting and makes a clear distinction between the self-system and the antiself-system. It exposes the alien system of thoughts (ego discordant aspects of the personality), deals with their sources and explains their relationship to self-destructive thought and action.

LF: Voice therapy includes techniques that help clients identify destructive thoughts and beliefs and also elicit powerful expressions of anger and sadness. It also includes a behavioral component that consists of therapist and client collaboratively planning corrective experiences to decrease the client's self-defeating, self-destructive behaviors, and increase actions that are in his or her best interests and that reflect his or her real self.

The most important difference is that voice therapy evokes deep feelings quickly and clients tend to develop spontaneous insights. In our work, we're not asking clients to simply talk about themselves; we're asking them to attack themselves, to give words to the hostility and derogatory things they're telling themselves.

In our approach, all the therapist does is to suggest to clients that they say their self-critical thoughts in the second person— that's about it. Just that transformation in itself brings out deep feelings and material that the client may not have been aware of before the session. The therapist may demonstrate the technique a couple of times. A man might say, for instance, "Girls will never like me." The therapist responds by saying, "Say that to yourself in the second person, 'Girls will never like you.'" We teach people how to verbalize their negative thoughts in this format, that's all. We don't interfere; we don't tell people what to say or what not to say, and we don't analyze what they say. People make their own interpretations. That's a significant difference between voice therapy and other more psychoanalytic approaches.

RF: Overall, there's a remarkable amount of feelings released in using this specific format of saying negative thoughts in the second person, because in reality, we really do talk to ourselves. Schizophrenic patients, like the ones I worked with when I first dealt with these voices, really talk to themselves. They're split and they actually hallucinate. The internal voices can be conceptualized as being a form of thought hallucination. It's almost as if someone were saying these things to the person. We help people put their destructive thoughts in those terms.

LF: I don't think Beck and Ellis ask clients to identify their self-critical thoughts in the second person. Their clients usually report their "automatic thoughts" or "irrational beliefs" in the first person, as "I" statements. But it's interesting that over the last few years, cognitive therapy has moved more toward incorporating certain techniques that would enhance the expression of feelings. They discovered that it was important for patients to identify the destructive cognitions in what Beck refers to as a "hot emotional environment" in order to uncover deep beliefs or core negative schema about the self and others.

In addition, cognitive and REBT approaches focus primarily on the individual's present-day life. Ellis, in particular, explores this kind of judgmental thoughts—the "shoulds" and "musts" that people think—but he tries to argue people out of these beliefs. Ellis also proposed that people, as he once put it, "have exceptionally powerful *innate* tendencies to think irrationally and to harm themselves." In contrast, we feel that the tendency to think irrationally or destructively is not innate; it is due to real frustrations experienced developmentally. It has its origins in the abuses of childhood—from actual physical and sexual abuses to emotional abuse and neglect—in the child's subsequent pain, and in the defenses he or she forms to protect against emotional pain and frustration. In our work, we are concerned with the dynamic origins of the voice rather than with attempting to argue the client out of his or her irrational point of view by using logic, humor or questioning as in cognitive therapy or REBT.

HR: *Why do you think so much feeling is released when people put these voices in the second person?*

RF: As noted, I was surprised at the degree of aggression toward the self that people harbor, that did not appear anywhere else in their everyday lives except in subtle ways. Most never know the degree to which they resent themselves but when they get into the voice dialogue, they say things like, " I hate you're guts," "You don't deserve to live" "Smash yourself!," vicious thoughts toward themselves that they don't even know about, or never think about, consciously. Once they get into it, they're surprised. It starts off with some small criticism like, "You're this or that," but if you encourage them to say it louder and get more feeling into it, it suddenly takes off and more and more feelings come out.

I believe the reason that the second person format releases so much affect is that it actually recapitulates parents attitudes and feelings that were originally so hurtful. They feel the way they felt as helpless, dependent children exposed to painful, hurtful mistreatment. Incorporated negative attitudes toward the self come to the surface in the dialogue. This intense affect reflects parental criticisms, rejecting attitudes and hostility that are retained as an alien element in the personality in the form of voices and internal prescriptions. These voices, an ongoing inner dialogue, influence both feelings and behavior. In some sense people are always telling themselves about themselves, praising, criticizing, or running themselves down. Voices reflect an internalized self-parenting process. In essence, we generally treat ourselves the way we were treated in our developmental years. This has far-reaching consequences.

LF: One interesting thing is that these voices really do predict people's behavior. In our research on the thoughts underlying self-destructive behavior and suicide, we found that if we could determine specific negative thoughts that a client is directing against himself or herself, we could more accurately predict the extent to which he or she is at risk for suicide. This ability to predict has been found to be true across cultures. For example, in a study conducted in Pakistan using the Urdu version of our scale for assessing suicide risk, researchers found they could distinguish between people who had made a previous suicide attempt and those who had not. These destructive thoughts may also predict violent behavior. Our research seems to indicate that people with a potential for violence tend to experience specific negative thoughts, for example, thoughts about being a social misfit, prejudicial thoughts and beliefs, and victimized paranoid beliefs as well as rationalizations for committing a violent act and injunctions to act out violent impulses.

We constructed a scale composed of negative thoughts we had gathered over the years from suicide attempters as well as "normal" individuals. The items on the scale are presented in the second person format, "you." In filling out the scale, clients are asked to indicate how frequently they experienced the negative statements, such as "You should just get alone so you'll have time to think" (thoughts leading to isolation), "See how bad you make your family feel. They'd be better off without you" (thoughts leading to hopelessness), "You have to get hold of some pills" (planning the details of a suicidal act).

HR: *I really like your video* The Inner Voice in Suicide. *I've shown it so many times that I often joke with graduate students and workshop participants that if I ever lose my job I could get a job acting in that movie. The movie depicts a woman who came painfully close to taking her own life. It also does a stellar job of illuminating the ambivalence of the suicidal personality. In the video the woman reveals her own inner voice, with statements like "I hate you, I hate you," or "You're so ugly. Who would choose you? Nobody, nobody." Is it too big of a psychoanalytic jump to assume that these were things that were actually said to her as a young child? In other words, did her mother's voice become her own?*

RF: Sometimes voices actually reflect words that were spoken by parents or caretakers but they are not necessarily that literal. They do reflect basic attitudes and feelings of parental figures. Voice therapy recapitulates the emotional climate that the child grew up in.

Some theorists have said that when there is a suicide, somebody, on a basic level, wanted the person dead. I have indicated that children tend to incorporate negative attitudes directed toward them under stressful conditions. These inimical thoughts become part of an ego alien aspect of the personality. In that sense the woman in the film, in talking about her suicide attempt, was actually acting out her mothers thoughts and feelings toward her. At one point in her real life, her mother had thrown her down a flight of stairs. Incorporated voices are analogous to the concept of being possessed. I think that's why they make films of demonic possession like *The Exorcist*.

Unfortunately, we incorporate negative parental attitudes when parents are at their worst, at those times we undergo the most stress. Therefore, voices may not reflect the overall parenting picture accurately. But this points out that parental lapses can be very damaging.

One interesting discovery was that when there's aggression in the parent, whether it's directed toward themselves or outward, the child picks up the aggression as though it's directed toward him or her. A self-hating or depressed parent will have a detrimental effect on a child, even though he or she may not act that out aggression directly on the child. In these cases, the parent's aggression has been turned inward and has contributed to his or her depressed mood. The child takes on the parent's inwardly directed aggression in the form of a destructive thought process with the associated angry effect.

Voices not only represent negative parental attitudes but are also influenced by existential realities. Even under ideal parenting conditions there would be a certain amount of stress and unhappiness. The voice supports defenses that are based on warding off pain and anxiety and includes defenses relating to existential anxiety. So the source of the voice is not only negative interpersonal experiences but involves the overall human condition.

LF: I have had the opportunity to show the video *The Inner Voice in Suicide* to hundreds of clinicians over the years when I conduct training workshops for professionals about dealing with suicidal clients. I feel that this film has been a valuable contribution to the profession and has helped educate many therapists about what it going on in the mind of someone who is suicidal. I have recently been exposed to interviews with suicide attempters from colleagues involved in a variety of research projects. It was striking that each of the interviewees talked about these voices and describe what they were telling themselves that led up to the attempt on their life, even though the researchers were not schooled in our theory or approach.

HR: *Could you give an example of how the voice works in terms of the existential issues?*

RF: We tell ourselves, "It's no use. You're going to die anyway. You'll always be alone." Reminders of death are conducive to incorporating destructive thoughts, incorporating the existential dilemma into yourself. "You're not going to survive, so what's the point?" "Why invest emotionally in a life you must certainly lose?" This attitude plays a significant part in relationships, when people wonder why they should invest personally and emotionally in another when they will only lose them in the end anyway. This refers to both skepticism about trusting the love object and the fact that we are certain to lose them eventually through death. Voices are an internalization of negative imprinting that come either from interpersonal interactions or simply realizations about the existential condition.

HR: *Lisa, do you and your dad ever work together as cotherapists? If so, what is it like?*

LF: We've never worked together as cotherapists, but in my research, I applied my father's theory to suicide assessment and prevention, and more recently to developing an instrument to assess violence potential in adult and adolescent populations.

RF: Although we've never worked together as therapists in clinical practice, we have collaborated on research projects and theory formation. We both developed The Firestone Assessment of Self-Destructive Thoughts (FAST), a self-report questionnaire that assesses suicide potential and a client's self-destructive thoughts and behaviors. After testing more than 1,300 subjects, our results showed significant correlations between elevated scores, in terms of the frequency that subjects reported experiencing these self-destructive voices, and suicide attempts.

HR: *How did you folks get interested in suicidal behavior?*

RF: It was a logical progression in our work. In our theory, voices are closely related to self-destructive ideation and behavior. Investigating the relationship between voice attacks and suicidal ideology, suicide attempts and actual suicide followed in sequence. In our clinical experience, patients who were suicidal or borderline exhibited serious voice attacks. Our film, *The Inner Voice in Suicide* (Parr, 1985) illustrated how voices predominate as a person vacillates in his/her suicide intent and action. Richard Heckler, in his book (*Waking Up Alive,* 1996) confirmed our findings, pointing out that among the fifty people he interviewed who had survived a serious suicide attempt, virtually all reported experiencing destructive voices. Negative-

voice attacks prevailed, not only revealing the fundamental ambivalence about taking their own lives, but also their voice attacks ultimately goading them to attempt suicide. We worked
with Richard Seiden, PhD, MPH, a suicidologist, to further develop the theory and construct the FAST. Seiden's ideas coin-
cided with our hypotheses and helped to stimulate our research.

LF: But it was Surgeon General C. Everett Koop who suggested
that our theories about self-destructive behavior and suicide required hard experimental evidence in order to be taken seriously. He also expressed how valuable it would be to have a
scale to predict suicide. After hearing his commentary, we set
out to developing our empirical research on the FAST.

HR: *I know that you've studied the inner voice and child abuse. Can
you comment briefly about your findings in this respect?*

RF: In part we see our children as extensions of ourselves and this is
conducive to projecting our negative traits or characteristics
onto our offspring. Our response is to either become excessively critical or punitive or attempt to compensate for these
projected negative qualities. Both types of responses are detrimental to the well-being of our children. Parents' voices about
themselves become the voices of their children. For example, a
father whose voices tell him he is not a real man will worry
about his son's masculinity and his son will grow up having
similar doubts. In this manner, voices are perpetuated through
the generations.

Our documentary film, *The Inner Voice in Child Abuse*, explores the role of the voice process in the repetition of both
physical and emotional child abuse from one generation to the
next. The program depicts parents revealing how they were
treated as children as well as describing interactions with their
own children. In the film, a group of parents illustrate their
voices and the personality dynamics underlying the perpetuation of a damaging cycle of emotional child abuse.

More recently, we produced another documentary, *Invisible
Child Abuse,* which shed additional light on patterns of emotional child abuse that have been largely neglected in today's

focus on physical and sexual abuse. The people in the film reveal that despite the success they have achieved in their lives, the damage they sustained in growing up, albeit subtle, had debilitating effects on their self-esteem, impaired their personal relationships, and limited their career pursuits.

My book, *Compassionate Child-Rearing* (1990) explains the dynamics of emotional child abuse. In the foreword, R. D. Laing eloquently explains why it is unlikely that parents can sustain a loving relationship with their children. In the book I go on to describe how children's freedom of movement, spontaneity, and self-expression intrude on parents' psychological defenses. Parents then react to the anxiety that is aroused by this disruption of their defenses and psychological equilibrium by inadvertently distancing themselves from their children or restricting or punishing them.

LF: The book explains the underlying dynamics in family relationships and how well-meaning parents unintentionally hurt their children's self-esteem, spirit, and personality. We then used the principles and methods from the book and excerpts from our films on parent-child relations to develop a parent education program. The classes focus on parents' personal development, and the films and class discussion help them gain compassion for themselves in relation to negative events they experienced in their childhoods. A small pilot study showed that there was an increase in parents' self-esteem and positive attitudes toward their children after participating in the classes.

HR: *Recently, when I've received requests to provide suicide prevention lectures, the persons contacting me have told me that other agencies and suicide centers have turned them down. The persons running these centers are worried that such lectures can do more harm than good. Personally, I have never experienced this. What's your take on this phenomenon that seems to be a throwback to the past? You know, if we talk about it, they'll do it.*

LF: I agree with you that this way of thinking is a throwback to the past. There is no evidence showing that educating young people about the signs of suicide (in themselves and their peers) increases their propensity for attempting suicide. In fact, the only way we can prevent suicide on a larger scale is to inform people about the danger signs or risk factors to look for in their friends and family members, and to encourage them to be open in discussing suicidal feelings rather than keeping them secret.

There was a small body of research showing that some suicide prevention curricula in certain high schools may have had some detrimental effects. However, lectures or classes conducted by clinicians who have expertise and experience in the field of suicide prevention can provide valuable information to adolescents and adults regarding significant signs of suicide and how to obtain help for themselves or for a friend or family member who may be at risk. There are many well-researched programs for educating youth about suicide that have demonstrated positive outcomes.

HR: *What is your position on using a verbal or written contract with the suicidal individual? I've heard experts assert that the procedure is worthless. Nevertheless, I've talked with individuals who insist they are only alive today because a therapist, or perhaps a school guidance counselor, made them promise not to commit suicide twenty years ago.*

RF: It's a good technique and also indicates a genuine spirit of caring. Clients get a very good feeling from entering into a no suicide contract, a sense that you're really in it together.

LF: I believe that therapists should make responsible use of antisuicide contracts. The client signs a written contract or agrees verbally not to kill himself or herself during the next period of time—a period that is decided upon by the clinician and client. The client also agrees to contact the therapist by phone any time he or she feels unsure of his or her ability to resist suicidal impulses, (leaving a voice message does not count). Antisuicide contracts help to establish a therapeutic alliance, but therapists should not be overly reassured by the contract to such an extent that they fail to continually reassess the client's level of risk or institute a more developed intervention strategy that addresses their clients' suicidality.

Like you, I have clients who feel that a therapist's contracting with them contributed to their being alive today. So while I agree it is one of the things we should do, it should be part of an integrated strategy for reducing the client's suicidality.

HR: *Any thoughts on how the media and mental health profession-als should handle the so-called Werther or contagion effect where the suicide rate goes up after a famous person commits suicide or down during a newspaper strike? We can't live in a perpetual world of newspaper strikes . . . although truthfully, with the papers and television broadcasts inundated with hor-rendous news, it is a comforting thought.*

LF: The media coverage following a suicide of a famous person or of a high school student, for example, can be handled effec-tively and responsibly. The American Association of Suicidol-ogy (AAS) and the Center for Disease Control (CDC) both pro-vide specific guidelines for media coverage of a suicide. The AAS also will provide contacts that schools can use for helping students, parents, and teachers cope with the feelings aroused by the tragedy. One of the guidelines states that the media should provide information about the help that is available in the community, together with telephone numbers of active "hot-lines" where people can be put in touch with counselors or ther-apists. Obviously any program or news story that dramatizes, glamorizes, or romanticizes a student's or star's suicide should be strictly avoided.

The contagion effect must be taken seriously. This effect was observed in the months following Marilyn Monroe's suicide in a 12 percent increase in suicides in the United States, particu-larly among young females. However, after this initial rush of imitative suicides, the rate actually fell. Possibly those individ-uals who were already engaging in suicidal thinking and behav-iors, in learning of Monroe's suicide, were influenced to act out the negative side of their ambivalence about living or dying.

A striking example of responsible press coverage can be found in the aftermath of Kurt Cobain's (the lead singer of the rock group Nirvana) suicide. One would have thought that dozens of young people might have been influenced and would have followed his example and attempted suicide. Actually there was a decrease in the suicide rate in the Northwest and Seattle areas in the months after Cobain's suicide. However, there was a significant increase in the number of calls from young people to hotlines. At each memorial and in each news story, the numbers of these hotlines and Suicide Prevention Centers were announced. In addition, rather than romanticizing her husband's suicide, Courtney Love expressed sadness about her loss and also anger about his needlessly wasting his life, hurting his friends, and abandoning his family. Her message probably also helped save lives.

HR: *A new therapist is just starting out and I've only given you ten minutes to spend with him or her. What important message would you convey to this neophyte helper?*

RF: I would emphasize that considering the lack of definitive scientific verification for any specific approach to psychotherapy theory and methodology, that the individual practitioner avoid dogmatic attitudes and doctor-patient role-playing, maintain absolute honesty and personal integrity with patients, and continually strive to understand and develop himself or herself in his or her own life.

Perhaps the most significant barriers to effective psychotherapy are the psychological defenses and defensiveness of the therapist and therefore, it is essential that the new clinician undergo a successful psychotherapy experience to minimize these effects. Ideally, this therapy experience would emphasize deep feeling release and the working through of transference distortions. Only by learning to fully feel and cope with our own emotions can we tolerate, respect, and allow our clients to express and understand their deepest feelings. We must emphasize the fact that all feelings are acceptable and only actions must be scrutinized in terms of moral considerations, reality testing, and other consequences.

Above all, the therapist must remain an authentic human being with real feelings. So many children have been hurt by immature, emotionally deadened, role-playing parents. Just as children learn more by example than instruction, clients reflect a similar identification with their therapists. Children suffer from contact with emotionally hungry parents who manifest needy attitudes toward them, and the same holds true for emotionally hungry therapists. Therefore, it is vitally important for the therapist to achieve a high level of emotional maturity and maintain positive, fulfilling interpersonal relationships. If a therapist's life is emotionally flat, and he or she is excessively dependent, hostile, or phony, these issues will inevitably spill over into his or her therapeutic encounters.

The ideal therapist is an artist who can sensitively imagine what his or her client would look like without his or her usual defenses and limitations and would never impose on or in any way damage his or her individuality. Ideally, we must constantly strive to become better human beings, with respect for the fragile nature of other people, their personal boundaries, and unique qualities.

HR: *Lisa, what was the most important thing your dad taught you about working with clients?*

LF: The most important thing I learned from my father was a compassionate way of looking at people. I learned this from observing how he treated people in everyday life. He always saw the real person, not just the person's defenses. He responded to the person underneath. He saw the armor or the defenses that people use to push others away. But he also realized that everybody is hurt to a certain extent and that people come by their defenses honestly. In other words, something happened to them early in life that made it necessary for them to protect themselves by forming defenses. He has compassion for people, which I believe is one of the most important elements necessary for establishing a therapeutic relationship. It helps in two ways: one, patients don't feel judged or criticized; and two, this attitude also tends to draw out the real self of the patient, his or her real wants and desires and priorities.

If therapists are compassionate, they are supportive of the patient's real self. When signs of the real wants and interests of the patient come to the surface during a session, therapists support that aspect of his or her personality and help the patient take chances on giving up his or her defenses. A major part of any effective treatment process involves the therapists' ability to communicate to a client their vision of what the client would be like without his or her defenses.

In fact, research has shown that the nature of the relationship that develops between therapist and client is the most important variable contributing to a positive outcome in therapy. Statistics can be cited that indicate that nearly 80 percent of a client's change is attributable to the relationship between the therapist and the client, whereas only about 7 percent is correlated with the type of therapy the clinician is practicing. So the personality characteristics of the therapist are significant factors that contribute to an effective therapeutic relationship, and I think my father exemplifies those qualities, being nonjudgmental and seeing the best in people. He is able to make contact with the most vulnerable part of a person. That ability has had a profound impact on me in terms of how I try to work with clients.

HR: *You work with some tough clients. What are your trade secrets for preventing burnout?*

RF: That's an interesting question, which I hadn't really thought much about. I believe that as long as the therapist remains a genuine, feeling person in the therapeutic encounter, constantly growing both personally and intellectually, his or her work will remain interesting and vital. Every session should be looked at as a fresh experience, never rigidly applying a theory to the patient; instead a theory should evolve for each individual. As long as a real experiential copresence is manifested in sessions, they will never be dull.

In relation to tough cases, and the possibility of therapeutic failure, it is wise for the clinician to have resolved any sense of his or her own vanity or omnipotence. A mature approach to psychotherapy involves a respectful awareness of the limitations of both parties. It's painful to hear a naïve and immature therapist boasting of successes or worse, of cures. A single person's psychological development is multidetermined and complex and its evaluation requires careful analysis and a good deal of humility.

LF: I am involved in some clinical work, however I am engaged in a number of other activities—teaching, training, and conducting research—which makes my career well-rounded. I know that I would find it difficult to be solely involved in psychotherapy practice.

I also think that it's important, as my father said, to stay in a feeling state while engaged in clinical practice. Therapy never becomes old or stale for me because I don't put people in the category of being "a patient."

I have advised therapists whose practices include high-risk suicidal patients to limit the number of suicidal patients they are treating at any one time, because working with that type of person can be really draining. In working with depressed or suicidal patients, you really do care, you really don't want them to die, and you really feel the struggle they're going through. You become deeply involved and concerned despite the fact that many people who are extremely suicidal are not that likeable. They are usually doing a lot to alienate you and other people in their lives, because they're living out the image of being a bad person who nobody likes and nobody cares about. So it's very draining work, because you may be continually fighting against their efforts to elicit a negative response or treatment failure that will fit their image and expectations.

HR: *I feel kind of like an old record stuck in a groove because I've been asking nearly every professional I've interviewed some version of this double-barreled question. What are your thoughts and feelings about (a) managed care and (b) psychologists getting the right to prescribe meds to patients?*

RF: I feel terrible that managed care is restricted to only a comparatively few psychotherapy sessions. It is ridiculous to imagine that a therapist can effectively help a depressed or anxious person in a short time. It leads to methods that are inadequate attempts to achieve quick cures. In addition, managed care demands that clients be considered mentally or emotionally ill in order to qualify for treatment and therefore implies medical remedies.

I believe that clinical psychologists with appropriate training should have the right to prescribe medicines to their clients. But I'm worried about the increased use of drugs in the general practice of treating people with emotional problems, attention deficit disorders, etc.

LF: I think that there is a serious problem with managed care today. The decision process is out of the hands of the professional treating the client. The most frightening example is with suicidal patients where the clinician may feel that the client needs more frequent sessions or longer-term treatment, yet gets their request to provide this treatment denied. This can have serious consequences for the client and the therapist.

I believe in parity for psychologists getting paid for treating patients just like other doctors. I believe in parity for mental health. I think that if you are dealing with mental health concerns, these are often reflected in physical concerns. There's a real argument for psychologists taking a more central role in managed care networks, and it is important that psychologists are brought in or consulted early in the treatment process.

The prescription rights issue is complicated, and I think that medicating patients is currently not being done particularly well. Much of the prescribing is being done by general practitioners, not by psychiatrists with extensive training in psychotropic medicine. In addition, I think many people in this country are on medications that may or may not be helpful. For example, currently we are prescribing medications for children before we have conclusive data on the long-term effects or side effects on the developing brain.

But do I personally want to be able to prescribe medication for patients? No. I think as a psychologist, you need a working knowledge of psychotropics, data about the impact the drug might have on a particular client. I believe therapists can provide a valuable service monitoring their clients' reactions to medications, their medical compliance, or abuse of such medicines. We should be wary of the belief that medications are going to solve everything for our clients. Research shows that in disorders like depression, where medication can be effective, it is the medication plus psychotherapy combination that has the best long-term outcomes associated with it. In treating a depressed client, for example, I would in most cases recommend a psychiatric consultation. At the same time, I would also provide quality psychotherapy.

HR: *Look into your crystal ball. What does the face of psychotherapy look like fifty or seventy-five years from now?*

LF: I hope that there will be a backlash toward a more humanistic view of people, but I don't know if or when that's going to happen. It's also true that these movements (the progressive and regressive cultural movements that Murray Bowen wrote about) have tended to occur in waves in the past. First we had the sixties where people were really interested in themselves and in looking into psychology, and now we've moved away from that focus to some extent. We focused on our physical health and exercise and today, many trends in our culture, for example, the continuing focus of terrorism threats in the popular media appear to be indicative of a movement toward the cutting off of feeling. Certainly since 9/11, with the terrorism attacks and continuing focus on political threats have created an atmosphere of fear. Research post–9/11 shows an increase in all types of vices, smoking, drinking, and other methods for numbing ourselves. Of course, the number of people seeking psychotherapy also increased. With the situation that we're creating in the world right now, it looks like we're going to have many more problems to deal with before things get better or before the field of psychotherapy moves in the other direction.

RF: It is difficult to imagine. Current trends suggest that psychotherapy, particularly depth therapy as we know it today or better yet, would like to know it today, is unlikely to exist. Psychotherapy would probably be conducted largely on the Internet or Web sites. Psychiatrists and psychologists would probably be administering more effective designer drugs to combat emotional ills, and their practice would be increasingly more pharmacological and less talk.

Brain research will offer the possibility of new and exciting treatment modalities that involve direct manipulation of the brain. Genetic theory and research will combine with brain research leading to a broader understanding of genetic predisposition and its effect on psychological development. Evolutionary psychologists will contribute a greater understanding of evolutionary determinants and their effect on human motivations. In spite of these other trends, group work, workshops, corporate retreats, lifestyle coaching, and other new approaches to human relationships will most likely continue to play a role in the future.

In my opinion, psychology must not and indeed, cannot simply be reduced to genetics, biology, and evolutionary preconditioning. These movements should not discount or minimize the effect of environmental conditioning or programming on the psyche. Environmental effects and in particular early environmental influences within the family will always be a significant factor in an individuals psychological development.

On an interpersonal level, there will always be a need for some form of psychological counseling. Marital therapy, sex therapy, seminars on child-rearing, and couples and family therapy will most likely prevail.

In conclusion, I would like to refer to my article, "The Death of Psychoanalysis and Depth Psychotherapy" (Firestone, *Psychotherapy,* 2002) and discuss some of my conclusions about what I consider a destructive reactionary trend in our society.

"Numerous attempts have been made to explain the demise of psychoanalysis and depth psychotherapy, placing blame on secularism among analysts, insufficient empirical research, prolonged treatment time, monetary considerations and managed care. I consider the primary cause to be an implicit cultural movement to squelch serious inquiry into family dynamics and interpersonal relationships, in particular information about the widespread manifestations of physical, sexual, and emotional abuse of children. To revive the humane practice of depth psychotherapy, therapists need to make use of the recent findings from neuropsychiatry and attachment research to support their clinical research, scientific work that emphasizes the importance of early psychosocial environmental influences on personality development. Clinicians must also have the courage to challenge restrictive societal pressure, sacred illusions concerning family life, and their own psychological defenses in order to reestablish a legitimate practice of depth therapy that moves away from quick fixes and over-reliance on the medical model." (from the Abstract)

"When one considers the paradoxical aspects of psychotherapy practice and its effects in relation to a culture characterized by denial, it is easy to understand the resistance to psychoanalysis and depth therapy. Societal forces combined with individuals' resistance have effectively extinguished this unique form of inquiry and conspired to shut it down as a source of insight and illumination."

"It is possible for psychoanalysis and depth psychotherapy to survive and find a resurgence if courageous individuals inside and outside the field of psychotherapy are willing to challenge cultural attitudes and illusions that cause so much personal damage. Energy must be directed toward understanding and improving emotional interactions within the family system. We must develop a more objective view of present-day family life, and critically evaluate dehumanizing child-rearing practices. Without this resurgence, much important meaning in life will be sacrificed, a uniquely valuable therapeutic tool will be lost, the future will be bleak for those individuals suffering from emotional distress, and a powerful methodology to help mankind move toward a truly compassionate and moral approach to life shall have been abandoned. . . . I am convinced that the tens of thousands of individuals who have benefited in life from depth psychotherapy share this concern."

HR: *Thank you for sharing your time, energy, and insightful ideas.*

Chapter 10

Samuel T. Gladding on Creativity

Samuel T. Gladding is the director of and a professor in the counselor education program as well as the associate provost at Wake For-
est University in Winston-Salem, North Carolina. He has been a practicing counselor in both public and private agencies. Gladding is the
past editor of the *Journal for Specialists in Group Work,* and the past
president of the Counselor Education and Supervision (ACES), the
Association for Specialists in Group Work (ASGW), and Chi Sigma
Iota (international academic and professional counseling honor society). Some of his most recent books are: *Becoming a Counselor: The
Light, the Bright, and the Serious* (2002), *The Counseling Dictionary*
(2001), *Counseling: A Comprehensive Profession* (Fourth edition,
2000), *Group Work: A Counseling Specialty* (Third edition, 1999),
The Creative Arts in Counseling (Second edition, 1998), and *Family
Therapy: History, Theory, & Process* (Third edition, 2002).

HR: *Sam, I was just updating my book the* Encyclopedia of Counseling *and there you were. I thought to myself . . . I better check out
the Gladding textbooks. There could be something critical I'm
overlooking. My colleagues said, "Oh, you're updating your
book, you need to check out the Gladding texts." When you first
entered this field did you ever dream that your texts would be
the staples or, dare I say it, some of the gold standards in our
field?*

This material first appeared in Rosenthal, Howard. 2002. "Samuel T. Gladding on
Creativity." From *Journal of Clinical Activities, Assignments, & Handouts in Psychotherapy Practice,* 2(2), pp. 23-33. Reprinted with permission.

SG: I think dreams are the underpinnings of change and during my life I have dreamed a great deal. However, even in my wildest dreams I did not entertain the idea, except briefly in a moment of euphoria and hope, that my counseling texts would do well.

I mainly started writing because I was not pleased with the texts I was using in my courses. When I griped one too many times, a colleague challenged me by saying: "Well, if you can do better, I'd like to see it." I could not let the challenge go unanswered. So, I decided I would like to write a book. I was pretty naïve and did not realize the enormous effort that goes into such a project. When I approached a rather large and prestigious publisher, I was firmly and rather quickly turned down. In fact, I remember the conversation I had with the editor of the company. It may have lasted two minutes at most. I went away discouraged, but not defeated.

I still thought I had something to say that was fresh and clean so I began writing my first book—*Counseling: A Comprehensive Profession*—without a contract. The second editor from a different publisher, who I talked with a year after my initial rejection, was most kind and encouraging. Her name was Vicki Knight. She was honest in her feedback with an intriguing British accent. I followed her suggestions for writing and my first book emerged. It was exciting and invigorating. I loved the process and actually got (and still get) mentally stimulated by the research. In summary, I actually exceeded my expectations (and probably well exceeded the possibilities my nineth-grade English teacher ever had for me). I am most fortunate.

HR: *If Freud truly analyzed Little Hans by mail then I ought to be able to pull off this question. If we had to perform a vest-pocket analysis of your childhood, what do you think was the catalyst for your superior creativity?*

SG: First let me say that I am flattered by your two final words "superior creativity." While I consider myself somewhat creative, I would never use a modifier like "superior" to describe what I do or who I am. That being said, I will try to give you a vest-pocket analysis of my childhood. Believe me, it was nothing like "Little Hans." We did not have horses in our neighborhood!

I think my creativity stems from both an innate tendency to enjoy play and from the challenges of my environment. Early in my life, I was an observer. I had disconnected hips and spent essentially my first two years in a hospital in a full-body cast. To be honest, I do not remember a lot from that time except I am sure it sharpened my tendency to be aware of what was around me and how things work.

Another early influence on my life was my grandmother, Inez Templeman, whom my older sister, brother, and I called "Pal," because she told us she was our pal. I remember hearing many family stories from Pal and it heightened my curiosity about people and their interactions with each other. I know my imagination kicked in during this time (ages four to sixteen) and I filled in details on my own, often creating several endings to a particular story.

The fact that I was small for my age also had an influence on the development of my creativity. I had to come up with clever ways to either outwit or win over bullies and those who judged me by size alone. Thus, I learned how to read different situations and people and how to verbally spar with humor. This interaction spilled over into other realms of my life and actually helped make me popular with my peers and adults. So I continued it.

Another important influence in my early life related to creativity was the fact that my family was anything but affluent. My mother and father were quite resourceful, having suffered through the Great Depression and the shortages of World War II. I was rewarded with smiles and words for being thrifty and innovative. I was taught to make everything stretch to its limit.

Finally, stubbornness, optimism, and encouragement were important factors in my becoming creative. As a child and adolescent I did not think there was anything I could not do. In addition, my parents rarely discouraged me from doing the impossible or improbable, including trying out for the basketball team when I was a foot shorter than anyone else. Through my childhood I learned rather quickly what I could not do but I tended to concentrate on the positives, avoid the negatives, and frequently tried the new and challenging (which I enjoyed).

HR: *Okay, Sam, define creativity. How will we know it when we see it in the psychotherapeutic setting and give some examples of how you have personally used creativity in the treatment process?*

SG: Creativity as a concept is elusive. Just when I think I know what it is, it changes. Maybe that is the nature of creativity or perhaps it is a part of human nature.

My latest thinking about creativity is that it involves divergent thinking where elements within the environment are arranged or rearranged so that a new and productive process or outcome occurs. In creativity there is a recognition, an "aha" experience, that what has been assembled has a usefulness that provides pleasure or possibilities that were not present before it came into being.

I think that all effective long-lasting psychotherapy is creative in nature. Counselors are catalysts. As such they are creative in their sessions and help their clients think, behave, and/or feel differently so that the clients are more aware, appropriate, and satisfied with life because they leave sessions with more choices than they began with. Sometimes the process of counselor creativity involves adding something to sessions that was not there previously—stimuli, such as thoughts. At other times, it is helping clients rearrange what they already have but may not be using effectively, such as words. Then, of course, there are times that to be creative barriers must be eliminated, for example, excessive behaviors.

In my own life, many times I have tried to be creative in sessions through using the expressive arts. Frequently, I will ask clients to draw lines that represent their feelings at the moment. Wavy lines often represent energy and optimism, while straight lines may represent a static state of being. Colors contribute to the emotion conveyed and help make clients more attuned to what is inside of them. This type of experience is an example of the additive approach I mentioned earlier. It can easily be converted into a rearranging experience where insight emerges with new or different drawings. At other times, I help clients by assisting them in highlighting features already in their lives, such as the art within their language. For instance, if clients tell me they are lost, I explore with them what roads they are on and which ones they might travel as well as avoid.

HR: *I'll never forget the first time I came across Haley's* Uncommon Therapy *(1973). I was convinced that Milton H. Erickson was doing something new, something exciting, and certainly something that was creatively different. I often had that same feeling when I read psychotherapy dialogues by Ellis, Lazarus, Salter (okay, in the case of Salter I realize I'm dating myself), and others. In essence, these folks became my role models. Did you have any creative heroes or heroines who influenced your work?*

SG: Leo Goldman, then the editor of the *Personnel and Guidance Journal* (today the *Journal for Counseling and Development*) and Arthur Lerner, a psychologist from Los Angeles, are probably the persons who have influenced my work the most. They are both heroes in my eyes for what they did and how they helped me develop.

Leo Goldman, as many professionals know, was a researcher scholar. He wrote extensively on methods of research, evaluation, and statistics. Yet, he was not afraid of creativity and actually welcomed the submission of poems into the journal he edited. My first published work was a poem that I wrote during my first clinical position. During Goldman's tenure as editor, I wrote and published many more. He wrote exceptional letters that helped me realize that counseling was multifaceted. I still have them and reread them every so often.

Art Lerner came into my life when I was making a presentation at the American Psychological Association annual convention in 1979. Never having met him, I quoted him that day not realizing he was in the front row of the audience. I was in my early thirties and just a novice at making presentations. He took me out to dinner that night and stayed in touch with me regularly thereafter. He got me involved in the National Association of Poetry Therapy and helped me realize anew the power of words and how creativity is so much a part of therapy.

HR: *The behaviorists and supporters of NLP praise the merits of modeling. Will sitting around pigging out on fat-free popcorn and watching reruns of Gloria and Rogers improve a counselor's interventions? In other words, is it helpful to watch videos or listen to tapes made by creative therapists? I guess we are back to the nature versus nurture thing: Are creative helpers born or are they made?*

SG: There is a great lyric by the rock group Meatloaf that goes "Baby we could talk all night, but that ain't getting us nowhere." While the use of English in the lyric is not wonderful, the thought is solid. I think it is important to watch highly skilled professionals in action. Bandura and company have the data that indicates modeling works (with or without fat-free popcorn).

However, Gloria Estefan is also correct and in tune with Meatloaf when she sings "Get on your feet. Get up and make it happen!" No one ultimately becomes creative as a counselor without practicing the helping skill arts basic to the profession. I think it is when we become comfortable with those skills that we dare to go beyond them and trust ourselves to tailor-make the therapeutic experience with our clients so that it becomes powerful, productive, and often creative. My father used to tell me as a young man that I could not be promising forever. I think that is the same with all of us. There is life beyond the Gloria films and we make our own mental videos every day through our counselor/client interactions.

HR: *Okay, say I want to become a more creative therapist. What's the paradigm? Is there some type of a paint by number, step-by-step process, or turnkey method? Will I need to sit on a mountaintop, meditate, and contemplate my navel for a year? I remember when I wrote my first book I couldn't come up with an innovative title. I tried and tried to no avail. Finally, I said the heck with it. I literally gave up. Then one day, while I was driving down the highway, thinking about totally unrelated issues, a terrific idea popped into my head. I swerved the car over to the curb and wrote down the idea. To this day, I always carry a sheet of paper in my pocket for creative moments like this.*

SG: I think that your car episode is a great example of what it takes to be a creative therapist. In your case, you thought for a long time on a subject that was important to you. Nothing happened, so you stopped concentrating. Then, it happened. An idea literally popped into your mind almost by accident (and it nearly caused an accident). The important point is that you incubated your thought and it came back to you in a brand new idea that literally moved you (and has helped move your book).

I think it is important to work hard on an idea and then in the words of the Beatles "Let it be, let it be." What happens when we let go of trying to control the idea is that our mind can relax and play with the thought in associating it with other experiences that move in and out of our lives. I am like you. I do not travel without paper and pen. I do not sleep without the same at the nightstand. Many times nothing happens during our down times of relaxing and incubating a thought. But when those times come, watch out!

HR: *Sam, I remember when I was taking the final courses for my doctorate and my advisor said I needed to have a more well-rounded education than I had at that point. Therefore, he placed me in a seminar on John Dewey's poetry. After selling the farm or at least taking a student loan for the next decade to pay for this privilege, we concluded that there was some reason to believe the fellow who collected Dewey's trash might have actually drafted the poetry. All I walked away with was the knowledge that it was the other Dewey (Melvil) who created the infamous Dewey decimal system for libraries. I know that you have written time and time again about the role of poetry in psychotherapeutic treatment. Since the course left me clueless, could you summarize your findings for me as well as the readers?*

SG: I think since antiquity people have had a premonition that literature plays an important part in our mental health and wellbeing. Unfortunately, there are some people who mean well, such as your doctoral advisor, who do not know exactly what to do with that universal hunch. As a consequence those who are around them suffer sometimes in multiple ways. (By the way, suffering also may produce more literature, especially poetry.)

In my own life, I was fortunate to discover early that it was not the Dewey decimal system (or even the Library of Congress system) that was important, but the books that they categorized. And I might add, I was blessed to realize that not all books are equal in speaking to us. (Maybe that is why there are so many books.) For instance, like you, I had a well-meaning but slightly misguided teacher who insisted that all of us in her class come to love a particular poet whose name I will not mention here. Well, the poet was probably okay if you had an experience in your own life that had some parallels to the poet's in regard to thoughts and events. Unfortunately, I did not. Thus, I found it painful and nonproductive to spend large quantities of time trying to decipher what I was reading. On the other hand, when I began my work in a small, rural mental health center I immediately became intrigued with the poetry my clients often brought me. The quality of their writing was not refined but the power of their feelings flowed in such a way that there was a universal dimension to it that was powerful and that persistently played in my mind. I think they were helped in writing and getting some of their pain out on paper. I, in turn, also benefited, for as a counselor I began to realize how much better I understood them.

I have been pleased to see in the last decade or so the work of James Pennebaker and other researchers who have documented both the physical and psychological benefits of writing. While not as well documented, reading has some similar benefits, too. That is especially true when there is identity by the reader with a character in the story. A therapeutic spillover effect is present also in lyrics, when clients and even ordinary people sing or say them. Human life with all its joys and tragedies is captured in words of poetry and sometimes in prose. At such times, clients and counselors can see as well as hear what they are thinking and feeling. What powerful moments!

HR: *Say a therapist is a strict behaviorist, reality therapist, REBT, or whatever. Is that therapist limiting his or her creativeness when compared to a helper who is eclectic?*

SG: I think the secret of being a good therapist is in knowing what you are doing. You can be true to one theory and still be creative. On the other hand, you can be eclectic and not worth very much. I used to work with someone who described therapy as "electric" (i.e., you did whatever turned you on).

Well, all of that said, I think the only limits to creativity in the therapeutic process are those that clinicians put on themselves. If they are strict adherents to an approach and do not believe in going beyond what the founder of the theory advocated, they will most likely not be creative. However, either purists or eclectic counselors can be quite creative. To do so they must know their approach or approaches well. They must also be attuned to themselves and their clients and be willing to take calculated risks that are appropriate within the context of a session. Thus, creativity requires a bit of courage along with clinical ability and an openness to possibility.

HR: *Is creativity ever a negative thing? I mean are there times when it can get you into trouble?*

SG: I think that like most things in life, creativity can be negative as well as positive. It depends on how it is used. For instance, I can see creativity being negative in people's lives if they think they must always be creative. Such a thought would become an obsession and be detrimental to one being creative. There are times, many times, when routine or the ordinary is just fine. I do not want to think about how I can have a creative breakfast every morning or counseling session every time, for it would be too taxing and tiring. Likewise, creativity can be negative if it is imposed on someone instead of generated within the person. What is helpful and creative for me may not be for you. As clinicians we need to realize that creativity is like a knife. In the hands of a surgeon it is a wonderful tool. In the hands of a criminal, it is destructive.

HR: *Let's talk managed care. Is it our friend or a foe? Is managed care mental health's worst nightmare or the savior of psychological treatment? Some experts insist that managed care has forced us to become more creative . . . to quit engaging in slow,* *insipid, treatment strategies. What is your take on this phenomenon?*

SG: I think there are user-friendly aspects to different elements in treatment. Managed care is probably not a factor that most therapists would say is one of those aspects because it can stifle spontaneity, creativity, and even the processes needed to help bring about change in the long run. On the other hand, managed care is not necessarily all bad. As you have pointed out, it has helped some counselors make the most use of the time they have and be more innovative.

I think that however we view managed care, we have to recognize that it is like the elephant in the living room. There is no way of getting around it for now for most of us. Whether the elephant will move or whether we will find a way to move the elephant is still undecided. However, I think that we should think of moving experiences with our clients, ourselves, and with companies or forces we do not necessarily agree with. If we set our thoughts in such a direction, I think we will find that we travel past the problem of today and into a potentially better future.

HR: *Sam, since I know you've done work as a university administrator, I must ask you this. Although licensing and certification are desirable we hear more and more that students only take courses that count toward credentialing. I recall an innovative graduate course in counseling that was so popular in the eighties that you needed recommendations from employers to get in. Everybody wanted it. The course is still relevant but it recently was dropped because nobody signs up for it. The students discovered that it wouldn't help put a sheepskin or a license after their name. Couldn't this trend stunt our professional growth in this field?*

SG: Your point is well made. Just taking what is required leads to probably less versatility and ability. I can remember in my initial counselor education program, for instance, that I took a course on the complete works of Shakespeare in addition to what was required. I cannot tell you how many times that course has enriched my counseling sessions. Clients usually come to us without ever having taken a counseling course. However, they have knowledge of life in many subject areas. If we are to relate to them effectively, we need to move beyond just therapeutic knowledge. Courses and life experiences either build bridges or erect barriers to our communication. I hope that both experienced and novice clinicians have expanded as well as continuing education on their minds. In my opinion, counseling is not just a process; it is a liberal art.

HR: *Sam, I've got to run in a minute since an old TV show with Bob Newhart as psychologist Bob Hartley is ready to come on and I'm hoping to pick up a few pointers. Please give our readers one final gem of wisdom to ensure that creative lightning strikes during the next session of therapy they perform.*

SG: I think my final thought about creativity in therapy is that it is usually something that comes with time, hard work, persistence, and playfulness. I think most clinicians can be creative but they have to be secure in their knowledge, open to themselves and their clients, willing to take calculated risks that expand the horizons of the sessions in which they are engaged, and have a tendency to be playful. Clients are allies in the process. If we listen to them we may learn much.

It is like author James Baldwin said: "Not everything that is tried can be changed but nothing can be changed unless it is tried." Creativity is worth trying. With it comes the possibility of change.

Chapter 11

One-on-One with William Glasser: Counseling with Choice Theory, the New Reality Therapy

William Glasser, MD, is so well known that he hardly needs an introduction. Dr. Glasser is the founding father of reality therapy (now the new reality therapy) and choice theory. His ideas regarding counseling and education have had a tremendous impact on the helping and teaching professions.

HR: *Young and Feller (1993) researched several divisions of the American Counseling Association and discovered that you were in a three-way tie with Albert Ellis and Salvador Minuchin as the second most influential therapist. The respondents also suggested that your1965 book* Reality Therapy *was the second most influential work in terms of their own counseling practice. When you were a child did you ever think you would grow up to be one of the most prominent psychiatrists of all-time?*

WG: I didn't think of becoming a psychiatrist as a child. That occurred while I was training to become a clinical psychologist as a young adult. I worked for a while as a chemical engineer my first short career. One of my psychology teachers suggested I go to medical school and become a psychiatrist, but I didn't think I would get accepted. But after I got into medical school and recognized that there are some real flaws in the way they taught psychiatry I got the idea I could do better. After I got into

Therapy's Best
© 2006 by The Haworth Press, Inc. All rights reserved.
doi:10.1300/5189_11

psychiatric practice I got the idea I could do better and I'm still trying.

HR: *Was your training in psychology and psychiatry basically Freudian?*

WG: I was totally immersed in Freudian psychiatry. It was during this time that I began to doubt the concepts and began to develop the ideas that became reality therapy in 1962.

HR: *Tell me about the evolution of reality therapy.*

WG: Reality therapy hasn't changed that much from where it was until about 1977 when I became involved with William Powers in a group of ideas that I initially called control theory but evolved into what I am presently working on, which in 1996 I began to call choice theory. The control ideas were good but the name was very misleading. It implied that the theory was about controlling others when it is actually about controlling ourselves.

HR: *When you wrote the book* Reality Therapy *was it an overnight success? Were agents and publishers fighting for rights to the manuscript or did it take a while for it to catch on?*

WG: No one fought over *Reality Therapy*. But I wasn't surprised by its success. By that time I was involved in an extensive lecture schedule and I could get a lot of feedback and it was all very positive.

HR: *Now that we've mentioned book publishing, let's talk about professional helpers. As a graduate student in the late seventies I remember hearing all these wonderful things about your approach, nevertheless, your name and your theory were conspicuously missing from my textbooks and class lectures. Were theoreticians biased against your approach in the early years? If so, why? Was it too commonsensical . . . too pragmatic? I mean you must admit that perusing Freud is a bit like reading a combination of Greek mythology and physics.*

WG: My professional helpers were G. L. Harrington, MD, instructor in my residency whom I stayed with mentor and pupil for seven years after my residency was completed. He was, essentially, the only psychiatrist who recognized that I had something to contribute. I never got a referral from a psychiatrist in all the years I was in practice. As far as the field of psychiatry is concerned I didn't exist then and I don't exist now. My helpers have come from the fields of corrections, education, and counseling. I have plenty of them.

HR: *Okay, let's fast-forward to the present. I want to acquire some insight into your newest and most innovative ideas. I know that you now assert that defining mental illness must be completely separate from defining mental health. Tell us about that.*

WG: As far as I am concerned, my ideas have been on a steady and expanding course since I published *Reality Therapy* in 1965. It has evolved due to my association with William Powers where I added control theory that later I changed to choice theory. The evolution was such that in 2001, when the book was reissued, I called that book *Counseling with Choice Theory: The New Reality Therapy.* All of my counseling is now counseling with choice theory, which means that I teach choice theory to the client along with the reality therapy, because what I'm really focusing on . . . and this brings me completely up-to-date . . . is what is called mental health. The problem is that when psychiatrists mention the two words mental health, what they are really talking about mental illness.

I now focus on mental health, which is basically not doing with your life what you want. I discuss this in my most important paper to date called "Defining Mental Health As a Public Health Problem," at my Web site at www.wglasser.com. And the subtitle of that paper is "A New Leadership Role for Counselors." It is available for everyone to read, copy, and talk about free-of-charge.

In the paper I talk about the medical model, which is very destructive to people's mental health since it stigmatizes them with a mental illness they don't have. Let me emphasize that in the case of psychiatry no pathology has ever been found that can be replicated with any kind of a test. There is no X-ray test, CAT scan, MRIs, blood tests, all the usual tests that discover pathology that ever found in any of the illnesses listed in the DSM-IV. If you push the psychiatrists who created that book they'll say, "We know the pathology is there, we'll eventually find it. But since we know it is there, we're going to act like we found it and use the medical model."

I'm now associating myself with counseling, because all I've ever done is counsel. I counsel with choice theory now, which is a new reality therapy.

Once again, psychiatrists have created a book that I think is an extremely harmful book—harmful to the mental health of many people—called the DSM-IV.

HR: *Let me be very blunt. Do we need to bury the medical model of mental health and its alter ego, the DSM, at this point in time?*

WG: Yes, that's what we need to do; that model is destructive. The DSM describes psychological symptoms, and of course in choice theory I change symptoms to verbs. I don't use nouns such as depression. Instead I say the client is depressing, panicking, compulsing, manicing, hallucinating, and obsessing. These symptoms are described reasonable accurately in the DSM-IV, but then psychiatry takes a huge leap in the wrong direction and states that these symptoms (either individually or as a grouped together as syndromes) should be called mental illnesses. The book then defines these as aberrations or pathologies in the brain caused by chemistry or the person's genetic structure. None of this pathology has ever been found. It is just assumed that it is there because we always thought it was there. It is just a common sense thing. There are a few neurological diseases such as Parkinson's disease that is thrown into the book to confuse people. You might say, "Well, if Parkinson's is truly a disease, then the other conditions like schizophrenia, depression, and all the other things psychiatrists diagnose must also be caused by pathology in the brain."

Parkinson's is a real illness caused by pathology in the brain: the others are not. There is no pathology in the brain. The diagnoses are wrong and stigmatize the person with the diagnosis.

It has gotten to the point where counselors and others who are not psychiatrists who treat these people are afraid not to recommend medicine to treat these people. They are also afraid not to diagnose these clients with the DSM, otherwise they will be accused of malpractice. In reality, drugs can't treat these things because drugs can only treat a pathology.

Pediatricians often diagnose kids with attention-deficit disorder (ADD) or attention-deficit/hyperactivity disorder (ADHD) and all of this is false and misleading and harmful and I am trying very hard to set the record straight.

What people are suffering from when they have symptoms is what I call unhappiness. I always say that the best way to describe these people is that they are not mentally ill, but rather less than mentally healthy. Just like a couch potato is not physically ill, but he or she is less than physically healthy. But a couch potato knows that if he or she exercises more and eats less, he or she can get back in shape. A person diagnosed with a mental illness is not mentally ill. The person is analogous to the couch potato in that he or she is less than mentally healthy. Since the beginning of counseling thousands of years ago people have come because they are unhappy.

Unhappiness is an appraisal of my life in which you say, "My life is not going the way I want it to go." You can have any or all of the symptoms in the DSM without being mentally ill. Even a schizophrenic who gets creative with symptoms such as hallucinating is not mentally ill.

HR: *Recently, you put forth the notion that mental health should be treated as a public health problem. This is seemingly a landmark approach that I don't believe any other psychotherapeutic theorist has espoused in the past. How did you come up with this position? Also, please give us the rationale why people with psychiatric symptoms should be treated as public health problems.*

WG: Yes, it is a landmark approach. What I'm now saying . . . and this is my latest part of what I'm teaching and believing . . . is that the model that should be used is the public health model. The public health model is different from the medical model. In the public health model, doctors may be involved but they are not in charge. For example, sanitation is a public health problem and many people would be ill if we did not clean up the water and dispose of sewage properly. The public health model is teaching people to live their lives differently and in doing so avoid diseases with pathology. In recent years the most prevalent disease that has been avoided in modern times is lung cancer, by teaching people . . . that's the public health model . . . to stop smoking. The number of people who smoke has been reduced by 15 to 26 percent in the past ten or fifteen years. This is a tremendous reduction and thousands and thousands of lives have been saved through the public health education process.

Depressing, manicing, obsessing, hallucinating, and deluding, are psychological symptoms with no pathology behind them and thus there is no medical treatment for them. Clients with these problems don't need a drug or a doctor since no pathology has been found.

The symptoms are real and people with them do suffer, and the clients need to be taught choice theory to improve their own mental health. Mental health is something you can be taught, just as you can teach a person to stop smoking.

I use the triple metaphor: mental health, is happiness, is choice theory.

I came up with this approach because from the very beginning I never thought that there was anything wrong with the brains of any of the people I dealt with, including those diagnosed with psychiatric labels from the DSM.

HR: *Am I correct that you have never prescribed psychiatric medicines for your clients?*

WG: I have never prescribed a psychiatric drug because I am credible in what I am saying. I never felt the need to prescribe a psychiatric drug. In some cases these drugs can be harmful and in some cases even kill people . . . the drugs cause people to kill themselves.

HR: *What about the notion that the patient has a chemical imbalance or low serotonin levels or whatever? Do we really, truly*

*have irrefutable, hard-core, ironclad scientific evidence to sup-
port the notion of giving medicines to clients? You know . . . I
hear it every day . . . there's always some big new study . . . or
perhaps from our clients who say, "I'm different than the rest of
your clients, my psychiatrist told me I have a chemical imbalance."*

WG: They are desperately looking for something because if they
can't find something then they have less and less reason to
prescribe the psychiatric drugs, which are now a billion-dollar,
possibly approaching a trillion-dollar practice.

Every day you read in the paper about a new gene, or a new
chemical that has been found, or a new flaw in the brain, or
something like that. Of course, they find things. I don't claim
that a person who is hallucinating or deluding has exactly the
same brain chemistry then a person who is not doing these
things. Just like I don't think we have the same brain chemistry
when we are unhappy. But a normal brain can have a difference
in chemistry without that brain being pathological.

HR: *Is it accurate to say that when psychiatric medicines work, they
are merely acting as placebos?*

WG: They are acting as two things. Obviously, the major action is
placebo and extensive studies have shown especially if people
are given in a large, warm-colored pill and told that these pills
will help you with these symptoms, it is probably better than
giving medications because the medications have harmful effects. I've used placebos myself with people. But, I've always
told the people (these were people who were experiencing severe pain) this is a placebo, it's not supposed to work, and nobody knows how they work, but sometimes it does work and I
think it could help you. I was working as a psychiatrist for Los
Angeles Orthopedic Hospital then and a lot of people with severe back pain said, "Dr. these placebos are absolutely the
greatest." Of course they work great, a lot of pain is associated
with belief. Unhappiness is one of the greatest causes of physical pain that has no pathological cause.

Also, some of the SSRIs [selective serotonin reuptake inhibitors] that are common drugs, act as amphetamines. They give you a lift and you feel better. Of course, amphetamines are addictive. I've worked with people and I've said things like, "Why don't you stop the Prozac now that you feel so well?" They will say, "I can't stop. The minute I stop I don't feel so well." So you can see the addicting effect.

HR: *As this book goes to press, psychologists in two states have joined the ranks of psychiatrists acquiring prescription pads. What impact will this have on the profession of psychology?*

WG: Psychiatrists will fight very hard against that on the basis that these are really medically ill people that only doctors can handle. But if psychologists do get this privilege then the effect on psychology will be just as powerful as the effect on has been on psychiatry. I would need to change the title of my book *Warning Psychiatry Could Be Hazardous to Your Mental Health* to *Warning Psychiatry and Psychology Could Be Hazardous to Your Mental Health*.

This is why I'm working with counselors now. Because all I've ever done myself is counseling. That is why I say that counselors should take the lead in mental health. This is something that counseling can do—counseling can be a public health program, teaching people how to get along better with the important people in their life.

HR: *Well, based on that last statement, let me ask you this. If you were first entering the field now would you become a counselor or perhaps a social worker rather than a psychiatrist?*

WG: I think I would probably become a counselor because social workers have a lot of other functions such as getting housing for people. Social work is a nice profession, but I think I'd rather counsel.

HR: *You often talk about the fact that humans are driven by needs. Tell us about that.*

WG: Other creatures are driven by four basic needs: survival, love and belonging, freedom, and fun. Human beings have a fifth need . . . a need that leads to war, to abuse in families, harming and hurting each other, and that need is the need for power. Power does not have to be harmful. We can certainly be powerful, as many famous people have done, by helping their fellow human beings. Albert Sabin, who developed the polio vaccine, became very, very powerful because other people respected him. The way to satisfy your need for power in a choice theory fashion . . . a way that helps you keep close to the important people in your life . . . is to gain respect from these people.

Many of the symptoms in the DSM can be caused by trying to change other people. Depressing and suffering from pain are the most common symptoms. These symptoms help us escape the control of other people or literally to escape the idea of controlling ourselves.

HR: *You recently urged American Counseling Association members to become involved in the mental health movement and in the process ditch the mental illness paradigm.*

WG: Counselors listen to me a great deal. I am giving the presidential address regarding mental health as a public health problem to the American Counseling Association in 2005. I figure 50,000 counselors who can't prescribe drugs, but have counseled successfully using a variety of counseling methods such as Albert Ellis's model, or that set forth by Aaron T. Beck, as well as success with the new reality therapy, counseling with choice theory, can take the lead in mental health. It is open for the taking and I say counselors ought to take it. Let psychiatrists have the lead in mental illness. And if psychiatrists criticize counselors for using the term mental health, the counselors will point out that the term is accurate, that these people are not mentally ill.

HR: *The new buzzword in our field seems to be integrative counseling and therapy. The notion implies that combining two or more psychotherapies yields better results than using a single approach. Can your methods be combined with others popular* *modalities, say Ellis's REBT or Beck's cognitive therapy, or would such integration only serve to weaken the treatment process?*

WG: I am not against other psychological methods such as Adlerian psychology, or Albert Ellis's REBT, or Aaron T. Beck's cognitive therapy. All of these can be taught to people as choice theory is taught to people and then they could use these to improve their own mental health. What I'm saying is that choice theory is not the only way. I doubt whether there is any single model that is any better than any other. The main purpose is to help people get along with other important people in their lives, literally to choose to behave differently as choice theory says. Every time we choose a behavior—and everything that we do from birth to death is to behave—then ask yourself: "Will this behavior get me closer to the important people in my life or get me closer to the life I want to live or will it separate me from those two goals?" If it gets you closer, then it is a good method of counseling, regardless of what it is called, and if it separates you from those two goals, then it is an ineffective method of counseling. Any counseling theory that uses the medical model is ineffective and is a harmful approach.

HR: *I'd like to ask you a personal question here. I've asked many of the therapists in this book how they use their own theory as self-help when they are having a day from hell or perhaps just a difficult situation. Can you give an actual brief example where you replaced external control with choice theory to deal with a particularly tough situation in your own life?*

WG: I use choice theory all day long. Choice theory is the basis of everything I do. I realize that my behavior has an important effect on other people and I want it to have a helpful effect. For example, in my marriage I get rid of the habits that harm relationships, and when you get rid of these habits all of your relationships improve. I get rid of criticizing, which is the worst; I get rid of blaming, which is bad; I get rid of complaining, which is also bad; I get rid of nagging, threatening, punishing, and bribing. These are very deadly habits. In fact, I use examples from my own life as I counsel people and teach people. I use choice theory to live my life and replace the external control theory most people adhere to.

HR: *Most of our readers are therapists. What is the biggest mistake therapists make and how can they improve their counseling and therapy sessions?*

WG: Using the DSM to diagnose problems that don't exist. Another mistake they make is talking about the client's past. Unless helpers focus on the present failing relationships in the client's life or the lack of present relationships, they are wasting the client's time and money. Talking about the past is a way to avoid the present.

HR: *Tell us about your work and interest in fibromyalgia.*

WG: I got involved with fibromyalgia because they [the medical establishment] call it a disease. It's not a disease. Fibromyalgia is a group of symptoms: pain, fatigue, and difficulty concentrating. About six or seven million women suffer from fibromyalgia and maybe a million men. Thus, about 90 percent of those who suffer are female. Since it afflicts so many people, I thought I ought to inform people that this is not a condition that can be treated by the medical model. It consists of symptoms that people can only improve by improving their mental health and when they do they recover from their symptoms. In 2001, I wrote a book called *Fibromyalgia: Hope from a Completely New Direction.* In the book, I talk about a woman who works for my office that is completely recovered from fibromyalgia. She put choice theory to work in her life as I do in mine. The severe aches and pains and even fatigue often result when individuals are trying to approach perfection. They have to be less demanding of themselves and they can certainly learn that with counseling with choice theory. Hence, my book applies choice theory to chronic pain. Pain, that has no physical cause as occurs in what is diagnosed fibromyalgia, is caused by unhappiness and is the same as any other symptom in the DSM-IV. I thought the book would become a big seller but the people who

have the pain would rather suffer than act differently in their relationships.

HR: *I know you just returned from lecturing in the Orient. I believe
you have several institutes in that area of he world.*

WG: Yes, you are correct. I have institutes all over the world. I received an unbelievably warm reception where I just lectured in
Japan, and in Singapore, where I have institutes. I also lectured
in Hong Kong and I got a tremendous reception there. I was
asked a question by an important person in the mental health
field in Hong Kong: "Dr. Glasser is there any place in the world
for psychiatry as psychiatry is practiced now?" And I told him
as far as I can see there is no place for psychiatry as long as they
follow the medical model. They are destroying the very thing
they are trying to help.

HR: *Thank you for taking time out of your busy schedule to share
with us. This interview has been a real eye-opener.*

WG: I wish to thank you very much, Howard, for you giving me a
chance to express these things. I'm looking for every chance to
put my new approach, treating mental health as with a public
health program. That's core to everything I stand for right now.
Thanks again.

Chapter 12

Les Greenberg:
Emotion Makes a Comeback

Les Greenberg, PhD, is professor of psychology at York University in Toronto, Ontario. He is the director of the York University Psychotherapy Research Clinic. He has co-authored texts on *Emotion in Psychotherapy* (1986), *Emotionally Focused Therapy for Couples* (1988), *Facilitating Emotional Change* (1993), and *Working with Emotions in Psychotherapy* (1997). He co-edited *Empathy Reconsidered* (1997), and the *Handbook of Experiential Psychotherapy* (1998). His latest book is *Emotion-Focused Therapy: Coaching Clients to Work Through Emotion* (APA press, 2002).

Dr. Greenberg is a founding member of the Society of the Exploration of Psychotherapy Integration (SEPI) and a past president of the Society for Psychotherapy Research (SPR). He has received the Distinguished Research Career award of the Society for Psychotherapy Research, an international interdisciplinary society. He is on the editorial board of many psychotherapy journals, including the *Journal of Psychotherapy Integration* and the *Journal of Marital and Family Therapy*. He conducts a private practice for individuals and couples and trains people in experiential and emotion-focused approaches.

HR: *Les, I'm really excited about this interview because I'm convinced that our readers are going to learn something new, exciting, and creatively different. So let's start at the beginning. How did you end up becoming a therapist?*

LG: From high school on I was very interested in working with people. I was involved in leadership roles at school that entailed working with people and I enjoyed that, and I had a group of male friends with whom I was trying to workout the "meaning of life" and we were all very psychologically minded. I think this is where it all began explicitly. I also came from a family that suffered external stresses and I was the resilient one. My friends and I were all outsiders, reading existential philosophy, critical of inauthenticity and of society, and in South Africa that was not difficult. And we all were interested in intimate relationships. Two these friends went to medical school and after a stint at being jazz musicians became psychiatrists and now are psychoanalysts, so our interest in psychotherapy was there early on in some nascent form even though we didn't yet know it. This sense of the importance of tacit knowledge, of knowing more than I could say has always been an important idea to me. I however did not want to be a doctor and worshipped math and physics. So I did an undergraduate degree in engineering to which I was guided by a counselor rather than in physics because supposedly in engineering one could work more with people, which in a limited way is true. Once in engineering I was not very happy and tried to steer my studies toward industrial engineering because this involved more consideration of people. I did not consider doing psychology in South Africa as it was not a recognized profession and I didn't see it as a science and I valued science. I left South Africa in 1968, for political as well as educational reasons, and completed a master's degree in engineering systems in Canada. It was there in the context of the inner exploration, taking place in the sixties in North America, that I decided to move to psychology, which looked much more attractive from a North-American perspective. My wife had graduated in psychology and through her I was exposed to counseling and went initially into a counseling PhD at York University. There I became a student of Laura Rice who had been trained at the Chicago Counseling Center with Rogers. I had heard that she believed that curiosity was an important motivation that led people to explore in counseling. This idea appealed to me as I already had formed views that behaviorism was too simplistic and Psychoanalysis was too pessimistic. My contact with Laura was the most important influence in my development as a therapist and a researcher.

HR: *What modalities were you originally trained in?*

LG: I first trained as a client-centered therapist and then as a Gestalt therapist. After seven years I also trained as a systemic therapist at MRI in Palo Alta.

HR: *On your Web site at www.emotionfocusedtherapy.org you say that cognitive therapy and medications may be overused. Tell us about that.*

LG: Although they can be helpful I think they often are more about symptom management or developing coping skills than about deeper emotional restructuring or dealing essentially with the causes of the symptoms. Sometimes I think medication is extremely useful and necessary but it is also often overused. Although the development of coping skills may in the long run lead to change by promoting self-efficacy and thereby leading to changes in the persons view of self this is not assured. The problems of relapse in both CBT [cognitive behavior therapy] and drug treatment troubles me as does the short treatment that results from their promotion

HR: *Some psychologists in the United States have been given medication privileges. Is this a good thing are a health hazard?*

LG: I am not sure this is a good thing, but do not have a clear understanding of all the issues.

HR: *Okay, how did you discover emotion-focused therapy (EFT)?*

LG: I am not sure it was as much discovered as invented. It is a humanistic/experiential therapy and draws on client-centered and Gestalt therapy and integrates these approaches with emotion theory and in our couples therapy we integrate this in addition with systemic/interactional perspectives. EFT predominantly was developed through research focused on what makes people change. It thus comes from a combination of my background experience and from research. Much of the individual therapy was developed from process research. Even the couple's therapy originated with my study of how people resolve conflict in two-chair dialogues and from looking at the process of conflict resolution in couples to see if it was similar. My focus on emotion also came from a combination of training and experience and from studying the process of change in which I repeatedly observed that emotion often seemed to signal that important change was occurring.

In the first book Laura Rice and I wrote, called *Patterns of Change* (1984), we were studying how people change. I then looked at these therapies I was being trained in for what seemed to be the most active change processes. We tried to look at how to measure these processes and so on. At this point I began integrating client centered and gestalt therapy and I was very interested in cognition at the level of cognitive science. I did my minor in cognitive development at that same time I studied with Pascual-Leone, a student of Piaget, and so I was very interested in the processes of cognition. But I wasn't interested in cognitive therapy, which held a very primitive view of cognition as thought and belief. Instead, I was very interested in the role of attention, in Piaget's notion of action and experience producing schemes and in constructive cognition, and then in emotion theory. So I was bringing all of that to bear on studying the process of change through the lens of cognition and emotion and how these processes take place. So I integrated all of these things, but essentially I was integrating a client-centered relationship with gestalt therapies more active interventions, with a type of constructivist view of how meaning is created in people. And then I was psychodynamically informed having read and been interested in British object relations theorists like Fairburn, Guntrip, and Winnicott.

I began to study specifically how people resolve intrapsychic conflict within themselves, or in gestalt terms splits which are more conscious conflicts, and I built my first model of a change process. The split-resolution process looked like the resolution of a conflict between two people, except it was between two voices in one person. I was simultaneously very interested in couples and family therapy so I trained in family therapy with people like Virginia Satir and then Minuchin, and then I later went to Palo Alto and studied with people there who used a systemic approach. After that I began to direct my attention to how couples resolved conflicts and built an emotionally focused couples therapy based on similar sorts of ideas that emotion was very important but now there was interaction as well. So what I did was integrate lots of different things. I began to feel comfortable with more therapist directiveness from family work where the therapist was more structuring and guiding and this fed back into influencing my approach to individual therapy, which had up to that point been very nondirective. From this I finally came up with the idea of the therapist as an emotion coach—that what therapists are actually doing is acting as facilitative coaches, helping people be more aware of their feelings, regulate their feelings, reflect on and transform their feelings. So EFT is an integration of lots of different strands but at its most fundamental it's an integration of client-centered and gestalt within a cognitive-affective science theoretical framework and the addition of an interactional perspective.

HR: *Can you give us a vest-pocket definition of EFT as well as the basic implementation process?*

LG: EFT is a therapy that as its name says focuses on emotion. In this view core emotions need to be brought into awareness to change them. In more general terms both the therapeutic relationship and the specific change processes are seen as important in promoting change. A warm, supportive, empathic, validating relationship is a crucial ingredient of both accessing affect and helping it transform via new relational acceptance. The dyadic regulation of affect is important from birth into adulthood. Distressed emotion is soothed by the presence of a responsive other. In addition to offering an emotion regulating relationship we attempt to help clients access adaptive emotions in order to promote change, resilience, and strength.

EFT thus is based on two fundamental ideas: empathic attunement to affect and differential intervention to promote emotional processing. Within the context of an affect regulating, empathically attuned relationship therapists pay attention to particular kinds of processing difficulties that emerge in the sessions and intervene differentially. The therapist as well as adopting a certain way of being outlined by Rogers also does different things at different times to facilitate different kinds of emotional processes. Doing different things at different times can involve either intervening at the level of the moment-by-moment processes or by asking someone to pay attention to what's going on inside his or her body which is making a specific moment-by-moment intervention. Or by suggesting a larger task such as asking someone to imagine a significant other in an empty chair and engage in a dialogue with the imagined other in order to facilitate a particular kind of processing found to be most helpful for that type of problem state. Initially we identified six or seven types of emotionally based problems and specific interventions designed for those states. States such as unfinished business involving an unresolved bad feeling toward a significant other, problematic reactions, and internal conflict. So we've defined different kinds of problems that are then worked on with a particular intervention with a focus on emotion. The therapeutic style involves a combination of following and leading, with the leading closely attuned to clients' current possibilities. Finally EFT suggests "you can't leave a place until you have arrived at it." Thus you have to experience the emotion you need to change and you need to experience new emotions to produce change. In our view *emotion is needed to change emotion* and we in addition need the wisdom to know which emotions we can trust and use as a guide and which we need to change, i.e., we need to know which emotions to change and which to be changed by.

We suggest that human beings' lives are profoundly shaped and organized by emotional experiences and that emotion is the creative and organizing force in people's lives. In therapy we work to enhance peoples emotional intelligence, which involves the recognition and use of one's own and others' emotional states to solve problems and regulate behavior. We focus on *increasing emotional awareness* and on *helping people with their affect regulation* (affect regulation refers to cognitive, affective, and behavioral strategies people use to increase adaptive more positive emotions and decrease maladaptive unpleasant emotions) with *reflecting on emotions to make sense of them* and on *transforming emotion with emotion*. Our goal is thus change in self-organization via increase in emotion acceptance, utilization, and transformation.

In EFT we help people become aware of what they are feeling, to find better ways of coping with their feelings, and to transform old emotional responses into new ones. It is not whether a belief is true or not that is at issue in EFT but rather whether it is useful or adaptive. Clearly negative beliefs about self generally are not adaptive. So beliefs are not disputed rather they are viewed as maladaptive and the work of therapy is not to disprove them but to generate alternative emotional states and different modes of processing that are more functional. EFT proposes working in domains of value and what is good for one rather than on whether something is true or logical. *Change in meaning,* however, is important in EFT and we have developed a dialectical constructivist view of self-functioning in which the person is seen as a dynamic self-organizing system always dynamically synthesizing many component process to form a current operating self-organization. This tacit dynamic process provides a bodily felt referent, the feeling of what happens. This when attended to and symbolized in awareness forms our experiencing process which then enters into a dialectical process with our more conceptual, linguistic, culturally informed explaining processes. We thus live in an ongoing process of making sense of our experience and thereby create the self we are about to become. This self we construct is constrained by biologically based emotional experience and by cultural forms of explanation. We thus create meaning by dialectically synthesizing influences from biology and culture.

Emotion, however, is neurologically primary. Messages from the emotional brain prepare the body for flight or fight and the prefrontal cortex for analyzing whether there is novelty, danger, attack, loss, and so on before we are consciously aware of what we are responding to. In people who are depressed, for example, the tacit evaluation is often one of diminishment/humiliation or insecurity/anxiety and this leads to the activation of core depressogenic emotion schemes which include bodily feelings of shame or fear as well possibly as dysfunctional beliefs and negative thoughts in language. In this view emotion is primary and beliefs are the tip of the iceberg that articulate rather than determine experience. The activation of emotion schemes occurs out of awareness and is synthesized into a feeling of what happens. When not attended to or avoided this leads to secondary bad feelings such as depressive hopelessness or despair. In EFT it is the core emotion and the fundamental evaluations and modes of processing embedded in affect that are the target of change. To change this basic emotion schematic processing the core emotion needs to be brought into awareness and provided an affective antidote.

EFT treatment can be broken into four phases. The first is bonding and awareness, which involves therapist empathic attunement and client emotional awareness. Second is the evoking and exploring phase, in which emotion is aroused based on the notion that you cannot leave a place without arriving at it, but evocation is not used until regulation is achieved. The third phase involves constructing alternatives. This involves making sense of emotions and generating new adaptive emotions to transform maladaptive emotions. The final phase involves consolidation of new meaning. New narratives based on experiential shifts in core organizing processes emerge. In summary, therapy ends with a new-told story that articulates the new-lived story of novel present moments of experience that emerged in sessions.

HR: *I want to go back to something I read on your Web site. You make the statement that, "Today too many people are cutting themselves off from their feelings—cutting themselves off from too much of what makes them feel human and truly alive." Could some psychotherapies inadvertently make us more disturbed by attempting to keep emotions in check? Are we, as a society, afraid of emotions? In fact, are therapists afraid of emotions?*

LG: Emotion phobia is a potential societal problem. Emotions, especially unpleasant and painful ones, can be frightening so people tend to avoid them. Ever since Plato there has been an attempt in the West to control the horses of passion with the charioteer of intellect. This image has promoted a view of the beast within that needs to be controlled. Eastern philosophical traditions have had a more accepting view of emotion. Some Western therapists, researchers, and academics I think are afraid of emotion or want to control them. In addition men generally are more afraid of emotion than women. People with high control orientation are afraid of the passions as we receive them passively, they occur whether we like them or not.

Psychotherapies that promote too much reflection and conceptualizing can destroy spontaneity and those that promote cognitive control or rationality can remove the joy and passion of living. As to whether these therapies inadvertently make us more disturbed I am not sure that being in these therapies does this but some of the philosophies that come from "feeling good" or "mind over mood" can, I think, promote emotion suppression or avoidance. This in the long run can be deleterious. Emotion informs and moves us and it needs to be listened to for the message it gives and its action tendencies and needs must be acknowledged. Acceptance of emotion is therefore the first step. Learning to tolerate and regulate unpleasant emotions is another step. Then we need to evaluate our own emotions as to whether they give us good information and organize us for adaptive action or whether they are maladaptive and need to be changed.

HR: *Do you view EFT primarily as a stand-alone therapy or does it work best when it is supplemented by traditional therapies?*

LG: I think it is a stand-alone approach for working with people with mild to moderate affective disorders and problems in living. With more severely distressed people I think integration with other approaches enhances treatment. For individuals and couples who are highly dysregulated I think a stage one treatment that focuses on behavioral regulation is helpful before embarking on an emotion-focused treatment and for long-term clients more focus on the therapeutic relationship becomes important over time. Not that these are excluded from EFT, which essentially is integrative, but they are not emphasized by, or unique to, EFT.

HR: *EFT has been researched at the York Research Clinic. Do you have any idea how it fares against competitive brands of psychotherapy?*

LG: In relation to the individual treatment there have been two major outcome studies of EFT of depression that have shown that EFT is more effective than the therapeutic relationship alone and more effective than CBT on interpersonal problems. Jeanne Watson recently ran a clinical trial showing that EFT was superior to CBT in reducing interpersonal problems and that there was no significant difference between treatments in reduction of symptoms in the treatment of depression. EFT has also been shown to be more effective than psychoeducation in resolving emotional injuries and unfinished business. In analyses of the components of EFT the addition of the process-directive tasks to the empathic relationship has been shown to enhance treatment effectiveness for both depressed and traumatized populations. In couple therapy EFT has been shown to be more effective than problem solving therapy, and more effective than wait list controls.

In terms of research on the process of change, emotional arousal and reflection on aroused emotion has been found to relate to outcome. Increase in depth of experiencing over therapy also related to outcome. Therapist depth of experiential focus was found to influence client's depth of experience in the next moment and predict treatment outcome. Finally the degree to which clients resolved major tasks like splits or unfinished business related to outcome and relapse prevention. This showed that deeper emotional restructuring relates to relapse prevention

HR: *Why does EFT lend itself to couples therapy?*

LG: Because emotion is at the core of intimate relationships. The bond between people is an emotional one providing security, love, and identity. Emotions are an important part of the glue that holds marital partners together. Without emotions couples probably would not exist. Our relationships with others are a wellspring of emotional experience. Emotions are fundamentally relational. They link mind and body, the social and the individual, and they give us information about the state of our social bonds. Emotional connectedness and separation are universal factors operating in systems, and are identifiable by the emotions expressed. Adult intimate relationships involve an ongoing struggle for connection and separateness, for attachment and identity, and are a major source of gratification of adults need for closeness and validation. When needs are met or not met emotion results. When emotions are not able to be accepted and expressed constuctively by self and partner problems ensue.

HR: *Is EFT successfully making its way into the graduate classes and the textbooks?*

LG: Slowly. Couples therapy, because of it's early empirical support, has I think been accepted into graduate courses in marriage and family. Individual treatment, with its more recent empirical support and because of the growing interest in emotion, is beginning to be recognized.

HR: *Are there times when EFT is decidedly not the treatment of choice?*

LG: When someone is too dysregulated, delusional, or highly fragile then the emotionally evocative aspects of EFT are not indicated, although the empathic component is suitable, especially for fragile borderline and narcissistic people. Couples who are violent or too emotionally reactive are also not suitable for emotion accessing. EFT is best for people who are not too functionally impaired such that they are unable to function in there world. If too severely impaired the first need is to create stability and order. EFT thus is most applicable to overregulated clients rather than underregulated people with impulse disorders or those engaged in self-harm.

HR: *Does your work with EFT support the age-old stereotype that men don't express their emotions as freely as women?*

LG: To some degree. Some men can access emotion but most find it more difficult. It is important, however, to understand that men do have emotions, they are just a lot less easily able to symbolize them in awareness and express them.

HR: *Is EFT a good multicultural therapy?*

LG: Although there is a general view that certain cultures are less emotionally accessible and require more directive processes such as advice, I am convinced that emotion is a universal human phenomenon. I believe that emotion can be worked on in all cultures in the way we suggest, in the context of a good working alliance, and with an appropriate understanding of cultural issues governing the expression of emotion. I have just returned from a four-month trip to East and Southeast Asia and found that EFT was highly applicable and drew a lot of interest from local therapists.

HR: *Let's assume you are personally having a bad day . . . worse yet, the day from hell! What EFT technique would we find you using on yourself?*

LG: I would breathe first and try and relax a little. Then I would focus on my body and attend to and describe the sensations and again check my breathing. This would all be by way of soothing or regulating. I would now try and focus on that place inside where I felt my feelings and try to find words to fit what I felt at my core. First emotion words, such as I feel sad, hurt or angry. These would become more differentiated and more meaning-laden, such as I feel rejected, abandoned, or violated. This would either lead to a felt shift, in which case I would follow the feeling where it went or I would feel stuck in the bad feeling, usually a feeling of fear or shame. Then I would reflect on this feeling, asking where it came from. I would view it as a wound and I would try and access a hot cognition or belief that accompanied the feeling and link it to where the feeling and belief came from. This would probably be some deep-rooted self-organization articulated in words such as I cant survive without support, I am nothing without validation, I feel empty, unlovable, in danger, all alone, or mad at the world or some such negative view. I would try and really feel the fear or shame or anger and again breathe. Now I might dialogue with an imaginary other or myself and make sure I articulate what I need. Then I would try to mobilize internal resources to meet my need and use my newfound more resilient state to transform my stuck feeling. I could do this either by explicitly challenging my articulated belief in words (e.g., I am lovable or I am not going to die). Or just see that that's the way I was seeing things, that it was a construction that was not useful and let the new feeling permeate the bad feeling in my body.

HR: *How would you describe yourself from an emotional standpoint?*

LG: I'm a somewhat open and trusting person but at the same time I am sensitive and can feel easily hurt in closer relationships. I am organized emotionally around feeling loved or abandoned or that I can't rely on people to be there when I need them. I am confident and yet anxious, jovial yet serious. I pursue closeness in intimate relationships and prefer to face painful emotions and conflict rather than avoid them. I am both demanding and empathic.

HR: *What is your favorite movie with a psychological slant and why?*

LG: From my past I loved films by Truffaut such as *Jules et Jim* and *Elvira Madigan*. I don't remember them clearly but they were about love, beauty, pain, abandonment in both senses of the word, and suicide. I liked *The Piano* a movie set in New Zealand, for its haunting beauty and mood which also ends in death! More recently I liked both *The Barbarian Invasions,* a celebration of love and life even in death and *Eternal Sunshine of the Spotless Mind,* about memory erasure and relationships. I like films that depict the pain of life and love and people's capacity for a great depth of understanding of themselves and others.

HR: *Now that are readers are enthused about EFT, what sources can they use to secure additional information?*

LG: Books. [See suggested references for this chapter at the end of this book.]

HR: *What's in store for the future of psychotherapy? Can you paint a picture of the discipline fifty years from today?*

LG: I hope the field will be based on principles rather than schools, and that the current dominance and marketing of brand names based on weak empirical support of effectiveness rather than a depth of understanding of how therapy works will end. My hope lies in a set of both common and specific principles that will unite the field.

HR: *Thanks for giving us something to get emotional about!*

Chapter 13

The Wisdom of Muriel James

Dr. Muriel James is the author of nearly twenty books, including the classic *Born to Win: Transactional Analysis with Gestalt Experiments* (which she co-authored with Dorothy Jongeward). The book—which introduced therapists and clients alike to transactional analysis and Gestalt—has sold over four million copies and has been translated in twenty-two languages. Dr. James studied with Eric Berne, who created transactional analysis.

HR: *Why did you decide to become a therapist?*

MJ: I became a therapist as a result of a course I was teaching at the University of California in Berkeley for graduate students who planned to be certified as adult educators. The course was, "Philosophy and Principles of Adult Education." It had a component in transactional analysis and 200 to 300 students took the course each time I taught it. I was also teaching communication skills to a number of government agencies and corporations.

Because of the kinds of questions that were asked I became increasingly aware of how psychological issues interfere with people's capacities to learn and to think independently. So I decided to learn more, have advanced supervision, and become state licensed. I did this.

My internships were in a private hospital in Berkeley and in a large state hospital and I asked one of my past professors to arrange for me to have the best supervision possible. He did, and I met with four psychotherapists weekly for two hours each time. Together, they critiqued my individual and group work with clients.

Therapy's Best
doi:10.1300/5189_13

I began to think of Friday afternoons as "Fry Muriel Days." It was challenging. When criticized, I was not allowed to defend my point of view or argue back until I said aloud, "I wonder if by any chance it could be true?" After saying that, it was okay for me to agree or disagree with the supervisors' comments.

I learned to think in new ways and it was a wonderful experience. However, as the supervisors had different psychological orientations, they often disagreed with each other. So I learned a lot more by listening and observing their similarities and differences of opinions.

Ken Everts, MD, a psychiatrist who was one of these supervisors, and later became president of the International Transactional Analysis Association, introduced me to Eric Berne, MD, at a small training meeting that Eric held weekly in San Francisco.

HR: *You studied with Dr. Eric Berne, the Founder of transactional analysis. What was he like?*

MJ: Although he had a psychoanalytic background, I believe Eric thought of himself as an independent thinker, a psychotherapist, and an innovator of a new theory. He seldom talked about himself and I did not experience him as a father figure nor as a showoff. I knew him from 1958 until his death in 1970, and to me he was always a friendly professional.

When I observed him working with other professionals in training, or with patient groups at St. Mary's Hospital in San Francisco, his manner was the same. Most often he used a Socratic method, which was to use questions that would encourage others to think for themselves.

He had clear ethical boundaries, was practical, and occasionally humorous. I asked him for clinical supervision when I was studying advanced transactional analysis and one of his questions was, "Muriel, what ego state do you think your patients should pay you for?" This alerted my to possibilities that my Parent ego state (an incorporation of parent figures) or my Child ego state (a "natural" child who is adapted in childhood) could contaminate the clear-thinking adult.

Another time when I commented on my commuting time and financial cost of his supervision he challenged me to remain in the program for six more months and I did. One day I reported, "Guess what, Eric, my income from therapy has doubled." His immediate response was, "Guess what, Muriel, so has my fee for supervision." We both laughed and I continued to learn from him. In fact he once said to me, "Stand on my shoulders and keep on developing theory and techniques in you own way."

Like others with transactional analysis specialty, I continue to discover and design new ways to use transactional analysis in education, organizational management, and clinical work.

HR: *I'm curious about your extensive writing. How did you get started?*

MJ: My doctoral thesis at the University of California was in education and ancient history. When I finished it I said to myself that I never wanted to write again but I did. Perhaps my interest in writing was reactivated when Eric Berne asked me to write a brief chapter on pastoral counseling for one of his early books. This could have been a subtle permission to continue thinking along theological lines as three of my books integrated spirituality and transactional analysis, culminating with, *Passion for Life: Psychology and the Human Spirit.*

My initial interest in writing was reinforced after he listened to a speech I made on "The Cure of Impotency with Transactional Analysis." It was at a non-TA conference for professionals at the University of California. Standing in the lobby immediately after I finished, he complimented me with, "Muriel get that published as soon as possible and keep on writing!"

I guess I added him to the parent figures I had incorporated into my Parent ego state. In transactional analysis theory, typical responses from the Child ego state to criticism, advice, or encouragement, are compliance, rebellion, or withdrawal. I complied, partly because I believe that good therapy is educational, and good education is therapeutic.

Nineteen of the books I authored or co-authored have been published. Two of my nineteen books are about history (one of my passions); the others are on transactional analysis and how it can be used in different ways in training or therapy with individuals, couples, families, and organizations.

I have also written many articles for magazines and journals. *Perspectives in Transactional Analysis* is a collection of my essays and one of my recent books. Incidentally, I have never taken a course in writing and I'm a terrible speller (hurrah for computer spell-check).

I am currently working on three more books in different subjects. It's a challenge I enjoy, probably because remnants of messages from critical parent figures in my Parent ego state are minimal. I like waking up early, fixing a cup of coffee, and taking it back to bed. I pick up a book of tablet beside my bed and write in longhand.

I sleep very soundly and guess that as some level of being my brain enjoys being creative while I sleep. Later I go to the computer and, with my hunt-and-peck, two-finger ability, I copy my poor handwriting.

HR: *Let's talk about the success of your classic book* Born to Win. *It has sold four million copies and is in twenty-two languages. How did you create this work?*

MJ: The idea for *Born to Win* began to develop when Dorothy Jongeward and I were on the same panel at a YMCA meeting. We recognized we had similar professional backgrounds, were both interested in transactional analysis, and lived only a short distance away from each other.

For about two years we worked together regularly at the same card table. However, when we sent the finished manuscript to the publisher it was returned with the comment that no one would be interested because Berne had already written a book on transactional analysis so we should write something else.

At the same time both of us were lecturing and leading various workshops for government employees and other organizations. At one of these, Jack Howell was present and became so enthusiastic over the concept and our manuscript that he submitted it the Addison Wesley Publishing Company for whom he worked. It was rejected. But he persisted so they published it, reluctantly, in 1971.

At that time interest in diversity was relatively new but our concern for it clearly showed in the photos and examples that we used. Universities became enthusiastic and to introduce it to the public Dorothy and I each made speeches to all kinds of groups. Eric Berne never read the manuscript; he died the year before it was published.

HR: *In an age when psychotherapy superiority reigned, why did transactional analysis and gestalt therapy blend so nicely?*

MJ: Both Eric Berne and Fritz Perls were trained as Freudian psychoanalysts and became iconoclasts. *Born to Win* is essentially a book about transactional analysis and supplemented by experiments we personally designed and other exercises derived from Gestalt therapy.

Gestalt is a German work that roughly means "organized whole." Both men had the same goal but different philosophies, theories, and methods. Both believed that people are often unaware of parts of themselves and need to reclaim and integrate their fragmented parts to become more self-reliant. My personal training in Gestalt therapy was in several workshops for professionals led by Fritz Perls. Mary and Bob Goulding integrated more fully the theories and techniques of transactional analysis and Gestalt in what is now known as redecision therapy.

HR: *When you consider you own contributions in the field of psychotherapy, what comes to mind?*

MJ: One of my contributions has been to write the spiritual dimension of life, beginning in the early eighties at a time when the word "spiritual" was seldom used. Another has been my development of the theory and process of "self-reparenting." Frankly, I wish I hadn't called it this. Instead, I wish I had called something like "self-remodeling your inner parent" because that's what it is. A bit like remodeling a house, it's a process for remodeling part of the personality by adding something new. Clients can learn to do this for themselves. They do not need a parenting-style therapist to act as a parent.

It can be done on a one-to-one basis, although I prefer using it in groups, with no more than twenty persons, in a concentrated five-day workshop in a beautiful location such as Lake Tahoe, on the California-Nevada border. Some therapists who use it do so on a weekly basis. Either way, self reparenting has been clinically proven to work effectively. People can cure themselves, often by learning how to solving their problems.

HR: *Recently, brief therapy . . . say six sessions or less . . . is being pushed. What are your feelings about this model?*

MJ: I think brief therapy, even shorter than six sessions, can be successful with some people with personal or interpersonal problems, but not with all. The basic motivation of a client for brief therapy often needs to be the willingness to clarify a problem, recognize the options for solving it, and deciding which direction to take.

HR: *I know this a very tough question, but when you were actively engaged in doing a therapy session what was the most common thing going through your head?*

MJ: When doing therapy I often, and silently, ask myself the old question I learned, "I wonder if by any chance it could be true, or partly true, what I and/or my client is saying?"

There are also three questions I often use with clients starting with, "What do you want that will enhance you life?" The word "enhance" is important because some things people want can destroy their lives instead of enhancing it.

The second question is, "What do *you* need to do to get what you want?" The third one is, "What are you *willing* to do?" If a client is willing to do what is needed, the action becomes the basis of a contract and is compatible with cognitive therapy.

If a client is not willing, another goal is more appropriate. For positive change, contracts to think of options, and organize a plan of action using the Adult ego state, are often useful and the self-reparenting process are in two of my books, *Breaking Free* and *It's Never Too Late to Be Happy.*

Now, at age eighty-six, I still have a private therapy practice, still give lectures, lead workshops, write books, and am interviewed for magazines, newspapers, and TV. I love my family, friends, and the natural world. I also believe that you, too, were born to win and I hope you know and enjoy it.

HR: *You have certainly cast more than enough gems of wisdom our way. You truly embody the born to win life strategy, as well, if not better, than anybody I have ever come across. Believe me when I say that this has been a rare pleasure and a treat for me. Thank you!*

Chapter 14

An Interview with Jeffrey Kottler

Jeffrey Kottler, PhD, is currently the chair of the counseling department at California State University at Fullerton. He is the author
of fifty books, including *On Being a Therapist, Compassionate Theapy:
Working with Difficult Clients, Travel That Can Change Your Life,
Doing Good,* and *Making Changes Last.*

HR: *Jeffrey, you write a book more often than most people change
shirts! Where do you get the time, the energy, and why do you
think you are so creative?*

JK: Well, hopefully most people change shirts more than a few
times a year. I write because I have to—for me it's the same as
eating, or breathing, or at least brushing my teeth. It's just something I do every day, without exception, no excuses. It's not
work for me but rather something I do to make sense of what's
happening inside me or around me. All of my book ideas come
from some intensely personal journey to understand or discover
something. When I can't find the kind of textbook I'd like to use
in class, one that is experiential and personal and engaging, I
write one. Or I look for a guidebook—not how to help people
change, but how to make the changes last. If I can't find one, I
do the research on my own and then write about what I've
learned. Or if I wonder why I stopped crying for a long period

This material first appeared in Rosenthal, Howard. 2002. "An Interview with Dr.
Jeffrey Kottler." From *Journal of Clinical Activities, Assignments, & Handouts in Psychotherapy Practice,* 2(1), pp. 65-71. Reprinted with permission.

of time and then begin a study of crying as a language. Another book. I can't help myself: there is just so much I want to understand. I'm just fortunate enough to have outlets for publishing what I write.

As for why I write so much, I get frustrated and impatient because the publishing process takes so damn long. I write the draft of a book then send it in for review. That takes three or four months, so I start another book and then send that one in. And wait. The first one comes back and I rewrite it and send it out again. I start a third book while I'm waiting for the other two to return. And so on. I think I need therapy to help me with all this compulsive productivity.

Actually, none of it feels like work to me. Writing, for me, is just an extension of doing or teaching therapy. There's just so much to talk about, so much to wrestle with, so much to make sense of what is beyond comprehension. Every day something happens that is so interesting to explore further.

The idea for a book about "bad therapy" that you reviewed is a good example of that. I've been so interested in learning from failures and mistakes and have been writing about that for decades. But the subject is inexhaustible. When I was asked to make a demonstration video for a series that involved doing three different interviews, I wanted to use my worst session. That is the one that can teach the most. The videos that are so often published look so flawless and effortless. When I've watched them I've felt humbled and insecure. I think to myself I could never do that, never be that skilled. The videos don't look at all like the work I do, which is often awkward and ugly. Well, the producer insisted on using the best example that will only give the impression to others that my therapy is smooth and effortless, just like the other so-called "masters." I thought it would be so much fun, so interesting and illuminating, if only we could see the "outtakes," the worst sessions of the best therapists. So it is questions like these that stir my curiosity. The writing process is a way to find some answers I can live with.

HR: *I know you wrote a best seller about serial killers. What is the bottom line so to speak on these folks? In other words, what is* *really going on in a serial killer's mind? Can the person be treated and can therapy be used as a preventive measure?*

JK: The book I wrote, *The Last Victim,* wasn't so much about serial killers as it was the true story of a young man who thought he could manipulate the likes of Manson, Ramirez, Gacy, Dahmer, Lucas, and others. He wrote all of them using himself as bait to attract their attention. As a young, overconfident, misguided psychology major, the boy believed he could get these killers to confess secrets they hadn't told police. I'm not particularly interested in serial killers but I was extremely intrigued with what motivated this boy to do what he did so successfully.

One of the things I learned from studying the subject, visiting some of the killers in prison, and watching my student work, is that any generalizations about the subject are pretty useless. A lot of what has been written about in "classic" texts is based on pretty flawed data. Some of these killers admitted that they are in contact with one another via the Internet and mutual friends. They exchange notes on the experts who interview them. They make up lots of stuff and tell the interveiwers what they want to hear. Ramirez, the Night Stalker, is a Satanist who enjoys power. Dahmer was terribly lonely and ate his victims for company. I know there are lots of generalizations in the literature that are supposed to predict their behavior but I didn't find a lot of similarities. I think what made Jason, the subject of my book, so successful at getting to these guys is that he understood that each one had to be approached differently.

HR: *What is the most common difficulty in working with the serial killer besides convincing a managed care firm that you can't cure him or her in six sessions or less?*

JK: Well, hopefully none of the readers are actually working with this population. Serial killers are not actually motivated to seek help. They enjoy their power and sense of control. They lack a conscience in the traditional sense. They are consistently deceitful and manipulative. I can't imagine a worst candidate for therapy.

HR: *I know you are working on a book about bad therapy. Can you describe what makes a bad therapy session so we can avoid the therapeutic land mines?*

JK: Jon Carlson and I are in the process of interviewing some of the most prominent therapists to ask them about their worst sessions. I know from prior experience doing similar interviews for *The Imperfect Therapist* that the main themes that crop up most often are related to being overly rigid. We think we know what is good for people. We insist that our strategy is effective because it has worked many times before, but the client doesn't want what we are selling. Rather than making adjustments, or abandoning the strategy altogether, we continually use our favorite homework assignments or structured activities. You and I have had a spirited dialogue about this a few times before in your important collections of techniques. I'm all for such structured activities but not when they fail to respond to what clients need at any moment in time. I think therapists most often get in trouble when they don't pay attention to what their clients are doing or saying.

Other themes that frequently come up are the times when therapists (1) operate on incomplete or inaccurate information, (2) ask clients to do things that they are unable or unwilling to do, (3) get their own buttons pushed activating personal issues, and (4) disown their mistakes and lapses. Failure or lousy therapy is just not a subject that is very easy to talk about publicly so we live in fear of being found inadequate or incompetent. Or at least I will own that this is MY fear. Because basically, deep down inside, I'm not really sure what I'm doing most of the time (like right now) I feel like a fraud who is about to be discovered.

HR: *I know I'm being a bit direct here, but does a seasoned pro like yourself ever do bad therapy? I mean even Tiger Woods hits an occasional ball into the rough.*

JK: Well, gee, most of what I've been writing about all these years is about how transparently and authentically I don't feel like a pro. Don't misunderstand me: I am really, really good at what I do. I work very hard at my skills and practice continuously. But when a session or class is over, I spend most of the time thinking about all the things I did wrong, the things I could have done differently, the ways I could have been more helpful and effective.

HR: *So are you saying that you are often very critical of yourself?*

JK: My core paradox (if you want to know) is that I am both extremely hard on myself and yet also very forgiving. I try to be as honest with myself as I can about what I've bungled or mishandled, and I feel flooded with so many mistakes, but then I let them go and try to move on. I think that's how I keep getting better as a therapist, teacher, and writer.

HR: *I'm a bit perplexed about your position on techniques, homework assignments in therapy and that sort of thing. I used you to play the devil's advocate in my books* Favorite Counseling and Therapy Techniques *and* Favorite Counseling and Therapy Homework Assignments. *Nevertheless, I notice that you were on the board of a journal that is pushing clinical activities of this nature. Can you clarify your position? Should we as therapists be seeking out techniques or avoiding them like the plague?*

JK: I LOVE techniques and structures. I want as many of them in my bag of tricks as I can find or invent. There can never be too many. Some of the best therapy books I've ever seen are those that provide lots of practical stuff; I get so sick of reading theory that all seems to say the same thing in different words.

My concern with the subject is the overreliance on techniques. They are just tools. I don't think it even matters so much which structures we use as long as several conditions are met: (1) the intervention is novel and attention-getting, (2) the therapist believes the technique is useful and powerful, (3) therapist can convince the client that the strategy is useful, and (4) the major theme of this journal—it provides some structure for completing tasks. I agree that in many cases talk is just not enough; clients have to do things. And I get so discouraged because even the most structured therapies that produce miraculous results in a few sessions still don't produce enduring effects.

So, I like to concentrate on (and teach) basics which, to me, is the relationship, the caring and respect implicit in that alliance. And I think that since the client does most of the work our job is to help motivate and guide that process. Structures, activities, and homework assignments are extremely helpful in that way. Where you and I got into a fun dialogue was that I don't subscribe to "favorite" techniques, which implies that I use them because I like them. Certainly there are favorite stories I use in my teaching and writing. Of course there are favorite methods I employ in my therapy. But when I'm really working optimally it is because I am creating, inventing, adapting something completely new. Sort of like these questions—which I've been asked many times before—I'm really struggling to answer them as if for the first time. I get bored hearing myself over and over again. Therapy and teaching become stale for me when I keep repeating the same things. But being exposed to new ideas and activities are what stimulate new ideas. They teach us all about what is possible.

HR: *Can you very briefly describe five major things our readers need to keep in mind to improve their therapy?*

JK: I'm smiling as I hear this question. I just did a series of lectures in Kathmandu, Nepal. I was propped up in front of an audience composed mostly of nurses and doctors and given one hour to tell them about the essence of counseling that they might use in their work. I was speechless and awkward: I mean, what could I tell them in an hour that could make a difference? I told them that their work was important. I said that because they had so few staff and so little medicine for so many sick people their love and compassion were even more important. Well, I stumbled on for some time and then someone asked me a question. He stood up, some doctor-looking fellow, and said, "I have heard there are seven stages of counseling. Can you tell us what they are?"

I started to panic. Seven stages? I could only think of four. Or maybe five. I looked at my watch and I only had four minutes left. In a rush, I said, "Look, basically there are just three stages, a beginning, a middle, and an end. But forget the stages. Forget everything I just told you. Just remember one thing: what you do really matters." Then I walked off the stage.

Now, given how hard I am on myself you can imagine how much like a failure I must have felt. I didn't give them any techniques they could use. I didn't even tell them about the stages of counseling. All I did was tell them that what they were doing was really, really important. I told them that no matter how discouraged and unappreciated they might feel, how underpaid they were, how hopeless they felt in the face of so much pain and suffering, their work was the most important thing in the world.

So, now I see that WE are out of time and I don't have a clue what five things matter most. I know what DOESN'T matter— and that's which theory we use or even which techniques we select. But we have to do something. And we have to believe in our power to help and heal. I know this is a very unsatisfying answer to your question. I'm convinced, though, that what makes a very fine therapist—besides being moral, ethical, kind, caring, and other such qualities—is that we've each discovered our own unique way of helping that fits our personality, interpersonal style, clinical situation, and client population.

HR: *I know this is going to be my last question since I'm starting to sound like Tony Robbins on* Powertalk! *or something, but how would you like to be remembered?*

JK: As a nice person.

HR: *Thank you for providing what is perhaps the most open and honest interview I have ever come across in this field. You are certainly a great therapeutic role model for all of us. Best of all, it's nice to know that even the masters in this field such as yourself are fallible human beings just like the rest of us.*

Chapter 15

Taking off the Gloves
with Al Mahrer, the Undisputed
Welterweight Experiential Therapy
Champion of the World

Al Mahrer, PhD, is professor emeritus, School of Psychology, University of Ottawa, Canada, where he still tries to write each day, including weekends. Since graduating from Ohio State University in 1954, he has written fourteen or fifteen books, four of which he is especially proud of, and around 250 other publications, in an effort to go about as far as he can to carve out a way of making sense of human beings, and a way of doing psychotherapy that he is finally getting the hang of. His current tiltings at windmills are in a friendly attempt to delve into the larger and deeper issues underlying the field, and to use philosophy of science as a magnificent tool to revolutionize as much as he can about psychotherapy, from its foundational beliefs to its theorizing, from its training to its research, from the origins to the deeper worlds of personality, from what psychotherapy can be, to how people can have sessions by themselves, from the very uses to the exciting future development of what we now think of as psychotherapy.

HR: *I think most people would agree that when it comes to psychotherapy, few people in the field could match the vast knowledge of Raymond Corsini. When I interviewed Dr. Corsini for this text I asked him to speculate on the future of psychotherapy fifty years from now. He said, "I guess over time that new and better systems will evolve and that Freudian therapy will retain its hold on perhaps five percent of the people. For example, no one* *now knows of Alvin Mahrer's experiential psychotherapy that I expect will take over the field eventually." Coming from Corsini, that's quite a testimonial. The maestro is basically saying that your ideas are indeed the future of psychotherapy! But before we get into the nitty-gritty about your innovative experiential psychotherapy, let's start at the beginning. How in the world did you go from wanting to become the next welterweight champion to ending up in graduate school and studying psychotherapy? That hardly sounds like a typical route one takes to get involved in the helping professions!*

AM: You are saying that boxing is not an ordinary route into graduate school? I thought it was! In Cleveland, in the 1940s, most of my boxing buddies naturally went from boxing to graduate school. Actually, the head of the clinical program spent the first year telling me I really had to make a choice, and my neurologist settled the matter by saying that I should concentrate on the doctoral program because I was showing signs of brain damage. So I did.

HR: *What was your fascination with boxing? Why was it so important in your life?*

AM: Picture five or six elementary school kids at a boxing gym, staring fixedly at a film of two legendary boxers. We were listening to a wizened trainer pointing out their magnificent skills, and we were absolutely entranced, in another world, eyes wide open, jaws dropped. We were in heaven. Does that same passionate fascination happen when kids are introduced to psychotherapy? That would be nice!

HR: *When you were boxing seriously . . . for blood so to speak . . . what precisely constituted a winning attitude in the ring?*

AM: When I was in the ring, actively doing what I was doing—which had little or nothing to do with "for blood" it seems—I had no idea of having a "winning attitude." I was just wholly involved in doing what I was immediately doing. Outside the ring, the main attitude I had was the excitement, the fun, the importance of actually boxing, and being very good at it!

HR: *And is it accurate to say that your initial readings of Freud, as a young man, were primarily for the sexual content, rather than the psychotherapy content . . . sort of an adjunct to porn?*

AM: Picture a sex-filled pubertal kid, hidden in a room devouring his cache of dirty photos and stories, a few written by a fellow named Sigmund Freud. This is somewhat different from a picture of a young man reading Freud for the psychotherapy content. At twelve or thirteen, I knew sex, but not psychotherapy nor Freud.

HR: *I have an unpublished manuscript of yours in front of me that you were kind enough to allow me to read. You are talking about your graduate studies in psychotherapy. Please indulge me while I quote you: "My fellow students learned the professional material. I was awestruck by what the course material told me* about me.*" What exactly did you discover about yourself?*

AM: In our doctoral program, the other students learned how to be the doctors who administered and interpreted tests, who learned how to detect the mysterious pathological processes lurking inside their patients. Not me. I learned how to be the patient who, after each subsequent class, was convinced that deep inside me were actualization forces, Adlerian social interest, Jungian polarities, deep-seated frustrations leading to aggressions, Allportian traits, behavior patterns shaped by positive and negative reinforcements, the unfortunate residue of pathological parents, the defining effects of my birth order, the sociocultural imprinting of my Czech background, and my unconscious wish to kill my father and have great sex with my mother. My fellow students learned the profession. I learned the contents of my psyche. The contents changed every week.

HR: *What kind of student were you? Was anybody in the graduate school considering your picture to use as the straight A's poster child?*

AM: When I was in graduate school, and now that you ask me to look back on those years, I felt kind of average, nondescript,

unspecial. I was exceedingly average. I was not unusual or dis-
tinctive, either in some good way or in some bad way.

HR: *When you were in graduate school at the University of Ohio in
the late forties and fifties . . . luminaries . . . giants of psychotherapy . . . such as Carl R. Rogers, Julian B. Rotter, and
George Kelly roamed the halls. Did you know any or all of these
gentlemen personally? If so, what were they like on a personal
level? I guess what I'm really asking is whether you ever went
out with Rotter or Kelly for a beer or perhaps dinner? And finally, what impact did they have on your career?*

AM: Just before I showed up as a graduate student, Carl Rogers had
left Ohio State, but his legacy was all over the department, alive
and well. Did I have any personal acquaintance with Carl Rogers or Julian Rotter or George Kelly? Not really. I would have
felt strangely out of place.

  What impact did these people have on my career? A great
deal. For many of us students, they were great leaders, our
heroes. We were challenged and inspired and galvanized as
they proclaimed, "Wake up! Carve out new territory! Welcome
grand new ideas! Create whole new approaches! Revolutionize
psychotherapeutic theory, research, practice! Be bold! Work
hard! Push and pull the whole field into more and more what
the field can become! Do it."

HR: *Can Joe or Jane average therapist next door ever really expect
to perform traditional psychotherapy on a par with Carl Rogers or is that merely a pipe dream . . . such as expecting to box
like George Foreman? Must one possess a gift, if you will, to
perform at that level of excellence?*

AM: I hope that more and more training programs and internship
sites can have a few teachers and supervisors who can welcome
and foster students with even a tiny glow of passion to become
master therapists, virtuosos of the craft of psychotherapy. And I
hope that more and more future students enter our programs
with that precious glow of passion. I know that I am looking for
this precious inner glow, rather than at some gift or talent to become a fine practitioner.

HR: *At one point in your career you seemed obsessed with acquiring audiotapes of efficacious psychotherapy performed by adept helpers. I'm assuming that you felt your graduate education was biased in favor of theory and did not emphasize the nuts and bolts of practice as much as you would have liked. You were truly ahead of your time. This was obviously before the days of catalogs packed with audio- and videotapes of fine therapists. How did you get your hands on the tapes? You must have been very assertive. Did you merely write the therapist and ask if he or she had some tapes?*

AM: When I graduated and tried to do psychotherapy, a few of us mutually confessed that we hadn't studied the fine practitioners doing real psychotherapy, and that we were far from being even average psychotherapists. The fortunate mistake we made was to ask, to plead, for audiotapes of any unusual sessions, uncanny sessions, remarkable sessions, with unexpected, impressive, unusual in-session changes.

Did we have big trouble getting audiotapes? Over three or four decades, my failure rate was uncomfortably close to the 95 percent range. I managed to end up with nearly 500 audiocassettes from about eighty psychotherapists largely because of (a) dumb persistence, (b) naïve enthusiasm, and (c) pleading with so many professional psychotherapists for the names of truly gifted, unusual, master practitioners, in or out of the profession, doing any version of the craft, credentialed or not especially, and known because of their remarkable work, rather than their nonexistent publications, high offices, workshops, or training programs.

HR: *Before the advent of experiential psychotherapy, what modality or modalities did you practice?*

AM: When I ponder your question, the picture I get is that I tried out different kinds of therapies, and then either turned to "experiential therapy" or tried to develop it for myself.

The picture I am more inclined to have is that, from the start, and over about four decades, I did a kind of homemade, gradually evolving mishmash therapy, made up of all sorts of bits and pieces from so many different therapies that, if you name a fair number of therapies, I can probably nod that I tried bits and pieces of those therapies. I was not very good at a large bunch of therapies that I tried to put together in a way that seemed to work for me.

HR: *How, when, and why, did you create experiential psychotherapy?*

AM: How did I create experiential psychotherapy? Now that I look back, I believe that I spent about forty-five years trying to find ways of having a magical, magnificent session that could do two things: (1) It could literally transform a person into the whole new person that the person is capable of becoming. Yes! (2) It could literally free the person of the painful feelings in the painful scene that was front and center for the person in this session. The "how" consisted of searching for and trying to put together whatever it took to achieve these two wonderful achievements in a session.

When was experiential psychotherapy created? Conception occurred from 1949 to 1954, when I was in graduate school. Birth began in the 1978/1989 volume presenting my "experiential theory" of everything. Birth was completed with the 1996/2004 volume titled, *The Complete Guide to Experiential Psychotherapy.*

Why did I create experiential psychotherapy? It seems to me now that I was always searching for some way of achieving the two magical changes I just described. I was searching for these two magical changes for myself, not just for the people the people I worked with in therapy. If there had been any other way of achieving these two wonderful changes, I would have followed that way instead of trying to spend so many years concocting a way that just might work.

HR: *I know you don't put a lot of stock in intake interviews, diagnostic assessments, or evaluation procedures. Would you say that for the purpose of doing efficacious psychotherapy, the DSM and traditional standardized psychological tests are basically useless? Tell us about that.*

AM: Here are some of the reasons why the usual intake interviews, diagnostic assessments, and psychological tests and evaluations are not especially useful:

- In an initial session or two or more, I have a choice between being an evaluator, assessor, and diagnoser, or working with the person to be free of whatever painful feelings in whatever painful scene is front and center for the person, and working with the person to become qualitatively transformed new person that the person can become. I prefer the latter.
- I think of each experiential session as its own "minitherapy," so that therapy begins and ends with that session, no matter how many sessions we have. "Intake evaluation" can make sense when "therapy" is a series of sessions, and you find it useful to see the person you will be working with for the whole series of sessions. In experiential sessions, the therapist sees what, hopefully new, person the therapist is working with in the beginning of each session.
- In the beginning of each session, the helpful guiding information is found by finding the "scene of strong feeling" that is front and center for the person, and by using that "scene of strong feeling" to find the person's deeper potential for experiencing.' I can get that information much better by the methods of an experiential session than by trying to do a standard intake, diagnosis, assessment, or evaluation.
- What assessments assess, evaluations evaluate, diagnoses diagnose, and tests test have essentially no meaning in experiential thinking, nor any usefulness in or for the successful carrying out of experiential sessions.

HR: *Since readers may be unaware of the experiential paradigm I am going to share the four steps that are included in each session: 1. Discover the deeper potential for experiencing. 2. Welcome, accept, cherish the deeper potential for experiencing. 3. Undergo a qualitative shift into being the deeper potential for experiencing in the context of recent, earlier, and remote life scenes. 4. Be the qualitatively whole new person in scenes from the forthcoming new post-session world. Okay, I'm a little confused about the experiential paradigm. Is it best to see an expe-*

riential therapist for a session and then follow up with sessions by oneself? I guess what I am really asking is whether a client is qualified to handle his or her own session after just one visit with an experiential therapist or would it take multiple sessions before someone attempts self-therapy?

AM: A person can have an experiential session, or as many sessions as he or she wants, by going through a session with an experiential therapist who goes through the steps with the person.

A person can have an experiential session by learning how to have his or her own experiential sessions, and going through the same steps by and for oneself. (The 2002 book is titled, *Becoming the Person You Can Become: The Complete Guide to Self-Transformation.*) The person can learn by studying the book by himself or herself or by being taught by an experiential teacher.

HR: *Your paradigm for the beginning of a session of experiential therapy is roughly the opposite of some interventions. For example, here in town, many of our addiction treatment centers begin each session with a relaxation exercise or a brief meditation. Your experiential therapy begins with a state of readiness for strong feelings. I was recently listening to your audiotape entitled* How To Have Your Own Experiential Sessions, Tape 1. *On the cassette the listener gets to play Peeping Tom and listen in while you actually perform experiential therapy on yourself. I was listening to the tape in my car. It was a delightful warm, sunny, delightful day here in St. Louis, Missouri. I had the windows down, the sunroof open, and the volume cranked up as you swung into step one with an onslaught of yelling, and breathing that rivals anything I've ever encountered in a Hitchcock movie. Next I heard what sounds like you pounding on objects, and bloodcurdling animal-like screams for literally one minute and forty seconds . . . nonstop . . . I know . . . I timed it. I swear the woman next to me at the stop sign jumped a foot out of her seat! I felt sorry for her and quite frankly if I had access to a hit of antianxiety medication I believe I would have reached over and handed it to . . . well, you know what I'm going to say! Give* *us the inside scoop. What is the therapeutic purpose of this maximum overdrive emotional purge?*

AM: Each session begins with both the therapist and the person leaning back in large comfortable chairs, right next to one another and pointing in the same direction, feet on large hassocks, eyes closed throughout the session. Both therapist and person put themselves into a state of readiness for a session by engaging in one to two minutes of open, free powerful, uncontrolled outbursts, noisemakings, shrieks and shouts, grunts and groans, wheezes and whelps, explosions that are hilarious and fierce, booming and blasting. Experiential therapists do this easily and well, and so do the people they work with. Most nonexperiential therapists prefer the controlled state of ordinary conversation between two ordinarily controlled people.

Whether or not the session is successful in achieving its magnificent and rather extraordinary goals depends in large part on whether the therapist and the person can open the session by being able to unlock the usual controls, set aside the usual state of vigilant self-awareness and self-consciousness, free oneself of rigidly clinging to the person one rigidly clings to being, entering a state of openness and readiness for deep-seated wholesale change. The bottom line is that this way of opening a session works!

HR: *There is a wealth of emoting here. Is experiential therapy by any chance a second cousin to Janov's primal scream therapy?*

AM: Here is a "yes" answer. If you listen to a session of Janov's primal scream therapy and a session of experiential therapy, there will be times in both when you can hear loud noises, strong feelings. In that sense, the sessions can be similar.

Here is a "no" answer. The purpose or aim or use of an experiential session is to enable the ready and willing person to become a transformed whole new person, base on the discovery, in the session, of what lies deeper in the person. The companion aim or goal is for the person to become free of the painful feelings, and the painful scene in which they occur, that were front and center for the person in the session. I do believe that Janov's sessions have their own fitting, legitimate, but quite different aims and goals and uses. We both count on some strong feeling, but we use them for quite different purposes, I think.

HR: *After the client is in a state of emotional readiness you have him or her pick a scene of strong feeling and fully live and be in the scene. If I understand it correctly the scene could be something recent, something from childhood, or even a dream. How does one choose an appropriate scene? Do clients ever engage in sort of a vest-pocket free association in order to come up with an appropriate scene?*

AM: Yes, you got it just right. In some sessions, the person already has a scene of strong feeling that is front and center: a scene from a recent dream, something delicious that just happened, some awful scene that happened or one from a while ago that is pulling the person's attention.

Often we start by putting two or three possibilities on the table, and the person can choose which to use in this session. Each session offers the person a chance to start with any scene of strong feeling that seems to say, "Please work on me."

HR: *Am I going too far to suggest that your goal of the psychother- apy experience is roughly the antithesis of, say, a cognitive therapy session with Ellis, Beck, Glasser . . . or for that matter even a strict behaviorist or Freudian analyst? Aren't these ex- perts striving for control of cognitions, emotions, and behavior during the session, whereas you are advocating one strive for emotional intoxication?*

AM: Oh! You are taking me into touchy territory of other ap- proaches' theories and goals. Each experiential session is an opportunity to become a transformed, whole new person, and to be essentially free of the painful feelings and their painful scene that were front and center for the person in the session.

The qualitatively new person is probably also a quantitatively new person, whether that means more feelings or quieter, or a little of both, or neither. I am inclined to believe it is really nei- ther of them.

I hesitate to try to see if what an experiential session tries to help bring about are the main goals of cognitive therapy or psychoanalytic therapy or any other therapy. If I were impressed that some other psychotherapy valued my two goals, and could achieve them better than they can be achieved in an experiential session, I would sign up as a student of that better approach. Ha!

HR: *All right, back to the actual experiential therapy session. In several (though not all of the sessions you present on your tape) you are dealing with issues of anger. For example, in the first scene that you are personally imagining, we hear you say things like: "I don't give a God damn. I'm really angry, I'm furious; I'm going to do it. The hell with it. The hell with it . . . here's this guy; I really do want to beat the crap out of him. Go for it Al, kick the shit out of this son of a bitch." You're very sincere, sound very mean, and are snarling as you say these words. You then analyze your behavior on the tape saying, "I love this, that's a wonderful, wonderful feeling. Let's get it on, I'm ready for a fight, go for it, attack, that's the thrill. And that is the deeper potential inside me . . . Do I admit there is something inside me like this? Half the time I feel bad about this . . . I wish it felt better . . . but damn right I do. I like this quality, I just wish I could give it a better home." Did you intentionally use examples like this because most people have issues surrounding anger? Also, can you clarify what you meant by this deeper potential you experienced?*

AM: You bring up several good issues that I hope I can try to clarify one at a time.

  (1) I believe you have tapes of two sessions. One involved digging deep inside and discovering a deeper potential for experiencing sheer loving, caring for, closeness, intimacy, oneness. The other discovered a different deeper potential for experiencing. Most sessions, even with the same person, discover a somewhat different or surprisingly different deeper potential for experiencing.
  (2) Friendly and useful description of what a deeper potential is like tends to go beyond one-word general labels such as

independence, strength, competitiveness, passivity, or "anger." Instead of a one-word label such as "anger" in one person there may be a potential for experiencing violence, wholesale destructiveness, smashing apart, explosiveness; in another person there can be a potential for experiencing cold withdrawal, hostile distancing, aggressive separation; and in a third person there may be a deeper potential for experiencing sheer cruelty, torturing, cold-blooded hurtfulness. Lumping these into a single tub called "anger" is virtually useless and uselessly inaccurate, in experiential work.

(3) In one of the in-session steps, you throw yourself wholeheartedly into being the whole new person who is the deeper potential for experiencing. Being the transformed new person is helped by being this transformed new person in scene after scene, in incident after incident. This can help you become increasingly "at home" as the whole person.

HR: *Your third step involves using the deeper potential in recent, earlier, and remote life scenes to undergo a qualitative shift. You then mention a boxing scene where a fellow sucker punched you, a court custody scene that infuriates you, and a disturbing scene at your grandmother's house at age fourteen, to name a few. In each scene you allow yourself to experience the anger. Seemingly, you throw yourself into each scene one scene at a time and nothing is held back. You say things like: "Come on let's get it on. I'm ready for a fight," or "I'm gonna take the God damn referee and slap the shit out of this guy . . . ," or addressing the judge by saying, "Fuck this judicial system you bastard." What's going on here? What precisely is a qualitative change or shift?*

AM: Thank you for bringing up such a core question. In each experiential session, the first step is to dig down inside and to discover what is truly deeper, truly inside. The second step is to welcome and to embrace what had been discovered. Then you can have the precious opportunity, perhaps for the first time, to (a) let go of, disengage from the continuing person you are and have probably always been, and to (b) throw yourself into fully and completely being the whole person who is the living, breathing deeper potential for experiencing that you had discovered.

Done well, this is a qualitative shift, a radical change, the birth of a whole new person, a magnificent transformation.

HR: *Have you encountered many situations where experiential psychotherapy has been effective, where traditional modes have proved futile?*

AM: I wish I could say yes, but there are at least two reasons why I have trouble trying to compare experiential sessions with other therapies:

(1) Your question almost brings along a picture of experiential therapy and some other therapies having similar enough aims and goals that you can see which one did a better job. I honestly know of very few if any therapies that were developed to achieve the two goals of each experiential session. The more carefully I try to clarify the two goals of each experiential session, the more the other therapies shake their heads and wonder why I ever referred to experiential sessions as psychotherapy. I am inclined to agree.

(2) A fair number of professional psychotherapists had and have experiential sessions even though they teach, supervise, write about, practice cognitive therapy, Jungian analysis, integrative therapy, Gestalt therapy, psychoanalytic therapy, person-centered therapy, Aldlerian therapy, and so on. I had trouble being secretly pleased when it became clear that these psychotherapists did not regard experiential sessions as "psychotherapy." I am inclined to agree.

HR: *What about couples or marriage and family counseling? Would you have the couple perform the experiential session together or during individual sessions?*

AM: I have no experience having sessions with couples or families in the office, but that is mainly because I have fallen into a groove of working only with individuals, even some who live together but have separate sessions, rather than because I am following some nonexistent principle or reasons.

I know of some fine practitioners who can get some fine performances out of this experiential psychotherapy when they use it with couples or families. On this issue, I take my place on the sidelines or in the audience, and leave the stage to seasoned experiential therapists who work with couples or families.

HR: *I know that you have practiced in the United States and Canada. Are there multicultural differences between the populations?*

AM: If I look at the people I have worked with in experiential sessions, I see no substantial differences between those who grew up or live in the United States and Canada, and I don't modifiy what happens in sessions depending on whether the person is from the United States or Canada. That is the main part of the question that I can answer with some confidence.

HR: *We constantly hear mental health providers in the United States complaining about insurance and managed care. Is the Canadian system favorable in terms of paying for psychotherapeutic treatment?*

AM: When you ask about the Canadian system paying for psychotherapy, and especially my views on comparing the United States and Canadian systems, I picture myself clearing my throat, looking wise and authoritative, and pouring out pronouncements of utter foolishness until you catch on that I am thoroughly ignorant about these topics, and can make a complete fool of myself. My answer is: "I don't know."

HR: *In the United States psychiatric drugs are being pushed to the hilt and psychologists are now allowed to give meds in several states. What is the Canadian stand on these issues?*

AM: When I was an adult, living and working in the United States, I remember being the president of a state association, president of a division of the APA, on some APA boards and committees, and being somewhat informed on professional issues. Today, when you ask me about the Canadian stand on important issues like prescription drugs I am more inclined to give you the names of some young psychologists who are chairs of committees, who have authoritative answers. My answer is, "I wish I knew enough to answer your question, but I don't. Sorry."

HR: *Okay, time for a few quick personal questions. An accomplished therapist one time told me you can tell a lot about a man by the car he drives. What are you driving these days?*

AM: My answer is proof that you can tell a lot by the kind of car one drives, because I haven't had a license to drive a car in about thirty years. How about a bicycle? I have a wonderful bicycle!

HR: *Wow, I'll think twice before I ask* that *question again. Okay, moving right along: What tape or CD would I find in your home cassette, CD player, or VCR?*

AM: I have and treasure audiotapes of luscious classical music, videotapes of great fights, and rented videotapes of great movies.

HR: *What is your favorite movie with a psychological plot and why?*

AM: I love seeing videotapes of great movies. I love seeing great movies so much that I can nod to fifty or 100 great movies rather than flag one or a few as my personal favorites.

HR: *What book are you currently reading?*

AM: There are books I use for particular projects. These books come and go. For example, I am looking at books on (a) "where" personality comes from in the first place, the origins of the essential person one is, and on (b) what may be called an "optimal" state, on optimal ways of being and behaving.
Perhaps a better answer to your question is that there are other books that I treasure, that I study as carefully as I can, that I take plenty of time to try and think about, that I depend on for lots of notes. For years and years, these are books on the philosophy of science. Now for two specific ones: (a) Joel Weinsheimer's *Gadamer's Hermeneutics,* a 1985 guide for dummies

who can't make sense of Gadamer's own texts, and (b) *Readings in Philosophy of Science* edited by Herbert Feigl and May Brodbeck, published in 1953, and populated with some of the classic contributors to philosophy of science.

HR: *You have mentioned that you are over seventy years young. Have you discovered any gems of wisdom about the best way to handle the aging process?*

AM: Since I am preparing to head toward becoming eighty years old, I do remember going through the aging process about a decade or so ago.

I have almost always counting on three things: (1) having my own experiential sessions about every other week, (2) trying to spend a part of almost each day trying to carry out "optimal" behaviors, and (3) exercising strenuously three times a week. I do these three things religiously and superstitiously because of a nameless terror of what would surely happen if I didn't.

HR: *What's the best book ever written on the subject of psychotherapy, your own notwithstanding?*

AM: I would have little confidence in my nominating any as the best book on psychotherapy, mainly because of my captivated fascination with devouring most of the works by Sigmund Freud. I was utterly compelled by the world he introduced me to.

HR: *Who was the best boxer of all time and why? What about the best therapist?*

AM: There were two boxers whose films I studied in rapture, hero-worshiping slow motion; Sugar Ray Robinson and Archie Moore. There were on such a high plateau that I was inspired to seek some other career, such as becoming a psychotherapist.

When I think of the "best therapist," what comes to mind are a few dozen or more practitioners whose audiotapes introduced me to excitingly new heights and depths of what psychotherapy can be, most of whom were neither published nor well-known, each of whom was suggested by colleagues I asked to please give me the name of the finest, most gifted, most notable, most creative, most unusual psychotherapist they knew.

HR: *Your Web site states that you are one of the first four recipients of the "Living Legends in Psychotherapy" awards conferred via the American Psychological Association's Division of Psychotherapy. Two questions come to mind here. Who were the other three recipients and did you expect to snare this accolade for your groundbreaking work in this field?*

AM: It is mistakenly easy to picture that the APA Division of Psychotherapy decided to honor their distinguished "Living Legends of Psychotherapy," and selected four noble recipients for the first year.

Here is my picture of what really happened: The Division wanted to have one final try at having a midwinter meeting like it had in the good old days. "The problem was lack of attendance, so how could we get people to attend?" Let's advertise special workshops by special people and we can call them "Living Legends." "Who can we get?" Anyone who gives workshops, and is willing to attend what may be our last winter meeting—and they have to be old. "Do we have to give them plaques?" Sure, that might help attendance. The Division found three worthy candidates: Al Ellis, Rachel Hare-Mustin, and Jim Bugental, and one old ringer: Al Mahrer.

HR: *I must admit I am overwhelmed by your modesty and your keen sense of humor. Finally, did Corsini hit a bull's-eye? Has he seen the future and is it your experiential psychotherapy?*

AM: Trust me. Corsini hit the bull's-eye. In fifty years, my experiential psychotherapy will take over the entire field of psychotherapy. Naturally that means those who gear up for the future of psychotherapy should read these books: (1) *Experiencing,* almost 900 pages of the experiential perspective on almost everything, published in 1978/1989; (2) *The Complete Guide to Experiential Psychotherapy* by Bull publishing in 1996/2004;

(3) *Becoming the Person You Can Become: The Complete Guide to Self-Transformation*, also by Bull Publishing in 2002.

HR: *Thanks for taking the time to enlighten us! Hats off to the undisputed welterweight experiential therapy champion of the world!*

Chapter 16

Psychoanalysis Now and Then: A Conversation with Nancy McWilliams

Nancy McWilliams is author of *Psychoanalytic Diagnosis: Understanding Personality Structure in the Clinical Process* (1994), *Psychoanalytic Case Formulation* (1999), and *Psychoanalytic Psychotherapy: A Practitioner's Guide* (2004), all with Guilford Press. She teaches psychoanalytic theory and therapy at the Graduate School of Applied & Professional Psychology at Rutgers, the State University of New Jersey, and at several psychoanalytic institutes. She has trained therapists throughout the United States and in several other countries. Dr. McWilliams sees patients and supervisees in her private office in Flemington, New Jersey.

HR: *Say a very wise analyst knew you as a child. Could he or she have predicted that you would become an analyst as an adult?*

NM: Probably. When I reconnected with my high school friends twenty years after graduation and told them I was a psychotherapist, a number of them said "Of course!" Like most people drawn to psychoanalysis, I have an empathic temperament as well as a driving curiosity about what makes people tick.

HR: *Tell us something about formal psychoanalytic training. Say one of our readers wants to go from being a psychologist, counselor, or social worker to becoming a full-fledged analyst. Can you give us a glimpse of the process? What kinds of coursework, training analysis, and time frame would a person be looking at?*

Therapy's Best
© 2006 by The Haworth Press, Inc. All rights reserved.
doi:10.1300/5189_16

221

NM: Such a person would be looking at a significant emotional, intellectual, and financial investment over a minimum of four years. Still, it's a part-time commitment; unlike most basic professional training, you can manage a full-time job while doing it. The most important part of analytic training is going through analysis yourself; it's critical to find an analyst with whom you feel good personal chemistry. Because this relationship is more important than the particular psychoanalytic institute where one studies, I often advise people that unless they have strong feelings about going to an institute with a particular theoretical orientation (Freudian, Jungian, self-psychological, relational, etc.), they should find an analyst with whom they feel deeply simpatico and then get training at an institution that accepts that person as a training analyst.

Next in importance is supervision, and again, it's important to pick supervisors with whom one can talk honestly, exposing one's feelings in the clinical situation and admitting mistakes and uncertainties. Personal qualities in a supervisor that make openness possible are a lot more important than the person's prestige or brilliance.

The least important part of analytic training is coursework, though that can be very stimulating. If I were looking for analytic training today, I'd try to get a feel for the tone of the seminars in any given institute: How safe is the atmosphere, how competitive, how open to differences of opinion, and so on.

HR: *Would it be a massive understatement to say that training requirements have drastically increased over the years? I remember reading that Erik Erikson had a single psychology course, some formal education in art, and as training as a teacher.*

NM: Licensing, certification, and continuing education requirements in all the mental health professions have become increasingly elaborated and demanding. Analytic training itself hasn't changed much since the mid-1900s in terms of requirements (Erikson was in the generation right after Freud, before it had been formalized), but it *has* changed in most places into a much less dogmatic, more pluralistic, and more inclusive kind of education.

HR: *One of my best friends desperately wanted to become an analyst and had immersed himself in the analytic literature for years. He had a doctorate and numerous achievements. He then applied to a psychoanalytic foundation and was turned down after they analyzed a battery of psychological tests and put him through some interviews. He was shocked. What exactly are the training institutions looking for?*

NM: That must have been a while ago. Until recently, most of the mainstream medical analytic institutes could be as choosy as they liked. They were considered the most prestigious sources of training, and they represented the dominant treatment paradigm. They were basically in a buyer's market and had the problem of keeping their student bodies to a reasonable size. They may have used psychological testing to try to assess the mental health of prospective students, but I suspect that in practice this did more to enforce a stifling conformity than to keep people with significant psychopathology out of training. We all know of analysts who could have been poster children for pathological narcissism; they acted arrogant and entitled in a way that many thoughtful people, including many mental health professionals who liked psychoanalytic ideas, grew to hate. Your friend would probably be welcomed with open arms by most institutes at this point.

HR: *If I recall, Freud's* The Question of Lay Analysis *defended Theodor Reik's right to be an analyst without going to medical school. Freud even commented that he knew he wasn't a doctor in the traditional sense, yet for many years lay analysts who did not have medical degrees were at some disadvantage in terms of getting into psychoanalytic schools. Why was Freud ignored when it came to this topic?*

NM: You recall correctly. Freud felt passionate about this (and, as a person trained in the institute that Reik founded after the New York Psychoanalytic Institute rejected him, so do I). It's been a problem mainly in the United States, and the answer to the question of why is complicated. When the first European analysts came here in the Holocaust exodus, many of the most eminent, including Reik, were not physicians. Douglas Kirsner's research suggests that American medical analysts were nervous that these talented people, some of whom had the imprimatur of training by Freud himself, would compete successfully for their patients. Making a medical degree a prerequisite for doing analysis solved that problem. I doubt that this was a conscious, calculating position. We all tend to feel that our own training is the best, and many physicians obviously felt quite strongly about the value of their medical training.

They were also worried in that era about "wild analysis." Some people, on the basis of having read a bit of Freud, were calling themselves analysts and making glib, pseudo-Freudian pronouncements at their clients. It seemed reasonable to many serious analysts to restrict practice such that people using this powerful method would have had at least enough intelligence and sanity to get through med school. And clinical psychology and clinical social work didn't really exist as disciplines when this decision was made, so it wasn't quite as discriminatory as it appears with hindsight.

HR: *Wasn't there some sort of class action suit initiated by four psychologists in 1985 against the American Psychoanalytic Association (APsaA) and the International Psychoanalytic Association (IPA) that evened the playing field? What is the current status of lay analysts not trained as doctors?*

NM: Yes. Bryant Welch and three colleagues, with the support of the Division of Psychoanalysis of the American Psychological Association and other friendly parties, got tired of APsaA's stalling over the question of admitting nonmedical candidates into their institutes on an equal basis with physicians and sued them on restraint-of-trade grounds. The lawsuit was settled favorably for the plaintiffs. It was a deeply moving historical moment for many of us.

Ironically, the settlement came just in time to save the APsaA institutes from going under, because when biological psychiatry replaced psychoanalysis as the dominant medical approach, those institutes suddenly were attracting few physicians. Currently, social workers and psychologists make up the majority of their students, and leaders of APsaA have acknowledged in print more than once that the lawsuit did them a big favor. I haven't heard any stories lately about discrimination against nonphysician analysts.

HR: *Have you ever been discriminated against for not having a MD or DO?*

NM: In the early 1970s, when my husband, a political scientist, got a job offer from Johns Hopkins, we considered moving to Baltimore. I contacted the Baltimore Psychoanalytic Institute to ask about being trained there. They said they were willing to take me as a candidate but that because my analyst wasn't a member of the American Psychoanalytic Association, I'd have to have a second analysis. I'd been living around New York all my young adult life, where there were numerous well-regarded nonmedical institutes, and it was the first time I realized that in other parts of the country, the institutes of APsaA controlled training. I said I wasn't interested in having a second analysis, as I had just terminated my first, which had gone on several years and had been deeply therapeutic. In response, I was told, "Don't worry. It's only a didactic analysis." I remember feeling dismayed—I was much more subject to the shock of disillusionment as an idealistic young woman—at the implication that one could undergo psychoanalysis in a sort of perfunctory way, to go through the required motions in order to comply with a rule. We decided not to go to Baltimore.

That's the only incident I can recall in which I've ever suffered for not having a medical degree, and even in that instance, they were willing to take me as a psychologist. They were just applying to me the rules that their medical candidates had to follow. So I can't claim I've ever been oppressed by the psychoanalytic establishment. I do notice in myself a subtle feeling of satisfaction or vindication, though, whenever a once *medically dominated institute or association invites me to speak.*

HR: *Some nights I see more ads on television for psychiatric medicines than I do for new cars. What do the analysts think about the emphasis on biochemical intervention?*

NM: There's probably as much diversity among analysts on this
question as there is among other mental health professionals. If
I had to generalize, I'd say we're grateful for many medications, especially those for the more severe mood disorders and
psychoses. Psychotherapy is not even possible for some patients unless they're medicated. We would emphasize, however,
the importance of the patient being evaluated carefully by a
well-trained psychiatrist. Too many people get prescriptions
from doctors with limited diagnostic skill and a couple of favorite medications, who often recommend dosages that fall short
of therapeutic levels.

 We also feel that some conditions are overdiagnosed (bipolar
disorder, ADD) and that psychotropic medications are overpre-
scribed. Complex miseries of the soul get ignored in equating
psychological suffering with discrete medical "disorders." Probably most important, we regard the research behind the claims
of pharmaceutical companies as flawed and believe that the
money they control has a profoundly corrupting effect on mental health practice of all kinds, not just psychoanalytic therapy.

HR: *Should psychologists have prescription privileges?*

NM: I have no objection to individual psychologists pursuing post-
doctoral training that will give them sufficient knowledge to
prescribe. Politically, however, I think it has been a disastrous
policy for the American Psychological Association to pursue
prescription privileges at this time. It alienates psychiatrists,
many of whom share with psychologists—despite the pressures of their biologically oriented colleagues—a commitment
to doing quality psychotherapy. We need them as allies in main-
taining and strengthening the tradition of psychotherapy training. If training with a view to prescribing becomes the norm for
psychologists, that will preempt other kinds of training, and
doctors of psychology will be as ill-suited to sitting down to listen to a suffering human being as anyone else without good
training in psychotherapy. And I don't buy the argument that
there is anything inherent in being psychologists that will inno-
culate us against the kinds of ethical vulnerability—for example,

being unduly influenced by the pharmaceutical industry—for which some psychologists criticize physicians.

HR: *Managed care firms seem enamored with treatment so brief if you blink you can miss it. Do any insurance companies currently pick up the tab for full-fledged psychoanalytic treatment?*

NM: Not that I know of. There may be a few indemnity policies left that cover a pretty hefty chunk of it.

HR: *By the way, how may days a week and how long do most of your analysands take to complete analysis with you?*

NM: I don't do too much psychoanalysis per se. I generally have two or three patients in traditional analysis at any given time, and they tend to come three or four times a week. That was true of my practice even when analysis was easier to afford, because I enjoy treating a wide range of people—different types and severity of problems, different ages, socioeconomic backgrounds, occupations, races, ethnicities, religious beliefs. I also feel that as a teacher and supervisor, I should stay in the trenches, working with patients like the ones my students see, so that I retain empathy with their experience.

As to length of treatment for analysands, it ranges from three to fifteen years. The few people I've worked with for over a decade were either therapists who wanted to get the most thoroughgoing treatment possible (not just for their own sakes but for the welfare of their patients) or severely disturbed people whom I could keep out of hospitals and crisis centers with devoted, intensive treatment. Despite the critics of long-long-term therapy, I think it's cost-effective. It conduces to better physical health, and it plays an important role in preventing suicide, child abuse, revolving-door hospitalization, crime, substance abuse, and other expensive consequences of any individual's lack of a reliable and knowledgeable attachment figure.

HR: *When I was in graduate school several professors painted a picture of the typical analysand as very bright, well educated,* *wealthy, and generally white. Moreover, the individual was not in crisis and did not suffer from severe mental illness. Was . . . and is . . . this stereotype accurate? Who is your typical client?*

NM: Most professors, even those who teach clinical or abnormal psychology, don't know much about what it's like to be a full-time practitioner. Many of my patients arrive in crisis, struggle financially, and don't have an easy time keeping their sanity. Even those who come to me sheerly for training purposes may have powerful internal demons. I consult regularly with about fifty therapists, individually and in supervision groups, and their cases are as challenging as mine, if not more so.

Analysts have always treated people with serious problems. It was an academic myth that we work only with those who are emotionally, intellectually, and financially well-off. Ironically, at this point the clinicians most likely to see the "worried well" are those doing research on "evidence-based treatments." Such therapies are frequently studied using as research subjects only cooperative middle-class, mostly white populations with no "comorbidity"—i.e., people who report one significant symptom and no complicating personality disturbances. I've rarely had a patient like that.

I don't think I have a typical client. When I take on somebody new, it's usually because something about him or her is atypical, challenging, fascinating, full of things I'd like to learn more about.

HR: *How does psychodynamic therapy differ from classical analysis?*

NM: There's been a lot of ink spilled on that one, and you'd get different answers from different analysts. The *Reader's Digest* version is that classical analysis is conducted at a frequency that makes it likely that a fully elaborated transference will emerge and be worked through. The patient is asked to associate freely and is usually encouraged to lie down while doing so. The analyst attends to resistances to free expression and otherwise tries to facilitate the client's self-understanding and self-expression. Psychodynamic therapy is more focused on specific problem areas and requires the therapist to be more active. The participants generally meet once or twice a week, usually face-to-face. While the process relies on psychoanalytic concepts such as transference and resistance, it is less ambitious and more circumscribed than classical analysis. But psychodynamic therapy is not just a poor man's psychoanalysis, it is the treatment of choice for many clients.

HR: *How do you feel about the proliferation of brief solution-oriented therapies that focus on the present moment and the solution rather than the problem?*

NM: I'm happy they exist, because some people respond well to them who would not have the temperament to collaborate in psychoanalytic therapy. I wouldn't want to do that kind of work myself, though, because my temperament isn't suited for it and I would not find it spiritually nourishing. I also think that the majority of people who come to therapists seek more than a quick fix. They want to understand themselves, to grow in maturity, to improve their self-esteem and their intimate relationships, to feel accepted with all their flaws and craziness. I see a lot of people who have tried solution-focused treatment and felt that they "failed" it. The downside of emphasizing the value of brief therapies is that those people who are not good candidates for them feel defective when they don't work.

HR: *Do you believe in symptom substitution? Let's say I'm an alcoholic and I go to a behaviorist or say an Alcoholics Anonymous (AA) group and quit drinking. The behavior therapist or the AA group will only look at the problem and not my unconscious mind. Will I become addicted to gambling, jogging, or perhaps develop an addiction to attending a different twelve-step group every night?*

NM: I don't believe that things are simple. I think people are complex systems, and when you make a change in a system, something happens to create a new homeostasis. But I don't assume that a symptom is inevitably replaced by another symptom. Sometimes it's replaced by the gratifications that come with change. In your alcoholic example, it is arguable that some people who drink compulsively shift their addiction from substances to AA. But after a few years of the gratifications of not drinking, and as they feel the benefits of the honesty and support for emotional expression that characterize AA meetings, they eventually notice that they aren't craving a drink. In that case, AA has been deeply therapeutic.

HR: *Let me ask you an "I just don't get it analytic historical question." According to analytic historians Freud was not exactly entranced with hypnosis and was hardly a consummate hypnotist. Therefore, he was searching for a way to do treatment without hypnotizing the patient. Freudian folklore has it that in 1889 Freud visited Nancy and saw a demonstration where Hippolyte Bernheim vigorously questioned patients in the waking state and was able to get previously hypnotized patients to remember things they had apparently forgotten. Bernheim's cajoling and coaxing seems . . . well . . . extremely active-directive to me. It makes me wonder why psychoanalysis didn't turn out to be more like Albert Ellis' REBT or perhaps Fritz Perls' gestalt therapy pumped up on steroids. Instead of utilizing a highly active-directive approach, Freud like Bernheim, chose to replace hypnosis with free association, the most nondirective surrogate one could possibly choose. Where was Freud coming from? Am I missing something?*

NM: Freud did start out by being pretty active. He tried various methods, including touching patients on the temples and announcing that something important would occur to them. After one of his more talented patients persuaded him to stop pushing her and just listen to her free associations, he backed off, but even then, his early work included a lot of persuading and cajoling. It took years before he learned what we all learn if we're paying attention; namely, that people change at their own pace. As therapists, we are midwives to the change process, but the amount of motivation, capacity, and courage it takes is different in different people and needs to be respected. Early in his career, Freud was not above saying "You're resisting!" when a patient ran into trouble associating. Only later did he learn just to explore what was going on. I think he came to emphasize a relatively nondirective procedure for many reasons, including his feeling that it was more respectful to the patient and ultimately more therapeutic than "suggestion," a bugaboo of the times.

It is also important to note that, in his few papers on technique, Freud preached nondirectiveness more than he actually practiced it. Perhaps his emphasis in those papers derives from at least two things that were bothering him at the time he wrote them. First, he was learning that some of his colleagues were sexually involved with patients, so he was importuning his fellow analysts to hang back and not exploit people in their care. Second, he was being accused of implanting his notions into his patients, of suggesting rather than "discovering" that we are sexual beings from infancy on—the debate was remarkably similar to the controversies in the 1990s about whether alter personalities in dissociative patients are preexisting or are iatrogenically created. By emphasizing nondirectiveness, he was protesting that analysts don't put ideas into people's heads; they only listen to what is already there.

HR: *Let's discuss ethics for a moment. I'm assuming that ethics, like training requirements, have been augmented over the years. For example, isn't it true that Anna Freud was psychoanalyzed by her dad? Today that would clearly qualify as a dual or multiple relationship.*

NM: True. Freud showed remarkably bad judgment there. I gather that at the time, few analysts knew about his analysis of Anna, but I'm sure that among those who did, all but the most worshipful Freudians thought it was nuts. Melanie Klein also analyzed her children, much to the eventual consternation of the analytic community. I guess I can understand the normal parental narcissism of "Nobody else is good enough for my child," and maybe in some ways we all use our kids as guinea pigs for our pet theories, but it's a truly spectacular blind spot. It's hard enough being the child of an analyst without undergoing "treatment" by a parent!

HR: *I found a curious entry in the APsaA ethical guidelines. It seems to say that an analyst can override standard breaches of confidentiality if it is in the best interest of the analysand. Thus, am I correct in hypothesizing that if a client tells you in analysis that she has abused her child you could chose not to report the incident to the child abuse hotline? And, if you decide not to report the incident, wouldn't you be in violation of a state law anywhere in the United States?*

NM: As I'm not a member of APsaA, I'm not familiar with their ethics code. I'm held to the code of the American Psychological Association and to the ethics policies of the analytic institutes for which I teach. But if your reading is right, I do find myself having some sympathy for APsaA's position. Yes, to my knowledge, not revealing a divulgence of child abuse would violate state laws. It is not a small thing to disobey a law. In this country, however, there is an honorable tradition of civil disobedience when one feels deeply that a particular law—slavery and segregation laws are the most vivid examples—has immoral or destructive effects. When one disobeys a law on moral grounds, one knowingly risks prosecution. I can imagine a therapist deciding to disobey the letter of a child abuse reporting law, knowing that he or she may be held accountable legally.

If we look at the actual effects of recent legal efforts to make informants out of therapists, they are not usually therapeutic to the family or the community. The person in therapy feels profoundly betrayed, no matter how well he or she has understood intellectually what the legal limits to confidentiality are. After a report, employees of overworked state protective agencies investigate the family, and if the abuse is found to be relatively minor, they make no further intervention. The family has suffered a humiliating intrusion and exposure, with no positive effects, and with the probable loss of the one relationship, the parent's therapy, that held out some hope of stopping the abuse. If the state investigators determine that the abuse is serious, they typically require psychotherapy as a remedy. But now the patient's faith in psychotherapy has been traumatically destroyed.

HR: *Speaking of abuse, in the 1980s Jeffrey Moussaieff Masson claims he made a landmark discovery that Freud copped out and changed his theory. Masson supposedly discovered that Freud knew that a lot of folks were truly sexually abused and not just fantasizing about it as postulated in his controversial Oedipus/Electra complex theories. Masson claimed at the time that the finding was so monumental that only a few analysts in the world were speaking to him. Masson now writes books on animals and thus was not fair game for an interview in this book. In your estimation, was his finding accurate and has it had much impact on the practice of psychoanalysis?*

NM: I was irritated myself by the tone of moral righteousness in Masson's claim. First of all, it was well known already that many of Freud's patients had been sexually abused as children. Freud initially said as much, and he never recanted those observations. What he changed was his original belief that *all* patients with neurotic symptoms had been molested. He knew of too many neurotic individuals, including himself, who showed no evidence of such experiences. So the analytic community felt that Masson set up a straw man and presented himself as having heroically demolished him.

Second, there was a feeling that Masson had manipulatively earned the trust and affection of Anna Freud and Kurt Eissler so that he could get into the Freud archives and use his findings for self-promotion, meanwhile devastating these elderly analysts who had been generous to him. I'm not uncritically supportive of Freud's daughter and Eissler; I think their efforts to control access to the archives were excessive. Their overprotective policies have been aptly lamented by historians and Freud scholars. But I do regard Masson's behavior in seducing and betraying them as inhumane.

Finally, I think analysts felt that Masson was completely without empathy for Freud's situation as the first analyst. Freud was treating the children of local people, many of them his acquaintances, at a time when medical confidentiality had no exceptions. I don't find it surprising that he didn't do more to expose his neighbors as child molesters, even early, when his theories were stressing the connection between childhood "seduction" and later psychopathology.

HR: *Marriage and family therapy has been the rage for the last several years. If a client is seeing you for psychoanalysis, can he or she concurrently be seeing you—or someone else for that matter—for marriage, family, or couples counseling?*

NM: Sure. Ordinarily, if someone I'm working with wants or needs family or couple therapy, I refer that client for concurrent work to a colleague who is better trained in those areas than I am.

HR: *I think I can safely say that most of our readers won't become psychoanalysts per se. Is there any way they can incorporate psychoanalytic principles into their therapy sessions?*

NM: There is plenty of evidence that most therapists already do. Even those who think they don't may find themselves referring to the therapeutic alliance or the patient's defenses or attachment style. They often don't know that these concepts arose in the context of psychoanalysis. Theory developers, who demonstrate their originality by contrasting their ideas with an existing paradigm, often take the position that different approaches are mutually exclusive. But practicing therapists tend to take whatever is valuable from any tradition to which they are exposed and try to use it in a way that helps their clients.

HR: *What is the biggest misconception therapists have about analytic techniques?*

NM: That analysts sit there silently for session after session and then accuse the patient of "resisting."

HR: *What is the biggest misconception clients have about analytic techniques?*

NM: That they're oriented toward figuring out what happened to you as a child so that you can blame your mother and feel better. Analytic therapy is very "here and now." It values emotional honesty over intellectual reconstruction, and it focuses mainly on the patient's experience of relationship with the therapist. It holds people responsible for making changes in their lives no matter how good or bad their parents may have been.

HR: *I know you've discovered that feminist theory can be integrated into traditional therapeutic modalities. Tell us about that.*

NM: I wouldn't say I discovered that. I'm only one of many psychoanalytic feminists, a number of whom have written much more directly and incisively than I have about feminism and psychoanalytic theory. Some have published brilliant critiques of prevailing therapy paradigms.

As for myself, I have never felt that traditional modalities—especially psychoanalysis—are inherently incompatible with feminism. My own experience as an analysand was that I felt empowered as a woman by the experience. Despite the fact that Freud was in many ways patriarchal and had some misconceptions about women, the movement he started created the only discipline I know of in which, from the beginning, female professionals have been valued as much as males. Freud set a tone that encouraged women to distinguish themselves not only as practitioners but also as theorists, hence the important contributions from Anna Freud, Melanie Klein, Karen Horney, Frieda Fromm-Reichmann, and many other "seminal" analysts, to borrow a male metaphor. Sabina Spielrein, an early patient of Jung's and the first regular female member of Freud's circle, was murdered in the Holocaust before she could contribute to the literature, but even she may have made a significant contribution via her influence on her analysand, Jean Piaget.

When I became an analyst, I took seriously the encouragement from my best teachers to integrate my own personality into my therapeutic art. The kind of treatment I offer can't be separated from my feminist sensibility because that's who I am. Parenthetically, I don't know how one can understand the phenomenon of sexism without some reference to unconscious processes. Psychoanalysis as a theory has a lot to say about that.

HR: *Do you see much difference in the way men and women conduct therapy or psychoanalytic sessions?*

NM: No. I'm more impressed by personality differences than by general sex differences. We each have to do this work in a way that is authentic, that is true to our idiosyncratic self. Perhaps the fact that I can't come up with any generalizations about sex differences in therapeutic style is related to my impression that psychotherapy attracts rather androgynous people. It appeals to women who identify with the stereotypically masculine qualities of ambition and competitiveness and to men with the stereotypically feminine qualities of emotional sensitivity and nurturance.

HR: *Your books* Psychoanalytic Diagnosis: Understanding Personality Structure in the Clinical Process *and* Psychoanalytic Case Formulation *are staples in many psychodynamic training programs. How does your innovative approach differ from the DSM and the insurance company diagnostic model?*

NM: Both books were written out of a nagging worry that the DSM/insurance diagnosis model would diminish and corrupt the difficult but quintessentially therapeutic process of trying to understand and respond to the complex subjective experience of a fellow human being. I didn't see my books as particularly innovative—rather the opposite: I wrote them in the hope of preserving the best of the older tradition. The DSM substitutes simple reifications for the much richer understandings that have been painstakingly collected by careful listeners over the past century. Its recent versions have made certain kinds of research easier, but that research all too often turns out to be methodologically rigorous and substantively vacuous, and I doubt that therapists have become better healers because of it.

HR: *Do you have a favorite self-help strategy you use on yourself when you are feeling a bit anxious or depressed?*

NM: I rarely get anxious. My relative freedom from anxiety is one of the nicest results of my personal analysis. On the rare occasions when I do feel anxious, I typically talk with someone I trust, and the anxiety dissipates. I'm somewhat prone to depression, however. I had a lot of childhood losses that can get psychologically revived when I encounter a loss or rejection. Again, I tend to talk to my husband and my close friends, and I look for ways to comfort myself, such as with music, novels, good food, and family gatherings. In recent years I've taken singing lessons and enjoyed performing with a cabaret group. I'm not very good, but the experience gets me completely outside my professional world, which is therapeutic in itself. I have a remote little cabin up in the Berkshire Mountains where I can escape ordinary stresses, write, see the stars at night, and get some exercise hiking through stunning scenery. Another precious outcome of my experience as a patient in analysis was the capacity to comfort myself rather than criticize myself when I'm down.

HR: *What movie with a psychoanalytic slant do you like best, and why?*

NM: I guess I'm not very original in saying this, but I thought *American Beauty* was brilliantly conceived, cast, and acted. The psychologies of not only the main character but everyone in his family exemplified the devastation wreaked in a culture where youth, beauty, money, and power count for more than integrity or devotion or wisdom. The movie captured all this warmly and with compassion, not with a heavy judgmental hand. Kevin Spacey's character could have been an advertisement for the psychoanalytic literature on pathological narcissism. And Chris Cooper's portrayal of a man whose unconscious homoerotic longings cause a devastating enactment was remarkable. Freud would have found it a brilliant example of "the return of the repressed."

HR: *I've been asking most of the experts in this book to gaze into their crystal balls and tell me what psychotherapy will look like in the next twenty-five or fifty years. I've had this pet theory that we might just see a backlash fueled by the brief present-moment therapies and analytic-like therapies could be making a comeback. What's your vision?*

NM: I'm mostly just trying to survive these difficult times, when mental health care, especially for people of lower income, has gotten radically worse than it once was. For the severely mentally ill, the existence of powerful medications in a context where psychotherapy is devalued means that those who suffer the worst get the least attention. Overtaxed practitioners can't do much more than to try to get seriously ill patients on an appropriate drug regimen, and even that may not go well if the person feels ignored except for discussions about medication compliance.

But I do have confidence that psychoanalysis—and analytic and humanistic therapies in general—will survive and even flourish. They help people. A satisfied customer passes on his or her experience to other people irrespective of the therapeutic fashions of the day.

HR: *Would you like to share your Web site URL in the event that our readers would like to take in one of your lectures or workshops?*

NM: Sure. It's www.nancymcwilliams.com.

HR: *Thanks a million. I know you are extremely busy and I really appreciate the time you took to share your wisdom. Best wishes in your career!*

NM: Many thanks. I've enjoyed this conversation.

Chapter 17

The Gambling Addiction Era Cometh:
A Thought-Provoking Interview
with Lia Nower

Lia Nower, JD, PhD, has researched gambling addiction both in the United States and internationally. She is an assistant professor of social welfare at the University of Missouri, St. Louis, a state- and nationally certified compulsive gambling counselor, and a clinical supervisor for the National Counsel on Problem Gambling in Washington, DC. The combination of her legal and mental health experience gives her a unique perspective in understanding this issue.

HR: *I know that you have conducted research and numerous seminars on this topic. How did you personally become interested in gambling addiction?*

LN: I had the good fortune to be mentored by Dr. David Ohlms, an addiction psychiatrist and medical director of Anheuser-Busch and his wife, Terri Ohlms, a clinical social worker who was the first certified compulsive gambling counselor in Missouri. When I joined their practice, they essentially said, "Pick an addiction." Sex, drugs, alcohol, shopping—so many options, so little time! Gambling was the most complex and challenging to treat (it was also a relatively new field) so I thought I'd try my hand.

This interview appeared as the cover story article in *Counselor, The Magazine for Addiction Professionals,* 5(4), August 2004, pp. 14-20, and is reprinted via their permission herein.

HR: *Share a few statistics with us. How common is gambling addiction? Is the incidence of this problem really increasing or is it merely that we are just hearing more about it now?*

LN: The general prevalence estimate is that 1.7 percent of adults (3 to 5 percent of youth) meet diagnostic criteria for pathological gambling and an additional 3 to 5 percent have serious gambling problems. Those figures are often higher in jurisdictions where gambling has been legal longer. Studies have yet to track the yearly incidence of pathological gambling, so it's anybody's guess how that number is fluctuating, though we believe that availability, accessibility, and acceptability tend to increase overall rates in a given area.

HR: *Is there a personality profile—say a cluster of personality traits—that makes one more susceptible to this behavior?*

LN: The research in this area is still in its infancy but, in general, individuals with certain traits and biopsychosocial predispositions are more likely than others to develop problems. Those at highest risk are impulsive, intensity seeking, addicted to other substances, and typically depressed or anxious. They start gambling or pursuing other risk-taking behaviors at an early age and report childhoods marked by abuse or neglect and caregivers with addictions.

HR: *Let's say that Joe or Jane average gambling addict hits the casinos and loses enough money to bankrupt a small financial institution. Moreover, he or she can't afford to do so. What is the mind-set that keeps him or her coming back for more?*

LN: The hope that some day, some how, Lady Luck will smile down again. To understand the insanity of that thinking you have to understand the cycle. Early on, people gamble for recreation and tend to win something. Statistically, the less you gamble, the more likely your wins will outpace your losses. Many problem gamblers report they had an early big win that left them hungering for more. This precipitates "chasing" behavior—

gambling more often in hopes of recreating that early win. The more you gamble, the more you lose. So, before long, gamblers have lost a lot of money. Bills aren't getting paid, the mortgage is behind. They're borrowing, taking out new credit cards just to meet their financial obligations. And they start lying to friends and family members with fantastic requests for loans. At this point, gambling is no longer a past time but a necessity. A big win represents the only foreseeable way of ever catching up and breaking even. So they gamble more and lose more—until they've lied, stolen, manipulated, and juggled so many things that they can't hide it anymore. The bank is foreclosing on the house, the repo man's coming for the car. That's why the risk of suicide is high with this population—by the time they've reached the desperation phase, they are faced with financial and social ruin with few options left. If they're lucky, they suddenly stop maneuvering long enough to ask: "How the heck did I get here?"

HR: *What about all those books and courses . . . you know . . . How to Beat the Slots . . . the horses . . . whatever?*

LN: A bunch of nonsense. Odds are odds and probabilities are probabilities. Even the games with the best odds like blackjack are still weighted in favor of the house. Unless you're a card counter, a cheat, or a real professional who gambles in tournaments, you're going to lose your shirt if you gamble all the time. Slots and video poker are hopeless, largely because the odds against you are astronomical. They are governed by random chance, which is, by definition, unpredictable. Without getting too technical, what you see on a slot machine is definitely not what you get. The computer is driven by a random generator that decides the outcome the minute you push the button. The wheels you see spinning—what we call the "virtual reel"—bear little relation to what's really going on inside the computer. So when you think you've only missed the three cherries by a fraction of an inch, it's actually an optical illusion. Depending on the setup of the "real reel" in the computer, you could have missed by hundreds of numbers or more.

HR: *What part does Internet gambling play in the overall picture?*

LN: Hard to estimate with certainty since Internet gambling is theoretically illegal so revenues aren't officially tracked. However, most people in the gambling field view Internet gambling as the fastest-growing segment of the industry, generating millions and, according to some, billions of dollars each year.

HR: *Let me hit you with a few casino questions. First, you told me a fascinating story about a pathological gambler featured on a casino billboard ad. The story illustrated that the glitzy ads don't always paint a realistic picture of the horror that lurks beneath the surface. Would you be willing to briefly summarize that story for our readers?*

LN: "Bill" was a divorced guy, government worker. Lonely, with some health problems. Started going to the boat with an elderly relative and playing slots. Before long, he had gambled away his pension and savings and started borrowing from loan sharks to cover the bills. One night, he got lucky and won a car. There was lots of fanfare—people coming out from everywhere congratulating him, buying drinks—and the casino asked to take his picture for advertisement. There he was, smiling and waving out of the door of this brand new sports car for all the world to see. What no one knew is he never drove the car off the lot. By the time he won, he was so in debt that the IRS took the cash value of the car for back-taxes and Bill was left to fend off the loan sharks.

HR: *I know you have traveled the world to study the phenomenon of gambling addiction. In the United States, casinos conjure up the image of luxury . . . miles of slots that sparkle so intensely you could comb your hair in the shiny chrome edges of the machines if need be. Is this luxurious, roll out the red carpet carnival atmosphere, par for the course when you visit casinos worldwide?*

LN: It depends. Some tribal casinos and/or temporary casinos are big, bare smoky rooms with lots of machines. Casinos owned by big operators, no matter where they're located, are typically opulent and filled with sights, sounds, and scents that make patrons feel pampered and welcome.

HR: *Are there multicultural differences in terms of problem gambling?*

LN: There probably are, but the few studies that have looked at these variables have too many methodological problems to generalize. We know that there are definitely socioeconomic differences. A disproportionate number of problem gamblers in some studies were underemployed, with lower-than-average household incomes. There is increasing concern regarding the percentage of older adults and persons with disabilities frequenting some venues. Several years ago, an investigative reporter in Minnesota wrote a story that tracked the large amount of public aid withdrawn at or near casinos. All these factors taken together suggest that lower income families may be disproportionately represented. However, we also know that pathological gambling is a disorder that cuts across all of society: No matter how much you make, you can still gamble it away.

HR: *Where do lotteries fit into the puzzle? Is society sanctioning a serious form of addiction?*

LN: On one level, lotteries are like any other form of gambling—totally dependent on random chance. There are three important differences though. Contrary to popular slogans like "Somebody's got to Lotto, it might as well be you," the truth is that it's much more likely to be anybody other than you. Unlike casino table games with predictable odds, you have a much better chance of getting struck by lightening twice than you do to win even a modest sum in the lottery. There are also those who say the lottery is a regressive tax on the poor; it's actually a regressive tax on the poorly informed. The lottery, particularly scratch-off variations, provides immediate gratification and arousal which fuels more impulse purposes similar to a slot machine. There are those who become addicted for sure and many who spend much more than they should. But problem gamblers who only play the lottery make up a very small percentage of those with serious financial and psychosocial problems.

HR: *I know you champion a three-phase model of gambling disorder. Tell us about that.*

LN: The pathways model proposes that gamblers are not all alike. They come to problem gambling from different pathways and, as a result, require different treatments to stop gambling. Pathway 1 gamblers play initially for socialization, to be part of a group. They are relatively healthy folks who fall prey to the addictive nature of variable ratio reinforcement: there's going to be a pay-off, and the longer the play the bigger the payoff, but you just don't know when. Elderly people who start gambling because they're lonely after their spouse dies are characteristic of this pathway. They are the easiest to treat and, typically, the only group who may be suitable for controlled gambling in the future. Most gamblers fall in Pathway 2. They have some history of family instability, low self-esteem or significant life losses, depression or anxiety, and/or comorbid addictions. They gamble initially for escape or arousal then, like the Pathway 1 gamblers, succumb to operant conditioning. Pathway 3 gamblers are the hardest to treat. They have serious personality pathology, mood disorders, terrible childhoods, histories of antisocial behavior, and comorbid addictions. There is strong evidence of a biological component—ADHD, risk-taking, impulsivity. For this group, the prognosis is very poor.

HR: *What is the first thing a counselor should do when confronted with a client who is addicted to gambling?*

LN: Be realistic with himself or herself and the client. The success rate is very low with these clients, in part because a lot of them aren't ready to get well. There will always be a lot more falls than slips, a lot more slips than walks with sure footing. Sometimes the most we can do is raise the bottom. Therefore, counselors can't get their egos invested in the client's level of success or they won't be effective. The counselor also needs to understand that, for most problem gamblers, gambling offers more than fun and excitement—it provides meaning and hope. And you can't take that away from a person without replacing it. It's like telling an alcoholic: "Stop drinking." The alcohol is more than drink; it's often the glue that holds the personality together. So when you say "Stop," the alcoholic hears a threat to his or her existence and fears that, without alcohol, he or she will simply fragment all over the place. The same is true of gambling. Gambling treatment is a partnership and I tell my clients: " If you want to get better, I'm here to help you stop gambling and find some meaning for your life. If you want to play me and use me to lie to your family or yourself, don't waste my time."

HR: *Do you always advocate abstinence after the individual begins treatment?*

LN: I don't typically advocate anything outright. Because as soon as you tell someone not to do something, that's exactly what he or she will do. It's human nature. Few gamblers come in saying, "I never want to gamble again." They all think deep down that someway, somehow, they can learn to control it. So what I do is set up a little behavioral experiment. Together we decide, based on their budget, a "reasonable" amount they could spend on entertainment, in this case, gambling. And we decide how many times a week they can afford to gamble with that amount of money. Then we agree that they will gamble that much and no more. The following week, we check the progress. If the person is a problem gambler, he or she will never stick to the plan. So, the next week, we change the plan, upping the ante and making it a bit more "reasonable." But, alas, once again, the person goes over the limit. Through this process the gambler comes to the conclusion that controlled gambling doesn't work for him or her. And if he or she thinks that revelation is his or her idea, the gambler is one step closer to abstinence.

HR: *What are your feelings about Gambler's Anonymous (GA) or perhaps AA? Are these modalities appropriate for everybody and do they constitute a treatment per se or merely a supplement to psychotherapy?*

LN: I'm a big advocate of GA and AA. I think that no one can talk to an addict like someone who's been there. Few counselors can effectively confront someone in denial like someone who's been in denial. I don't see support groups as a treatment in the traditional sense, though I do believe some people are able to quit gambling without attending formal counseling. The best prescription is counseling plus GA. That way, the counselor helps the gambler address the reasons behind the excessive behavior and the illogical cognitions that sustain it, and peers in GA provide support, guidance, and accountability.

HR: *What is the biggest mistake counselors make with this type of addict?*

LN: Treating gambling with a substance abuse model. There are some similarities between the two behaviors—the level of dependency, the reported tolerance and withdrawal symptoms, the desperate maintenance behavior. But gambling disorder is much more complex. Unlike substance abuse, gambling becomes "addictive" as a result of a multifactorial constellation of factors: predisposing psychosocial and neurological vulnerabilities combined with a highly addictive variable ratio reinforcement schedule. There is a high level of reported suicidality and, sometimes, homicidality, so there is little margin for error. With gambling, there is no physiological dependence on a substance, though the psychological dependence and differential effects of the behavior on the individual can generate those changes on PET [positron-emission tomography] scans. A smart counselor refers pathological gamblers to a specialist—someone with the skills and training to address the neurobiological predispositions, behavioral reinforcement, underlying psychosocial issues, gambling-related illogical cognitions, and meaning-centered deficits that lie at the heart of the disorder.

HR: *I know you treat a lot of folks in your private practice. Are insurance and managed care companies sympathetic to your treatment needs or do you need to fight for an appropriate number of sessions?*

LN: Things are getting better. Some states like Missouri, where I practice, contract with providers to offer state-funded treatment to gamblers. Insurance companies vary depending on the company. It used to be that an Axis I mood disorder was required for treatment approval. Happily, this is changing.

HR: *Are most counselors who deal with gambling addicts properly trained? Specifically, what type of training do you recommend?*

LN: No. As I said previously, I take a hard line with regard to treatment qualifications. Just as I believe counselors without special qualifications shouldn't treat anorexia or bulimia, I also believe the only counselors who should be treating pathological gamblers are those who are state and, preferably, nationally certified. Most states offer a certification, which consists generally of sixty hours of gambling-specific training for licensed clinicians. The National Council on Problem Gambling in Washington, DC, offers a national certification which requires state certification, two years or twenty-four hours of supervision by a certified clinical supervisor, passage of a national exam, plus 2,000 direct practice hours with gamblers. That's the only person I would trust with my family member.

HR: *In some areas of the nation politicians are pushing casinos to secure gambling taxes as a remedy for our ailing schools, which have been assaulted by budget cuts and related ills. Should we replace Charlie Wilson's 1955 adage of "What's Good for General Motors is good for the rest of America" with "What's good for Harrahs is good for the country's educational system"?*

LN: I try to stay out of politics and deal with the realities that exist. The facts are that most states—and most prosperous countries around the world—are invested in and dependent on the gaming industry for revenue. Whether that's good or bad is an issue for politicians and radio commentators. Whether schools ever see a dime of the theoretically earmarked tax dollars that are actually spent on general fund budget deficits is an issue for accountants. What concerns me is that any state, province, or country that's going to legalize gambling has a social obligation to provide enough money for counseling and research to offset the level of devastation to the 1.7 percent of the population and their families who will invariably be affected in a permanent way.

HR: *Any feelings about hotlines and helplines sponsored by casino funding? The whole thing sounds . . . well . . . a little paradoxical.*

LN: Like putting the vampire in charge of the blood bank? That may be true in some cases. In most instances the hotlines are run by independent, ethical organizations irrespective of funding. Personally, I think any state with legalized gambling should budget for treatment, research, and hotline costs before legalizing gambling. But, often, in the United States, we do a lot of reactive damage control rather than proactive prevention. So, given the current nature of things, I'd rather have the casinos funding a hotline than no hotline at all.

HR: *Thank you for taking time out of your busy schedule to share your knowledge and expertise.*

Chapter 18

An Encounter with EMDR Pioneer Francine Shapiro: The Eyes Have It

Francine Shapiro, PhD, the originator and developer of EMDR, is a senior research fellow at the Mental Research Institute. She is also the founder and president emeritus of the EMDR Humanitarian Assistance Programs, a nonprofit organization that coordinates disaster response and pro bono trainings worldwide. Dr. Shapiro was designated as one of the "Cadre of Experts" of the American Psychological Association & Canadian Psychological Association Joint Initiative on Ethnopolitical Warfare, and has served as advisor to numerous trauma treatment and outreach organizations. She is an internationally invited speaker and has written three books about EMDR: *Eye Movement Desensitization and Reprocessing* (Guilford Press), *EMDR* (BasicBooks), and *EMDR As an Integrative Psychotherapy Approach* (American Psychological Association Press). She is a recipient of the International Sigmund Freud Award of the City of Vienna, for distinguished contribution to psychotherapy, and the Distinguished Scientific Achievement in Psychology Award presented by the California Psychological Association.

HR: *Francine, I understand that you discovered eye movement desensitization (EMD), which has evolved into eye movement desensitization and reprocessing (EMDR) while strolling through the park in 1987. Evidentially you picked up on the fact that the shifting movement of your eyes helped you abate some distressing thoughts. That sounds fascinating. What actually transpired on that fortuitous day?*

FS: It would be more accurate to say that EMDR evolved from that initial discovery. EMDR is an integrative psychotherapy that contains eye movements, or other forms of bilateral stimulation, as one of its elements. The day in the park was fairly straightforward. I noticed that some disturbing thoughts I was having disappeared, although I hadn't done anything consciously to dispel them. When I brought them back they didn't have the same "charge." Curious as to the cause, I paid very careful attention and noticed that when the same type of thoughts arose, my eyes starting moving in a certain way. The thoughts disappeared and when I brought them back they were not as disturbing. So I tried doing the eye movements deliberately and found that the same thing happened. Later that week I experimented with some friends and started to discover the possibilities and the limitations. The procedures that became EMDR began to evolve in the ensuing months and years.

HR: *I know there have been about twenty published studies now on EMD. Has anybody put his or her finger on the precise mechanism that makes the eye movements curative? I know that some research indicates that any source of dual attention . . . say auditory stimuli . . . or finger tapping . . . can accomplish the same thing. Can you bring us up to speed on this and share how you are incorporating this information in EMDR sessions?*

FS: The entire field of neurobiology is in its infancy, so there is no way of knowing why any form of psychotherapy, or even most forms of medications, work. There are currently about eight controlled studies that show a positive effect for the eye movements, which test theories that are concerned with working memory and the orienting response. The best elucidation of possible neurobiological mechanisms can be found in an article by a Harvard researcher who thinks EMDR links into the same processes that occur during rapid eye movement [REM] sleep. The rapid learning, memory associations, and emotional processing of REM are a direct parallel to EMDR treatment effects (Stickgold, 2002).

HR: *In the actual therapy sessions do you rely on devices, similar to those a hypnotist might employ, to help abet eye movements or to create a condition that requires dual attention?*

FS: No. I am personally very low-tech. I simply have clients follow my fingers with their eyes. I should also point out that the eye movements used in EMDR are in no way similar to those used to induce a hypnotic state.

HR: *I remember hearing that EMDR has received more attention (twenty-five outcome studies) than any other treatment for post-traumatic stress disorder (PTSD). Have you and your colleagues seen EMDR work in a significant number of cases for PTSD where traditional therapies proved futile?*

FS: It is generally accepted that most forms of therapy have not had a good track record with combat veterans. A number of exposure therapy advocates have stated that exposure is not suited to issues involving anger or guilt. Nevertheless, EMDR has been very successful with combat veterans. A study conducted by the Honolulu VA, which used a full course of EMDR treatment, found that in twelve sessions, 77 percent of the Vietnam vets no longer had PTSD. EMDR has been successful with veterans of the Korean War, World War II, the Gulf War and, most recently, veterans of the war in Iraq, who were successfully treated in very few sessions.

HR: *Was EMDR used extensively after the 9/11 World Trade Center terrorist attacks?*

FS: The nonprofit EMDR humanitarian assistance programs (HAP) came into existence after the Oklahoma City bombing to aid clinicians in that area. After 9/11, HAP funded the Disaster Mental Health Recovery Network to help coordinate clinicians offering pro bono treatment to victims, family members and emergency service workers. Over 900 people were treated, including 600 firefighters. HAP is trying to prepare for these types of emergencies worldwide. [http://www.emdrhap.org]

HR: *Is it true that some celebrities such as Barbara Walters endorse EMDR?*

FS: We do not ask for celebrity endorsements. Barbara Walters was simply commenting on the EMDR segment presented on the *20/20* program she hosted a number of years ago.

HR: *Okay, here's the $64,000 question. There seems to be a faction of the mental health community that is hell-bent on proving that EMDR is unethical and quackery. I still see Web sites that malign the technique and make personal attacks on your character. Why do you think that your work has generated so much controversy and . . . at times . . . seemingly hatred? Isn't it true that the APA does indeed list EMDR as an accepted form of intervention for PTSD?*

FS: I've been told by people who have been in the field for many years that this is quite typical. Psychodynamic psychology was greeted the same way by the medical community; behaviorists got a similar reception from the psychodynamic camp; they in turn attacked the cognitivists, and now EMDR is attacked by some in the CBT group. Some have been quoted as saying "the EMDR clinicians are too enthusiastic/nothing is that good." Unfortunately, this type of knee-jerk response is a common form of "turf war." The unfortunate thing is that clients needlessly suffer because of the misinformation. Thankfully, instead of being swayed by nonsense, the pertinent APA committee evaluated the actual research and decided that continuing education credit should be given to EMDR courses. Likewise, many scientific committees charged with setting mental health practice guidelines have also given EMDR the highest levels of recommendation.

HR: *EMDR has some commonalities with Joseph Wolpe's systematic desensitization. Just curious, when EMDR is pitted against systematic desensitization, CBT, hypnosis, flooding, and related therapies how does it fare? Also, when Wolpe was alive, what were his thoughts about EMDR? Didn't he actually test EMDR and give it a clean bill of health?*

FS: The resemblance between EMDR and systematic desensitization is superficial. We continue to use Wolpe's subjective units of disturbance scale, but we do not return repeatedly to the image, and the initial target can be extremely disturbing, rather than at the low end of the spectrum. Since the days of "EMD," the emphasis has been on reprocessing rather than desensitization. The desensitization (decrease in emotional disturbance) is viewed as a byproduct of the reprocessing which results in a comprehensive shift on cognitive, emotional, somatic, and behavioral levels. It is true that Wolpe was very supportive of EMD and published an article about his success. He introduced EMD as a "breakthrough" at the Association for the Advancement of Behavior Therapy in 1990. When EMDR is compared to CBT therapies, such as flooding with and without cognitive therapies, it is generally able to accomplish equal or superior treatment effects with in-session work, while the CBT conditions require an additional thirty to sixty-five hours of homework. Although these studies evaluated overt symptoms, also of interest are the quality and nature of comprehensive clinical changes. The latter needs more rigorous study. However, the kinds of differences are indicated in a chapter written by experts in chronic pain. They examined differential effects and concluded that EMDR is able to achieve outcomes not previously available through CBT. In this instance, pain is eliminated, instead of simply monitored or reduced [Ray & Zbik, 2001].

HR: *Can you give us a list of problems that respond well to EMDR as well as the type of difficulties that are not suited to this mode of intervention?*

FS: Simply put, EMDR is used to address the experiential contributors of clinical complaints. Difficulties that are of organic origins, such as certain kinds of learning problems (such as ADHD) or certain types of depression, would not be amenable to EMDR. The same would be true of organically based psychoses. On the other hand, what we call "small 't' traumas" that are ubiquitous throughout childhood can cause attention and learning problems similar to symptoms of ADHD. Once these troubling experiences are processed the symptoms disappear. The same may be the case with lifelong depressions that turn out not to be genetic, but rather the product of earlier experiences that contain affects and impressions generating feelings of "helpless" and "hopeless." There, too, remit with adequate processing. Some "delusional" states are also the product of experiences rather than chemical imbalances. Basically, whenever a condition is caused or exacerbated by earlier experiences, these experiences are stored in the brain as memories. It appears as though these unprocessed memories contain the cognitive, emotional, and somatic information that underlie the symptoms and comprehensive dysfunction. These memories, the present circumstances that trigger disturbance, and templates for appropriate future action are targeted and processed through EMDR.

HR: *Can a client perform self-induced EMDR? Say, for example, a Vietnam Vet is having a traumatic flashback. Can he be taught to use EMDR as a self-help technique outside of the therapy sessions?*

FS: EMDR is not simply eye movements. It is an eight-phase integrative psychotherapy that needs a clinician to guide the client through the standardized procedures and protocols.

HR: *Would the treatment protocol for a recent trauma differ from a situation where an adult was struggling with a childhood memory?*

FS: There is one protocol used for recent memories and another used for memories over two months old. It is also important to attend to the potential developmental deficits that may hamper an adult who was assaulted as a child. Basically, EMDR clinicians are trained to address the entire clinical picture.

HR: *Say you are personally confronted with a client who has a problem that is not suited to EMDR. What theory of therapy do you turn to?*

FS: Assuming a nonorganic origin, if a problem is not suited to EMDR, it will generally be a systemic issue to be dealt with via education and interactional interventions.

HR: *Let's say that you are counseling a client and not using EMDR. Do you have a favorite technique or homework assignment that you could share with us?*

FS: Whether or not I am using EMDR, I believe it is important for everyone to have a baseline of relaxation. Therefore I help the client begin a routine of meditation and/or guided imagery, which includes access to positive affects. These techniques help the client feel a greater sense of self-mastery and control. They are not a substitute for processing experiential contributors to a problem, and eliminating the habitual negative emotions, sensations, and thoughts through EMDR. However, they do serve as useful tools until processing is complete. And, we all occasionally need to deliberately return to equilibrium when life is particularly "messy."

HR: *Some of our readers might wish to become EMDR therapists. Tell us about the training process.*

FS: The training programs should be approved by the EMDR International Association [http://www.emdria.org] or by EMDR-Europe [http://www.emdr-europe.net]. The basic course is approximately forty hours, with additional coursework to attain certification. The courses include didactic instructions and supervised small group exercises with one trainer for every ten participants. The supervised practice gives each clinician the ability to actually experience the processing effects before using EMDR with clients.

HR: *What factors led you to become a therapist?*

FS: I was finishing up a PhD in English literature when I was diagnosed with cancer. This changed my focus of attention to mind/body issues and the nascent field of psychoneuroimmunology. I felt there was a need to identify useful tools and make sure they were available to the general public. I dropped my English PhD and started investigating everything that was known in the area, including entering into a program in clinical psychology. As I was about to launch into my dissertation, I took the walk in the part and noticed the effects of the eye movement. As I developed EMDR and saw the potential for healing, I decided to devote my life to it. That is what led me to become licensed as a therapist.

HR: *Will insurance companies and managed care firms pay for EMDR treatment? I've heard that EMDR sessions can often last ninety minutes, which of course, would be in contrast with the usual fifty-minute hour that third-party payers have become accustomed to.*

FS: A number of insurance and managed care companies give specialty payments to EMDR clinicians to handle the ninety-minute sessions. They find it is less expensive in the long run since the treatment is efficient and the effects stable. Other managed care companies are behind the curve and don't know the EMDR research base. A study funded by Kaiser Permanente indicated that the HMO would save millions of dollars by offering EMDR. I'm sure comparable companies will move in that direction if they haven't already.

HR: *I know you conduct a lot of workshops and training sessions. What is the biggest mistake you see therapists making?*

FS: The biggest error is mistaking "state" and "trait." There are numerous "state change" techniques that can make a client feel better immediately. Therapists need to understand that memory consolidation continues to occur outside the office. Just because a client feels better in the moment does not mean that the change will be comprehensive or permanent. Clinicians often are too ready to jump in to cause a state change, when what they need to do is make sure that comprehensive processing has occurred.

HR: *Time for a few quick personal questions. Excluding books you wrote yourself, what is the best therapy book ever written?*

FS: Viktor Frankl's *Man's Search for Meaning*. EMDR is dedicated to helping people to be capable of choosing their attitudes—rather than being driven to them by inner forces they cannot control.

HR: *If I went out to your car, what CD would I find in the CD player?*

FS: You'd find five, a mix of old rock (Youngbloods), new (Ilse de Lange and Donna the Buffalo), Italian arias (Puccini, Cilea, Verdi, Leoncavallo), and a rhythm and blues mix a friend put together for me.

HR: *What direction will psychotherapy take in the next fifty years or so and what part will EMDR play?*

FS: My hope is that psychotherapy will be widely available and as accepted as physical care, in order to prevent children from being derailed and ending up in institutions because of earlier experiences that prevent them from becoming healthy and happy adults. I also hope that attention will be given not only to physical, but mental health in developing countries. Only then can we hope to stop the cycle of violence that cascades from one generation to the next. My hope is that the EMDR humanitarian assistance programs can help bring pro-bono treatment to where it is needed most, and help train local clinicians so that all people are given the opportunity to "choose their own attitudes" and their own destinies.

HR: *Thank you for sharing your knowledge and experience related to this innovative form of treatment!*

Chapter 19

A Psychological Approach
to Psychotherapy with Suicidal Patients:
An Intellectual Exchange
with Edwin S. Shneidman

Edwin Shneidman, PhD, was born in 1918. He is professor of thanatology emeritus at UCLA. He has been visiting professor at Harvard and the Ben Gurion University of Negev; and research associate at the Karolinska Hospital in Stockholm. In the 1950s he was cofounder and codirector of the Los Angeles Suicide Prevention Center; in the 1960s he was charter chief of the Center for the Study of Suicide Prevention at the National Institute of Mental Health in Bethesda. In 1968, he founded the American Association of Suicidology. He is the author of *Deaths of Man* (nominated for a National Book Award), *Voices of Death, Definition of Suicide, The Suicidal Mind,* and *Comprehending Suicide,* and has edited ten books on suicide and death. He is widowed and has four children and six grandchildren.

HR: *Let me begin with a bit of personal self-disclosure. Although all , of the interviews in this book are with accomplished therapists, I must confess I was especially intrigued with the prospect of interviewing you. Although I was never a serious suicidologist like you, I served a brief stint as the program coordinator of Life Crisis Services, Inc., in St. Louis, Missouri, where I ran a rather large survivors group. My first book was on the subject of suicide prevention and I have lectured to over 100,000 people on this topic. Hence, what I'm really saying to the young up-*

Therapy's Best
© 2006 by The Haworth Press, Inc. All rights reserved.
doi:10.1300/5189_19

starts reading this is that if you are interested in suicide, an interview with Ed Shneidman is as good as it gets! Okay, first things first. Did something occur in your childhood to spawn your curiosity about death or suicidal behavior?

ES: My lifelong concern with the topics of suicide and suicide prevention has been strictly professional. There is nothing in my personal life nor of my family or collaterals that touches on this lugubrious subject. What *did* influence me enormously was a course in logic which I took at age sixteen at UCLA and where I learned and understood John Stuart Mill's method of difference as the heart of inductive science.

That understanding and those insights came to my mind (and handed me a career) when I stumbled onto a repository of thousands of suicide notes in the vaults of the coroner's office in Los Angeles in 1949.

Permit me an aside. In general, I have been taught to value conservative assertions in science, New England understatement. I am a little leery of hyperbole and florid language. In general, I tend to be careful with archenthusiasts—even though I recognize that it is we hypomanics that make the world go round. I am mildly embarrassed with book titles with words like gems, insightful, accomplished, but apparently my narcissism is not sufficiently tamed to have me totally eschew them. So here I am.

HR: *Did you personally have any heroes, heroines, or role models who influenced your professional work?*

ES: Anyone who knows anything about me knows that the absolute center of my intellectual life is Henry A. Murray whose influence I reach for in every sentence I utter. Dr. Murray, who died in 1988 at the age of ninety-five, was a surgeon, a physician, a PhD in physiology, a psychoanalyst, a student of Jung, author of *Explorations in Personality,* head of the Harvard Psychological Clinic, Boston Brahmin, handsome, independently wealthy, and the brightest, most generous man I ever met. Among his thousands of memorable utterances, he said to me, "Never disparage a fellow human being in fewer than two thousand words." This led me to eschew simple labels like "Schizophrenic reaction, paranoid type" and in general to stay away from DSM-ese. Please see my edited book, *Endeavors in Psychology, Selections from the Personology of Henry Murray* (Harper and Row, 1985).

HR: *Do you put much stock in the biochemical aspects of suicide? In my neck of the woods, psychiatrists are doling out antidepressants like they are greasy french fries and electroconvulsive shock therapy is about as common as our daily commute to work.*

ES: In my mind's eye, there is a grand circle or pie of etiology. It has various sectors or pieces: sociocultural, biochemical, psychological, etc. A priori, I am absolutely unwilling to see that etiological pie of suicide without a genetic or biological piece. I do, however, believe firmly that in its essence, most suicides are storms of the *mind* with concomitant activities in a living brain. No brain, no mind. However, I believe in the autonomy of the mind, that the mind has a mind of its own, and that the main business of the mind is to mind its own business. The core of suicide is psychological pain, what I call *psychache*. There is a great deal of psychological pain in the world without suicide but there is almost no suicide without a great deal of psychological pain. I have no vendetta against the biologically oriented suicidologists. I just wish they did not have the chutzpah to think that their sector of the pie is the whole enchilada.

HR: *I was preparing to teach one of my college classes some years ago and I picked up a vintage 1951 copy of the Carl R. Rogers classic* Client-Centered Therapy. *I figured I would simply open the book to a random page and read a therapeutic dialogue to my class. Then my students could go out and model their sessions after the maestro. Well low and behold, I began reading on page forty-six and Rogers was confronted with a suicidal client. He did not conduct a lethality assessment nor did he deal with the client's suicidal ideation. Of course, we now know that is wrong . . . dead wrong. I'm certainly not criticizing Rogers who was indeed a true trailblazer in our field. I'm merely point-*

ing out that I wasn't that long ago that we knew very little about
suicide and were doing the wrong things. Was it your work that
changed everything? Were you the pioneer who taught us that
the best plan of action is to ask the client if he or she is suicidal,
conduct a lethality assessment, and then to deal with the issue
head on?

ES: Conceptually, there is a continuum between "directive" and
"nondirective." "Directive" has a kind of pejorative overcast, it
seems bossy, dictatorial, abrasively assertive, yenta-like. On
the other hand, a life in balance calls for something more than
nondirection. If I could, I would direct individuals not to kill
themselves, but I would recognize that coercion and shrillness
are often ineffective and even counterproductive. The therapist
is never neutral. At the least he's on the side of life and is vitally
proactive as often and as much as the patient will permit. The
therapist can tolerate the patient's perturbations but needs to
keep a vigilant eye on the patient's *lethality,* and then be forth-
right in dealing with it. If I recall correctly, our few losses in the
early days (a half century ago) at the Los Angeles Suicide Prevention Center were with people of special status (like a judge
or an actress or a physician) from whom we withheld more active modes of intervention (like hospitalization or even ECT—
electroconvulsive therapy) which we might have considered for
ordinary citizens.

HR: *What are your feelings about written or verbal contracts with*
suicidal clients? I've heard world-renowned experts assert that
contracts are useless. Nevertheless, I've talked with a number
of individuals who say things like, "I'm only alive today be-
cause twenty years ago my eighth-grade science teacher made
me sign a contract saying I wouldn't kill myself," or something
like that.

ES: My feeling about contracts is that they are a kind of peripheral
issue. The best contract in my mind is the therapist's saying
"I'll see you next time" or the therapist increasing the intensity
of the interaction with more frequent sessions or telephone
calls or written communications. Suicide always involves bro-

ken promises—on both sides—and contracts are only as good as the quality of the transference.

HR: *You have postulated ten commonalities of suicide. Do these commonalities apply when performing multicultural counseling with clients from other cultures?*

ES: I believe that my ten commonalities of suicide (please see Exhibit 19.1) are applicable and usable with any patient I might see in the United States, but in my discussion of suicide (in *Definition of Suicide*) I begin by saying "Currently in the Western world . . ." I would be satisfied to have some impact in the prevention of suicide even if it were restricted to the Western world. I make no claim to understand suicide on other continents with radically different languages, cultures, and patterns of logical mentation.

EXHIBIT 19.1:
Ten Psychological Commonalities of Suicide

   I. The common STIMULUS in suicide is unendurable psychological pain
  II. The common STRESSOR in suicide is frustrated psychological needs
  III. The common PURPOSE in suicide is to seek a solution
  IV. The common GOAL in suicide is cessation of consciousness.
  V. The common EMOTION in suicide is hopelessness-helplessness
  VI. The common INTERNAL ATTITUDE toward suicide is ambivalence
  VII. The common COGNITIVE STATE in suicide is constriction
  VIII. The common INTERPERSONAL ACT in suicide is communication of intention
  IX. The common ACTION in suicide is egression
  X. The common CONSISTENCY in suicide is with lifelong coping patterns

Source: E. S. Shneidman, *Definition of Suicide.* New York: Wiley, 1985.

HR: *What is the biggest mistake therapists make when dealing with the suicidal client?*

ES: Granted that this is a minor quibble but I think that it is a mistake to conceptualize a needful suicidal person as a client rather than a patient. Attorneys see clients; clinical suicidologists see patients. The task is a serious one. It's not the treatment of a tic or a stammer, it's a life and death issue. Essentially at its roots is a philosophic question. Is pain worth enduring? Is the tie to life worth reaffirming? The biggest mistake might be the lack of consultation with professional persons with greater insight and even greater wisdom. Of all specialties, clinical suicidology is the least well adapted to solo, isolated practice.

HR: *What is the most important factor to keep in mind when counseling suicidal clients?*

ES: Still in the same mood, I would say that I eschew counseling suicidal clients. That is not in my vocabulary. I think the difference between therapy and counseling is the recognition of the potent role of transference. Theoretically, the concept of transference need not be invoked in counseling, but it is indispensable in therapy. A working, positive transference relationship is what, in my opinion, keeps chronically dysphoric pessimistic patients alive. What is needed is not advice (certainly not exhortation). What is needed is a safe sanctuary for exploration, for nonjudgmental disputation, for modeling with someone who affirms life's values.

HR: *Most experts would have us believe that intervention with the suicidal client should be active-directive and present moment oriented. I have heard you mention psychoanalytic concepts before in your work. Are analytic principles helpful with self-destructive clients? If so, can you share a brief example from your own clinical work?*

ES: Psychoanalytic therapy is, at the core of its id, longitudinal, that is, it goes back to earliest childhood, but that doesn't preclude its having an emphasis on present moment and the present situation. Longitudinal and cross-sectional orientations can exist simultaneously. I think one can be both proactive and operate as the patient's ombudsman (in both the therapy room and the larger world) and at the same time understand the patient (and attempt selectively to share some of these understandings in terms of psychoanalytic concepts). I am a proactive, psychoanalytically tilted, life-oriented psychotherapist.

Using one of the psychoanalytic concepts (perhaps Adlerian in its flavor) I believe that there is a kind of almost sibling competition between me and each of my patients: that *I* will win the patient over to life, to a less crazy way of seeing things, to less aberrant notions of life and of choice; and that the life-affirming elements of the exchange will win out over the death-wish elements that are active in the patient. I think my clinical work has had excitement of this tension and my investment is not losing a life.

Oftentimes the element in a highly suicidal patient's mentations that deserves the most immediate and urgent attention is the patient's proclivity for *constriction* of mental thought, a tendency to think dichotomously in terms of black and white, A or non-A, *Aut Caesar Aut nihil,* all or nothing. The therapist should have his third ear attuned to the word *only,* perhaps the most dangerous word in the suicidal patient's vocabulary ("It's the only thing I can do . . . It's the only way to do it . . ."). What is called for is to break up the binary way of thinking and to widen the patient's conceptual blinders.

Here is an example: I recall a college student who had told a friend that she had purchased a revolver with the sole intention of killing herself. The friend encouraged her to see me at my university office. The student was twenty, single, attractive, demure, well-to-do, and filled with Victorian sensibilities; she had had sexual intercourse once in her life a few months before, and was pregnant. She told me (in the language of the unconscious) that she "couldn't bear to live." The choice she presented to me was that she somehow had to be unpregnant—to turn the clock back to before the fateful night—or dead. A punishing dichotomy for her—impossible to fulfill. At that moment, given these two choices, suicide seemed her *only* option.

I did several things. For one, I took out a legal pad of paper and began,with her reluctant help, to generate a list—"Shneidman's lousy list," I called it. Our exchange went something like this: "You could bring the child to term and keep it." ("I couldn't do that.") "You could bring the child to term and put it up for adoption." ("I can't do that.") "You could have an abortion here locally." ("I'm not going to do that.") "You could go away and have an abortion." ("Not that.") "You could involve your parents." ("I won't do that.") "You could talk to the young man involved." ("I definitely won't do that.") "And you can always commit suicide, but there is no reason to do that today." (No comment by her.) The won'ts, the can'ts, the have-tos, the musts, the nevers, the alwayses—the person's initial unnegotiables—these are the main topics of therapy. "Now," I said, "let's look at our list, and would you please rank order them from the absolutely least acceptable on up to the least distasteful."

The very making of this list, the nonjudgmental attitude, had already had a calming effect on her. We had broken the dichotomy and enlarged her view. She actually ranked the list, mumbling dissent at each item. But what was of critical importance was that suicide was no longer a first or second choice. She put a "1" and a "2" with some tears, but when she wrote "3," I knew her life was saved and we were then simply haggling about life—which is a perfectly viable state, and for some people, at least at some times, the normal state of affairs.

It was possible to achieve the assignment of the moment—to loosen this young woman's suicidal resolve by reducing her confusion, her shame, and her panic, and by widening her constricted perception of her range of options. Her original dichotomous choice involving only suicide gave way to some viable choices within the scope of life's realistic options. There was now some hope.

I also did a number of practical things on her behalf, including making some telephone calls (in her presence), to set in motion what she had chosen as the least-undesirable-choice-under-these-circumstances; the reasonably best that one could do. She could live with that.

HR: *Are you a fan of Martin E. P. Seligman's notion of learned help-lessness? In essence, are suicidal folks like Seligman's dogs who were restrained and shocked, ergo concluding that struggling is seemingly useless or perhaps makes the situation worse?*

ES: I am certainly an admirer of the work of Martin Seligman but I have my own paradigm to follow, that of the central role of psychache in the suicidal drama. I do not see learned helpless-ness as the central pivot in the suicidal drama, although I am willing to believe that some instances of suicide can usefully be conceptualized in this way.

HR: *What about school suicide-prevention programs . . . are they lifesavers or health hazards?*

ES: I endorse suicide-prevention programs in the school, especially at the secondary school level. They are part of the prevailing zeitgeist where it appears that almost nothing is taboo, the problems with drugs, guns, condoms. There is no reason to in-terdict suicide prevention as a taboo topic. This means that school personnel, especially school nurses and school psychol-ogists, must be ready to deal forthrightly with self-destructive urges when students bring them to their attention.

HR: *Why is postvention (a term you coined if I recall) important for a suicide survivor who has lost a loved one via suicide? And just for the record, do you buy into grief theories that push stages such as Elisabeth Kübler Ross?*

ES: Apropos postvention I have said—which makes it a quasi-truth—that postvention is also prevention for the next genera-tion. Grief and mourning (admixed with guilt and shame and perplexity) are not diseases but in a sense their abrasive and del-eterious effects are almost as great as though they were. I have read with keen interest the several published accounts of survi-vors of tragic suicidal deaths. In every case the person who commits suicide puts a psychological skeleton in the survivor's closet and the survivor is sentenced, as it were, to obsess about

THERAPY'S BEST

the death. Any help, any "vention" which can be offered is all to the good. About Elisabeth Kübler-Ross: I never saw her five stages in any case I touched, and I felt from the beginning that they were more a mnemonic device for undergraduates to memorize rather than a set of clinical insights for practitioners to pursue.

HR: *Finally, why are you such a superb mentor? So many people who have studied with you have gone on to achieve notoriety.*

ES: It may be that one of the reasons that I am sometimes effective is that I pay close attention to the language of my patients and try carefully to distinguish between being notorius and being well-known. Careful use of language is the key to effective therapy. And note also that the therapist's task is often not to take the question at face value but to change the question—as I am doing now—so it can be answered in a more life-affirming way.

HR: *Thanks for sharing your knowledge and expertise. If it helps us save at least one life . . . and it will . . . then it was worth it.*

Chapter 20

What We Can Learn
from Accomplished Counselors
and Therapists: A Baker's Dozen
of Insightful Gems of Wisdom

The quintessential question in my mind is: What insightful gems of wisdom can we glean from our panel of hardworking and gifted experts that will make us more effective helpers?

I offer my own observations only with the hope that they will challenge you to look deep within and come up with your own conclusions. My list is in no way, shape, or form exhaustive, and I would not be surprised if your list was longer, contained different material, or even included commonalities and differences that are diametrically opposed to mine. Every therapist comes to the session with a unique background and perspective and that is what makes each of us creatively different—special, if you will—from the person in the next office. Thus, in one sense, this exercise is like a self-projective test that can reveal nuances about our own personalities.

Hard-core statisticians will not be impressed by my low N (only twenty therapists), the fact the therapists were not picked randomly, or by the obvious fact that the practitioners were not asked identical questions—and even when they were, the wording varied greatly. Nevertheless, I, for one, am convinced beyond a shadow of a doubt that our cast of characters did provide us with a valuable real-world education.

The first two observations, as well as observation number nine, might not readily appear on your list since they were acquired strictly because of my unique role as the editor.

1. *Accomplished therapists are modest.* My original title for this work was *The Best and the Brightest,* which I borrowed, of course, from David Halberstam's Vietnam-era classic. Several of the most accomplished contributors were squeamish about participating pointing out that they didn't fit into either "the best" or "the brightest" category, hence, the title of this text was revised. Many of our experts seemed to downplay their stellar accomplishments. Consider the response of Al Mahrer when I asked him about the "Living Legends of Psychotherapy Award" that he snared.

2. *Accomplished therapists seemingly enjoy enhanced longevity.* Neophyte readers may be unaware of the fact that several of our experts are hovering around the ninety-year-old mark. The amazing part is that these individuals haven't retired from the field or even necessarily slowed down to catch their breath! Albert Ellis might well be diagnosed as a veritable therapeutic Superman, still seeing over 100 clients a week at times, writing or contributing to numerous articles or books (such as the one you are holding this very instant), conducting workshops, and keeping up with a lecture circuit that would wipe out the average twenty-five-year-old fresh out of graduate school! When I initially contacted Ray Corsini to see if he could contribute, I was dumbfounded when he related that he was working on multiple books himself and has worked on as many as five at one time. A feat, I might add, that he claims "is easy" (his words, not mine), all of this *without* using graduate students or research assistants. Not to be outdone, TA and gestalt pioneer Muriel James told me prior to her interview that she wakes up each morning at 5:30, surrounded by about fifty books, and sips on a cup of coffee as she writes her latest history book. "I've branched out from just writing psychology books," she tells me.

Even more perplexing is the fact that although these folks all seem to lead fairly healthy lifestyles, none seemed obsessed with counting cholesterol, exercise, or popping the latest antiaging mineral or freeform amino acid supplements. Could it be that their love for helping others is true secret of their fountain of youth?

Research has clearly demonstrated that one's profession can have an impact on longevity. Perhaps more research needs to be conducted on outstanding therapists.

3. *Accomplished therapists enjoyed, repected, and valued their education although they often went in totally new directions after grad-*

uation. Al Mahrer speaks of the tremendous influence Freud and Rogers had on him. However, his existential psychotherapy system bears no resemblance to a session of classical analysis! Ellis was trained as an analyst and broke away. Glasser is obviously a psychiatrist who clearly does not believe in the medical model of psychiatry and so on.

4. *When accomplished therapists created their novel ideas or systems of therapy, they were initially ostracized by their peers.* Ellis readily admits that most therapists in his day actively tried to keep him from talking, speaking, and writing about his rational approach. Years ago I personally encountered graduate school professors and textbook authors who refused to discuss Glasser's reality therapy on the basis that it was too simplistic and therefore not a legitimate modality of treatment. As we speak, Francine Shapiro must deal with Internet hate sites and colleagues who are critical of her EMDR therapy although numerous research studies seemingly attest to the effectiveness of this intervention.

5. *Accomplished therapists truly believe in their strategies even when they are diametrically opposed to other experts.* Thanatologist and suicidologist Ed Shneidman is not a fan of the Elisabeth Kübler Ross stages of death and dying. Shneidman is not a huge fan of suicide prevention contracts with patients while Lisa Firestone is. Job-hunting specialist Richard Bolles does not believe in the magic résumé or vocational counseling inventories espoused by so many career counselors. Ray and Dorothy Becvar praise the genius of Milton H. Erickson, while Albert Ellis puts little or no stock in his methods. Les Greenberg, unlike Ellis, and those who favor CBT, does not believe that cognitive therapy is the answer to nearly every problem. Nancy McWilliams advocates long-term analytic methods that focus on one's problems while Bob Bertolino favors therapy that focuses on the solution.

6. *Accomplished therapists often became famous or achieved uncommon notoriety after the publication of a highly successful book.* Consider: Robert Alberti's *Your Perfect Right;* Albert Ellis' *Reason and Emotion in Psychotherapy* and *Guide to Rational Living;* Ray and Dorothy Becvar's *Marriage Counseling;* Richard Bolles' *What Color Is Your Parachute?;* Ray Corsini's *Current Psychotherapies; Sam T. Gladding's Counseling, The Comprehensive Profession;* William Glasser's *Reality Therapy;* Muriel James' *Born to Win;* Jeffrey

Kottler and Jon Carlson's recent *Mummy at the Dining Room Table;* and Edwin Shneidman's *Deaths of Man,* to cite a few choice examples.

7. *Most accomplished therapists do not support the current insurance, managed care, and health care payment system in the United States.* With the possible exception of Bob Bertolino, who practices brief therapy, most of the practitioners were extremely critical of the third-party payer system. For example, Ellis mentioning that many good psychologists can no longer make a satisfactory living as a clinician any longer or fact that that even his own institute is not on many of the provider panels! Or consider the Becvars who readily admit that they do not take clients with insurance. Nancy McWilliams acknowledged that it would be rare to find a third-party payer, who would foot the bill for a course of psychoanalysis. Ray Corsini once told me that he saw one client under a managed care system "and that was it."

8. *Accomplished therapists believe their strategies are effective when performing multicultural counseling.* Without exception, our seasoned practitioners felt that their methods would be effective with persons from other cultures.

9. *Accomplished therapists often don't take their theories as literal as academians.* My interviews included only a handful of "off the record" before and after questions. Nevertheless, as a college professor myself and an author of counseling licensure and certification exam materials, I couldn't help asking my experts a few sample exam questions regarding their theories put forth by professional organizations. These were questions I personally found challenging or questions in which I was downright unsure of the answer. I was amazed when a few of my interviewees *who created the theory* either didn't know the answer or in one instance remarked, "I created that concept years ago and can barely remember it. It's irrelevant now."

My point is certainly not to criticize the experts in question. Instead, it behooves us to stop and think: Are we in the helping professions focusing too heavily on the minutiae to the point where the student might be missing the big picture? I would contend that this is a distinct possibility.

10. *Accomplished therapists—like successful businesses—position themselves in the therapeutic marketplace.* Some readers are no doubt familiar with the landmark work in the field of advertising and

marketing by Al Ries and Jack Trout who proposed the concept of positioning in business. Ries and Trout insisted that a good business should never attempt to be everything to everybody. A concept that turned the traditional wisdom of "try to be everything to everybody" concept on its ear. Today, because of the validity of their admonition, we have shampoos for blondes, redheads, fine hair, dry hair, colored hair, damaged hair, and nearly any other type of hair you can think of. We have deodorants for men, women, and even those who are athletically inclined.

Let's look at our field. When you say the name Albert Ellis you think of REBT or perhaps CBT—not career counseling. When you say the name Richard Bolles you think of job-hunting and career counseling rather than REBT, CBT, or marriage and family counseling. Say Becvar and Becvar and the topic of marriage counseling comes to mind. And the list goes on: Lia Nower, gambling addiction; Robert Alberti, assertiveness training; Francine Shapiro EMDR or perhaps PTSD; Muriel James, TA and gestalt; Lisa and Robert Firestone, voice therapy, etc.

Our accomplished counselors and therapists (either consciously or unconsciously), have positioned themselves well in the therapeutic marketplace.

For those who see this as a trivial point, I beg to disagree. Open any phone book in virtually any big city and count the number of therapists who profess in their ads to treat everyone from those with from those who suffer from anorexia and depression, to crack addiction, to trichotillomania and everything in between. Their ads, brochures, and marketing materials often mention a myriad of treatment modalities they practice that will cover the waterfront from behavior therapy, to grief counseling, to primal scream therapy.

Clearly such practitioners and agencies just don't get it and are still trying to be everything to everybody.

11. *Accomplished therapists are split on the issue of whether nonmedical practitioners should have prescription privileges.* This should be a heated issue in the coming years with political, professional, organizational, psychological, medical, and business ramifications.

12. *Since highly accomplished therapists are often highly critical of rival modes of treatment they are only selectively eclectic or integrative in their approach.* Therapy wars are alive and living in the

field of psychotherapeutic intervention. The integrative therapy era may be right around the corner, but based on our interviewee's responses, it isn't totally here yet.

13. *Accomplished therapists often didn't set out to be an expert in their particular area of expertise.* Lia Nower discovered the field of gambling addiction while working with noted addiction specialists Terri and David Ohlms. Francine Shapiro discovered EMDR serendipitously while taking a stroll. Al Mahrer had dreams of becoming a boxer until he was injured and was fascinated with what he learned about himself in graduate school. Raymond Corsini was originally an industrial psychologist rather than a psychotherapist, and so on.

The reader might also want to analyze our experts positions on good therapy, bad therapy, best tip for practitioners, their childhoods, or other pertinent factors based on the information herein.

Perhaps the key is that we *need* psychotherapeutic diversity and should embrace it. Human behavior is infinitely complex and a "one psychotherapy fits all" approach may be highly unrealistic. One person's phobia may respond to the cognitive interventions of REBT, another makes immediate progress with EMDR, while still another will require the extreme abreaction of Mahrer's experiential therapy or the interpretations and transference provided by a long course of psychoanalysis.

Moreover, since therapists are human beings (at least the last time I checked) they too are infinitely complex and therefore may feel more comfortable or adept using a certain style or styles of helping. Certainly, each and every one of our experts after doing considerable soul searching now extols a paradigm that seems to work well with his or her personality. A model he or she truly believes in. Now, it's your turn.

The task is an important one. The readers of this book will be the leaders and experts of tomorrow, forming the new cast of characters for similar texts in the future. Hence, my final interview question: Will your name and theory grace the pages?

I'll be watching.

References

Chapter 4

Bertolino, B. (2003). *Change-oriented therapy with adolescents and young adults: A new generation of respectful and effective processes and practices.* New York: Norton.

Bertolino, B., & O'Hanlon, B. (2002). *Collaborative, competency-based counseling and therapy.* Boston: Allyn & Bacon.

Duncan, B.L., & Miller, S.D. (2000). *The heroic client: Doing client-centered, outcome-informed therapy.* San Francisco: Jossey-Bass.

Duncan, B.L., Miller, S.D., & Sparks, J.A. (2004). *The heroic client: A revolutionary way to improve effectiveness through client-directed, outcome-informed therapy* [Revised Paperback Edition]. San Francisco: Jossey-Bass.

Garfield, S.L. (1989). *The practice of brief psychotherapy.* New York: Pergamon.

Gurman, A.S. (1977). The patient's perceptions of the therapeutic relationship. In A.S. Gurman & A.M. Razin (Eds.), *Effective psychotherapy* (pp. 503-545). New York: Pergamon.

Horvath, A.O., & Luborsky, L. (1993). The role of the therapeutic alliance in psychotherapy. *Journal of Consulting and Clinical Psychology, 61,* 561-573.

Horvath, A.O., & Symonds, B.D. (1991). Relation between working alliance and outcome in psychotherapy: A meta-analysis. *Journal of Consulting and Clinical Psychology, 38,* 139-149.

Kopp, S., Akhtarullah, S., Niazi, F., Duncan, B., & Sparks, J. (2001). The seamless use of measures: The nuts and bolts of accountability. In B. Duncan & J. Sparks (Eds.), *Heroic clients, heroic agencies: Partners for change* (pp. 88-94). Davie, FL: Nova Southeastern University Press.

Koss, M.P., & Butcher, J.N. (1986). Research on brief psychotherapy. In A.E. Bergin & S. L. Garfield (Eds.), *Handbook of psychotherapy and behavior change* (3rd ed.) (pp. 627-663). New York: Wiley.

Lafferty, P., Beutler, L.E., & Crago, M. (1989). Differences between more and less effective psychotherapists: A study of select therapist variables. *Journal of Consulting and Clinical Psychology, 57,* 76-80.

Lambert, M.J. (1992). Implications of outcome research for psychotherapy integration. In J.C. Norcross & M.R. Goldfried (Eds.), *Handbook of psychotherapy integration* (pp. 94-129). New York: Basic Books.

Therapy's Best
© 2006 by The Haworth Press, Inc. All rights reserved.
doi:10.1300/5189_21

Lambert, M.J., & Bergin, A.E. (1994). The effectiveness of psychotherapy. In A.E. Bergin & S.L. Garfield (Eds.), *Handbook of psychotherapy and behavior change* (4th ed.) (pp. 143-189). New York: Wiley.

Levitt, E.E. (1966). Psychotherapy research and the expectation-reality discrepancy. *Psychotherapy, 3,* 163-166.

Miller, S.D. (1994). The solution conspiracy: A mystery in three installments. *Journal of Systemic Therapies, 13*(1), 18-37.

Wampold, B.E. (2001). *The great psychotherapy debate: Models, methods, and findings.* Mahwah, NJ: Lawrence Erlbaum.

Chapter 7

Recommended Reading

Calia, V.F., & Corsini, R.J. (1973). *Critical incidents in school counseling.* Englewood Cliffs, NJ: Prentice Hall.

Cassel, P., & Corsini, R.J. (1984). *Challenge of adolescence.* Toronto: Amberly.

Cassel, P., & Corsini, R.J. (1990). *Coping with teenagers in a democracy.* Toronto: Lugus.

Corsini, R.J. (1966). *Roleplaying in psychotherapy.* New York: Aldine.

Corsini, R.J., & Painter, G. (1975). *The practical parent.* New York: Harper & Row.

Dreikurs, R., & Corsini, R.J. (1974). *How to stop fighting with your kids.* New York: Ace.

Dreikurs, R., Corsini, R., Lowe, R., & Sonstegard, M. (1959). *Adlerian family counseling.* Eugene, OR: Oregon U. Press.

Dumont, F., & Corsini, R.J. (2000). *Six therapists and one client.* New York: Springer.

Painter, G., & Corsini, R.J. (1990). *Effective discipline in the home and the school.* New York: Taylor and Francis.

Phillips, C., & Corsini, R.J. (1982). *Give in or give up.* Chicago: Nelson-Hall.

Standal, S.W., & Corsini R.J. (1959). *Critical incidents in psychotherapy.* Englewood Cliffs, NJ: Prentice Hall.

Chapter 9

Firestone, R.W. (1990). *Compasssionate child-rearing: An in-depth approach to optimal parenting.* Santa Barbara, CA: Glendon Association.

Firestone, R.W. (2002). The death of psychoanalysis and depth therapy. *Psychotherapy, 39,* 223-232.

Parr, G. (Producer & director). (1985). *The inner voice in suicide.* [Video]. Santa Barbara, CA: Glendon Association.

Chapter 10

Haley, J. (1973). *Uncommon therapy: The psychiatric techniques of Milton H. Erickson, M.D.* New York: Ballentine Books.

Chapter 11

Young, M.E., & Feller, F. (1993). Theoretical trends in counseling: A national survey. *Guidance and Counseling, 9,* 4-9.

Chapter 12

Suggested References

Elliott, R., Watson, J., Goldman, R., & Greenberg, L. (2004). *Learning emotion focused therapy.* Washington, DC: American Psychological Association Press.

Greenberg, L. (2002). *Emotion-focused therapy: Coaching clients to work through feelings.* Washington, DC: American Psychological Association Press.

Greenberg, L. (2004). Being and doing in psychotherapy. *Person Centered & Experiential Psychotherapies, 3,* 52-65.

Greenberg, L. (2004). Emotion-focused therapy. *British Journal of Clinical Psychology and Psychotherapy, 11,* 3-16 (special issue).

Greenberg, L., & Angus, L. (2004). Emotion and narrative. In L. Angus & J. Mc Leod (Eds.), *Narrative in Psychotherapy.* Thousand Oaks, CA: Sage.

Greenberg, L., & Elliott R. (2002). *Emotion focused therapy: A process experiential approach.* In J. Lebow & F. Kaslow (Eds.), *Comprehensive handbook of psychotherapy* (pp. 213-241). New York: John Wiley & Sons.

Greenberg, L., Elliott, R., & Lietaer, G. (2003). Humanistic-experiential psychotherapy. In G. Stricker & T. Widiger (Eds.), *Handbook of psychology Vol. 8— Clinical Psychology* (pp. 301-326). Hoboken, NJ: John Wiley & Sons.

Greenberg, L., & Geller, S. (2001). Congruence and therapeutic presence. In G. Wyatt & P. Saunders (Eds.), *Rogers' therapeutic conditions: Congruence* (Volume 1, pp. 131-149). PCCS Books. Ross-on Wye. Herefordshire.

Greenberg, L., & Johnson, S. (1988). *Emotionally focused couples therapy.* New York: Guilford Press.

Greenberg, L., & Paivio, S. (1997). *Working with emotion in psychotherapy.* New York: Guilford Press. (Translated into Spanish and Italian.)

Greenberg, L. Rice, L., & Elliott, R. (1993). *Facilitating emotional change: The moment-by-moment process.* New York: Guilford Press. (Translated into Spanish, Italian, and German.)

Greenberg, L., Watson, J., & Lietaer, G. (Eds.). (1998). *Handbook of experiential therapy.* New York: Guilford Press. (Translated into Italian.)

Rice, L. & Greenberg, L. (Eds.). (1984). Patterns of change: An intensive research handbook. New York: Guilford Press.

Chapter 18

Ray, A.L. & Zbik A. (2001). Cognitive behavioral therapies and beyond. In C.D. Tollision, J.R., Satterhwaite, & J.W. Tollison (Eds.), *Practical Pain Management* (Third ed.) (pp. 189-208). Philadelphia: Lippincott.

Strickgold, R. (2002). EMDR: A putative neurobiological mechanism of action. *Journal of Clinical Psychology, 58,* 61-75.